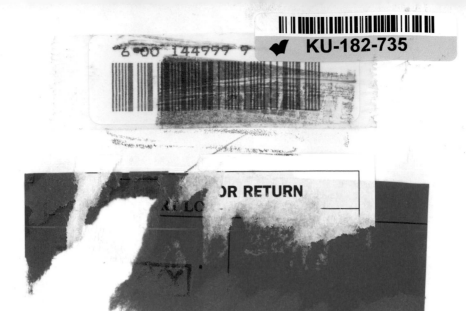

MARKET INSTITUTIONS AND ECONOMIC PROGRESS IN THE NEW SOUTH 1865–1900

Essays Stimulated by
*One Kind of Freedom:
The Economic Consequences of Emancipation*

MARKET INSTITUTIONS AND ECONOMIC PROGRESS IN THE NEW SOUTH 1865–1900

Essays Stimulated by
One Kind of Freedom:
The Economic Consequences of Emancipation

Edited by

GARY M. WALTON

Graduate School of Administration
University of California–Davis
Davis, California

JAMES F. SHEPHERD

Department of Economics
Whitman College
Walla Walla, Washington

ACADEMIC PRESS

A Subsidiary of Harcourt Brace Jovanovich, Publishers

New York   London   Toronto   Sydney   San Francisco

The chapters appearing in this work are edited versions of papers originally published in Volume 16 of *Explorations in Economic History*, 1979.

ACADEMIC PRESS, INC.
111 Fifth Avenue, New York, New York 10003

United Kingdom Edition published by
ACADEMIC PRESS, INC. (LONDON) LTD.
24/28 Oval Road, London NW1 7DX

Library of Congress Cataloging in Publication Data
Main entry under title:

Market institutions and economic progress in the New
    South, 1865-1900.

    Bibliography: p.
    1. Southern States--Economic conditions--Addresses,
essays, lectures. 2. Southern States--History- 1865-
--Addresses, essays, lectures. 3. Afro-Americans--
Southern States--Economic conditions--Addresses, essays,
lectures. I. Walton, Gary M. II. Shepherd, James F.
HC107.A13M37   330.976'04   81-15031
ISBN 0-12-733920-5   AACR2

PRINTED IN THE UNITED STATES OF AMERICA

81 82 83 84   9 8 7 6 5 4 3 2 1

Contents

List of Contributors

Numbers in parentheses indicate the pages on which the authors' contributions begin.

STEPHEN J. DeCANIO (103), Department of Economics, University of California–Santa Barbara, Santa Barbara, California 93106

CLAUDIA DALE GOLDIN (3), Department of Economics, University of Pennsylvania, Philadelphia, Pennsylvania 19104

ROGER L. RANSOM (59, 127), Department of Economics, University of California–Riverside, Riverside, California 92502

JOSEPH D. REID, JR. (33), Department of Economics, Virginia Polytechnic Institute and State University, Blacksburg, Virginia 24061

RICHARD SUTCH (59, 127), Department of Economics, University of California–Berkeley, Berkeley, California 94720

PETER TEMIN (25), Department of Economics, Massachusetts Institute of Technology, Cambridge, Massachusetts 02139

GARY M. WALTON (ix), Graduate School of Administration, University of California–Davis, Davis, California 95616

GAVIN WRIGHT (85), Department of Economics, University of Michigan, Ann Arbor, Michigan 48109

Regenerative Failings of the New South:
An Introduction

The issues of economic growth and social change in the Postbellum American South have fascinated and perplexed both scholars and laymen for more than a century. Periodically a substantial study surfaces, such as C. Vann Woodward's classic *The Origins of the New South, 1877–1913* (Louisiana State University Press, 1951), that significantly advances our understanding of the issues. A monumental effort was orchestrated years ago by Roger L. Ransom and Richard Sutch to break new ground and lift further our understanding of the painful aftermath of the American Civil War. As co-directors of the Southern Economic History Project supported by the National Science Foundation, they focused their attention primarily on the "deep South" or "cotton South," giving particularly close scrutiny to the census data of some 27 counties, located principally in South Carolina, Georgia, Mississippi, Alabama, and Louisiana.

This effort, which ultimately culminated in *One Kind of Freedom* (Cambridge University Press, 1977), was followed by a number of other studies, of which some were independent and some were in reaction to their book.

The professional debate that ensued, on issues too numerous to tally here, has been lively indeed, and there can be little doubt that the participants have succeeded in advancing our understanding of the Postbellum South.

The collection of essays comprising this volume present either directly or indirectly the views and findings of nearly all of the major participants in this advance. Besides the chapters and earlier writings of the contributing authors, the works and evidence of many others are discussed in these chapters, including such leading scholars as Woodman (1968, 1977), Higgs (1972, 1973, 1974, 1977, 1978), and Kousser (1974, 1972); recent dissertations, such as those by Hopkins (1978), Mellman (1975), Shlomowitz (1975); the social histories by Swartz (1976 and 1978); and many other contributions, old and new.[1]

However, the principal force behind this professional interchange, as the subtitle to this volume suggests, has been *One Kind of Freedom*. Its primary aim is to

[1]Complete citations are given in the list of references following Chapter 7.

untangle two critical problems: the persistence of economic subjugation of the mass of free black Americans, most of whom lived and died in the Deep South, and the emerging relative backwardness of the Southern Cotton Belt. As Ransom and Sutch state at the outset in *One Kind of Freedom*:

> We were intrigued, first, by the fact that while economists had given considerable attention to the institution of slavery and the economic exploitation of Blacks before the Civil War, they had virtually ignored Black history in the post–Civil War period. It seemed obvious to us that the economic institutions that replaced slavery and the conditions under which ex-slaves were allowed to enter the economic life of the United States for the first time as free agents were of crucial importance to an understanding of the Afro-American experience. We were intrigued also by an as yet unresolved paradox in American economic history. The period between the Civil War and World War I was one of unparalleled economic growth and development for the United States as a whole. Yet the South did not share in this expansion. Southern agriculture stagnated while an agricultural revolution transformed the rest of rural America. The South's industrial sector remained small and backward during the age of American industrial growth. And Southern people—white as well as Black—were among the poorest, least educated, and most deprived of all Americans at a time when America was becoming the richest, best educated, most advanced nation in the world [p. xi].

Focusing first on the initial adjustments and economic results of Emancipation, Ransom and Sutch proceed to explain the subjugation of southern blacks in terms of institutional arrangements allegedly formed for that purpose, namely, share-tenancy and merchant-credit-territorial monopoly. In combination, these institutions harnessed individual tenant farmer's (blacks and whites) efforts and "locked-in" their specialization in cotton farming. Because debt-burdened, tenant farmers were directed by credit merchant "monopolists" to emphasize cash-crop (cotton) production, or were self-motivated toward cotton specialization for the lack of skills in alternative activities, resource use stayed tied to cotton cultivation. In combination, Ransom and Sutch attest, the "lock-in" and "over-production" of cotton stifled economic advance by preventing the process of economic diversification characteristic of other sections of the country.

Most of the debate generated by *One Kind of Freedom* has concentrated on Ransom and Sutch's "institutional explanation" of the methods of coercion and their microeconomic effects. The interchange comprising Part I of this volume adds to this segment of the debate, and focuses specifically on the market institutions affecting credit, labor effort, land use, and management.

Perhaps the relative concentration on micro-issues merits no comment, but Ransom's and Sutch's "institutional explanation" is a curious one, especially for two cliometricians. The continued specialization in cotton in the Deep South in the late nineteenth century is apparent, but was it the result of directives from credit monopolists? Indeed, as Peter W. FitzRandolph has stated:

> The Mercantile Agency data showing that stores were an average of five to nine miles apart, that most storekeepers were neither wealthy when they began store-keeping nor able to accu-

mulate much wealth over time, and that the rates of market entry and failure were both high, is also consistent with, and perhaps better explained by, the hypothesis that Postbellum rural store-keeping was competitive[2]

And, although interest charges on credit were high—precisely how high is a major facet of the debate—if they were monopolistic and not due to risk, what would have prevented entry to exploit the monopoly earnings? As the evidence indicates, entry into merchant-credit activities was high. Alternatively, the persistent specialization in cotton may have stemmed from institutional factors such as illiteracy, poor communications, and immobility, which in combination perpetuated a vicious cycle locking-in labor and hindering economic diversification.

There is a second curious argument, concerning alleged overproduction, that is made by Ransom and Sutch, and reemphasized by Wright (Chapter 5) and by David who argue that the South failed to exploit its position in the world market for cotton:

These price movements during the cotton famine suggest that the South might have benefited through a policy of restricting output during "normal" times. Gavin Wright has estimated that the nature of the demand for American cotton in the antebellum period was such that any price increase stimulated by a reduction in supply would have been approximately proportional in magnitude to the decline in output. This means that a restriction in supply would have increased prices sufficiently so that the total revenue generated by cotton sales would remain largely unaffected despite the reduced volume of production. There would have been a large gain, nevertheless, from adopting a policy of output reduction. Resources would be freed from cotton production for use in other pursuits (such as food production and manufacturing) without reducing the revenue generated from cotton. Moreover, since the same total revenue would have been generated by a reduced quantity of inputs, the profit margin on cotton production would have risen.[3]

Accepting the elasticity measure as unitary and the ironclad logic of their contention, it still remains true that the South had no institutional or governmental means (or political awareness) to effectively coerce and police crop restrictions. It certainly was not in the best interests of individual farmers to restrict cotton production and no means of control existed to realize the aggregate gains to farmers from such restrictions. In short, their economic point is valid and yet unrealistic and ahistorical.

In contrast to Part I, Part II emphasizes that portion of the debate which is far less complete and which offers the most promise for further research. These issues are largely macroeconomic in nature and focus primarily on the questions of sav-

---

[2]Peter W. FitzRandolph, "The Rural Furnishing Merchant in the Postbellum United States: A Study in Spatial Economics," unpublished paper presented at the Twenty-First Annual Cliometrics Conference, University of Chicago, May 15, 1980 (p. 3).

[3]Paul A. David (1979) "Review of *One Kind of Freedom*," *Journal of Economic Literature* **17**, 1469.

ings, investment, and growth in the South and alterations in the distribution of income and wealth by race.

The rapid regeneration of war-torn economies is a phenomenon that is both unique and commonplace. The rapid recovery from war destruction is well documented by economists in modern times, and John Stuart Mill noted it as typical as early as 1848:

> The great rapidity with which countries recover from a state of devastation: . . . an enemy lays waste a country by fire and sword, and destroys or carries away nearly all the moveable wealth existing in it; all the inhabitants are ruined, and yet in a few years after, everything is much as it was before. . . . The possibility of a rapid repair of their disasters, mainly depends on whether the country has been depopulated. If its effective population have not been extirpated at the time, and are not starved afterwards; then, with the same skill and knowledge which they had before, with their land and its permanent improvements undestroyed, and the more durable buildings probably unimpaired, or only partially injured, they have nearly all the requisites for their former amount of production.[4]

And yet when compared to a country's long-run trend rate of growth, the rate of advance in the regenerative period appears uniquely rapid.

The theoretical expectation for rapid regeneration is based on the likelihood of responsive postwar investments in areas suffering disproportionate losses of particular resources such as certain types of capital.[5] For example, the South's railroad network had nearly totally collapsed by war's end, largely due to the lack of rolling stock and partially destroyed track. The roadbed, specialized labor expertise, and considerable track, however, remained in good condition. A region similar to the South in every way, but without a railroad would require an investment in rolling stock, in a complete roadbed, in an entire system of track, and in labor skills. The South, however, required investment in only that track in need of repair plus the rolling stock.

The regenerative spurt is temporary, of course, and comes largely from reemploying existing resources (labor, roadbed, and usable track) temporarily idled for the lack of essential complementary resources (rolling stock and damaged track). When those resources that were destroyed disproportionately are restored and input combinations return to normal the regenerative period ends and the slower long-run trend rate of growth is resumed.

The evidence presented in Chapter 3 of *One Kind of Freedom* confirms the forces of regeneration in the manufacturing and transportation sectors of the South. In agriculture, however, the percentage withdrawal of labor by freed

---

[4]John Stuart Mill (1848), *Principles of Political Economy*, 2 vols. (Boston: Charles C. Little & James Brown); Vol. 1, Chapter 5, Section 7.

[5]For elaboration on the theory of regenerative growth see Donald F. Gordon and Gary M. Walton (1981), "A New Theory of Regenerative Growth and the Post–World War II Experience of West Germany." In R.L. Ransom, R. Sutch, and G.M. Walton (Eds.), *Explorations in the New Economic History: Essays in Honor of Douglass C. North.* New York: Academic Press.

blacks apparently exceeded the losses of physical capital, land, and animals due to war destruction. In this vast sector, the forces of regeneration were snuffed out by reductions of labor effort. Moreover, the fall in output exceeded the labor withdrawal and the gap between actual output and the long-run trend rate of output throughout the 1870s and 1880s exceeded that which can be explained by black labor reductions alone.

Reinforcing the loss of production capacity from labor was the demise of the plantation system, a point stressed by Goldin in Chapter 1. The combination of factors, such as labor intensity, specialization of tasks, and the like, which raised plantation efficiency well above that of small-scale farms, was lost forever. In addition, there were significant losses of entrepreneurial and managerial talent due to the war, and such losses were at least semipermanent in character. A particularly intriguing inquiry awaits the scholar who disentangles these and other sources of lost production capacity and places them in quantitative perspective.

These and other issues, such as why growth rates lagged in the Deep South, will undoubtedly continue to demand the attention of scholars. This volume offers sophisticated yet readable analyses of a host of issues critical to our understanding of the postbellum era and points the way toward needed further research.

GARY M. WALTON

PART I

Market Institutions in the New South

CHAPTER 1

Credit Merchandising in the New South: The Role of Competition and Risk

CLAUDIA DALE GOLDIN

The Thirteenth Amendment provided for an immediate, uncompensated, landless emancipation of an uneducated and substantial population. No one could have expected the transition from slavery to freedom to have been easy, and the historical record substantiates this expectation. The American South was not alone in its difficulties with emancipation. The West Indies, for example, also underwent similar economic changes, including significant declines in per capita income, reductions in the scale of farms, and decreases in the supply of labor.[1] As in the United States case, recovery in terms of the level of per capita income and relative economic position came many decades later. The South is unique, in terms of its postemancipation economy, only in the maintenance and expansion of cotton, its major export. The West Indies moved in the opposite direction diversifying after emancipation, in part because of declining demand for its export, sugar. The economic ills shared by most former slave regions, in particular the sharp drop in measured income followed by an apparent slow recovery, are of primary interest and have been the subject of many works, especially for the American case.[2]

The author gratefully acknowledges the comments of Stanley Engerman, Robert Fogel, William Parker, Roger Ransom, Richard Sutch, and Gavin Wright, on an earlier draft of this paper.
[1] See Engerman (1977a,b) for a discussion of the literature on the West Indies and for comparisons with the United States case.

[2] In addition to Ransom and Sutch's volume, other recent books include DeCanio (1974a), Higgs (1977), and Wright (1978). See Woodman (1977) for an excellent review of this and other literature on the postbellum South.

MARKET INSTITUTIONS AND ECONOMIC PROGRESS
IN THE NEW SOUTH 1865–1900

The latest of these volumes is Roger Ransom and Richard Sutch's *One Kind of Freedom* (1977), a book which attempts to substantiate a dramatic hypothesis about the economic consequences of emancipation in the United States. Their theory, a resurrection of an old theme in American Southern history, is that by 1880 the South had fully recovered economically from the Civil War, but a lack of appropriate institutional arrangements caused it to stagnate for decades after.[3] Within the South, blacks fared far worse than whites, both absolutely and in terms of rates of change. A combination of tenant farming and the need to obtain credit from monopolistic, racist merchants were the main factors keeping a close check on the economic advancement of freedmen:

> Without an endowment of land, capital, or specialized skills, blacks sought to establish their credit in a market controlled by monopolists who refused to accept the possibility that black farmers could be as successful as whites. . . . That the gains were so small and the successes so few can be attributed to the failure of the southern economy to develop a set of institutional arrangements that might have allowed the freed slaves to participate fully in American society (p. 13).

The three primary issues in the book can be outlined, somewhat skeletally, as follows:

1. The Southern economy recovered fully from the Civil War by 1880, and two factors are primarily responsible for changes in measured income per capita between 1860 and 1880.
    (a) Black labor supply declined by 28% to 37% after emancipation.
    (b) The 1860 cotton crop was atypically high and comparisons with that year, in the absence of adjustment, are in error.
2. Tenant farming involved various economic inefficiencies with respect to the allocation of resources, land improvements, and crop production decisions. The burden of these losses fell most heavily on blacks.
3. Merchants extracted surplus income from black farmers, forcing them into perpetual debt peonage.
    (a) Merchants were territorial monopolists in the provision of credit.
    (b) Merchants caused "cotton overproduction," lowering Southern incomes, and charged astronomically high credit prices, keeping black farmers at or near subsistence.

Although much of the book pertains specifically to these issues, data and discussion are presented as well on peripherally related topics: the break-up of the plantation system, the contractual arrangements for vari-

---

[3] Ransom and Sutch's pessimistic portrayal of the Southern economy is remarkably similar to that of M. B. Hammond (1897), Holmes (1893), and Otken (1894), who wrote during particularly bad years for Southern agriculture. The Georgia Department of Agriculture documents (1878–1891) from the 1880s contain, in contrast, optimistic impressions of cotton farming, and even their worst portrayals of farmers' dealings with merchants stress, not the power of the merchant, but the improvidence of the farmers in overextending themselves on frivolities.

ous forms of agricultural tenure, and the changes in the Southern credit and banking sectors after the war. It should also be noted that this book is extremely rich in newly-mined data: The authors have sampled the Federal Population Census manuscripts and linked them to those on agriculture; they have exhaustively searched the Dun and Bradstreet Archives for data on the merchandising business; and they have used several Southern state Department of Agriculture documents, untapped since the late nineteenth century.

I will discuss much of the controversy surrounding issues (1) and (3) but will leave issue (2) to Reid and Wright. The disproportionate space I have allotted to issue (3) reflects its key position in Ransom and Sutch's argument that the failure of the South to develop and of Southern blacks to advance economically were largely the results of malfunctioning credit institutions. Temin's chapter in this volume does further justice to this crucial topic.

Without a doubt the most prominent datum in the economic history of the postbellum South is the striking drop in Southern income and agricultural product per capita following the American Civil War (Engerman, 1966). Although many scholars have attributed this change to the war itself, other factors related to the war, mainly those associated with emancipation, appear at fault (Goldin and Lewis, 1975).[4] Ransom and Sutch contend that the decline in income can be fully explained by just two factors, the reduction in exslave labor and an atypically large cotton crop in 1860. They estimate the withdrawal of labor by freedmen on the dawn of their emancipation to have been between 28 and 37%, and they claim that the 1860 cotton crop was as much as 30% too high (p. 7).

Their thesis on the decline in the black labor supply is part observation and part conjecture, but although the absolute magnitude of this change may be debatable, the direction is clear. A shift to the left in the black labor supply is fully consistent with postbellum planter complaints of a labor shortage, if wages had failed to adjust sufficiently after the war.

The transition from slave to free labor elsewhere was also accompanied by a decline in the supply of labor (Engerman, 1977a,b). But the 28 to 37% figure for the American case may be inflated by an overstatement of the decline in agricultural labor by black women, who spent a portion of their time at household tasks in both slavery and freedom. Ransom and Sutch allow one hour per working day in the 1850s for the caring of children, including nursing and performing of "some of the extras and odd jobs . . . women might have performed after the abolition of slavery (p. 235)." Although it is difficult to know whether slave women working in agriculture spent more than one hour per working day caring for their families, Ransom and Sutch's figures for working time in the 1870s imply

---

[4] Wright (1974) and Temin (1976) stress the role of cotton demand in reducing postbellum Southern incomes, but see Goldin and Lewis (1978) on the possible magnitude of this effect.

that freedmen's wives either engaged in substantially more leisure or spent substantially more time working at household production. Their data (Table C.1) show an increase of 628 hours of leisure per year for adult males but an increase of 1433 hours for adult females. It is difficult to believe that the wives of freedmen so dramatically changed their working time, and it is more likely that in 1870 they spent a substantial fraction of their time engaged in household and garden tasks that were performed when they were slaves by themselves and by other family members.[5] The impact of the decline in the labor supply on per capita income is eventually dependent on the form of the production function. By assuming one of fixed proportions, Ransom and Sutch overstate the importance of their labor supply thesis in rationalizing the change in income per capita.[6]

Not all students of the postbellum South agree with Ransom and Sutch that income per capita stagnated for decades and that the 1860 cotton crop output must be adjusted for abnormally high agricultural productivity. Disagreement on the first point has resulted from varying definitions both of the South and of income. Engermen's per capita income figures (adopted from Easterlin and Gallman) are for commodity output in the entire (Confederate) South.[7] These data are shown in Table 1.1 which gives, as well, Engerman's implied figures for agricultural output only. Goldin and Lewis' estimates of consumption per capita (also based on Easterlin and Gallman) in the Confederate South are listed in column 3. Although all three sets of data show a sharp decline in income per capita from 1859 to 1869, they demonstrate as well substantial growth from 1869 to 1879. The numbers in column 1, for example, yield a decline in commodity output per capita of 4.78% from 1859 to 1869 but an increase of 2.60% average annually from 1869 to 1879. Note that the increase from 1869 to 1879 is diminished to 1.88% average annually if agricultural output, as opposed to all commodity output, is considered. Commodity output produced in the manufacturing and mining sectors grew substantially faster in the postbellum period than that from agriculture.

Ransom and Sutch consider only the five-state rural cotton South for their income per capita figures, which measure crop output per (rural) capita.[8]

[5] The one hour per working day allotment is the difference between the adult male and adult female average hours worked per day in 1850. The figures of 628 and 1433 hours are the differences between the upper bound estimates for hours worked by adult males and females in 1850 and 1870 (*One Kind of Freedom,* Appendix C). If adult females withdrew an amount of labor equal to that for adult males, the labor supply in male equivalent hours would have declined by 20% instead of 28%. The use of the lower bound estimates for hours worked results in a figure of 27% instead of 37%.

[6] See Zepp (1976), for example, on substitution of factors in the antebellum production function. Ransom and Sutch later alter their assumption of a fixed factor technology in their discussion of changing factor ratios under different land tenure arrangements.

[7] Engerman (1966) notes that there is a small difference between income per capita in the Confederate South and in the group of Southern states included in the Easterlin data.

[8] Ransom and Sutch (Appendix F) discuss Easterlin's income estimates, Engerman's use of them, and their own figures for agricultural output for the five-state cotton South.

TABLE 1.1

Per Capita Income Estimates for the Entire South and Five-State Cotton South

	1	2	3	4	5	6	7
	Entire South commodity output, 1879 prices (Engerman)	Entire South agricultural output, 1879 prices (Engerman)	Entire South consumption, in 1860 dollars (Goldin and Lewis)	Five states[a]: crop output, in 1910–1914 dollars (Ransom and Sutch)		Five states: crop output, 1899–1908 prices (Ransom and Sutch)	
Year				Point estimate	Three year average	Point estimate	Three-year average
1859	77.7 (56.7)[b]	69.9(51.0)	86.2 (63.2)	89.4 (65.3)	89.4 (65.3)	71.4 (52.1)	71.4 (52.1)
1869	47.6	42.5	48.5	48.4	48.4	34.8	37.1
1874			52.0	47.9	48.1	38.8	40.6
1879	61.5	51.2	62.0	58.1	53.1	46.2	45.3
1884			68.6	48.2	49.1	43.6	45.1
1889			67.4	63.0	61.1	54.1	52.3
1894			64.8	56.1	55.0	59.6	53.7
1899			78.4	52.7	56.5	51.7	53.7

Notes: Columns 1, 2: Engerman (1966). Population figures for the per capita agricultural output figure are those implied by commodity output data. Column 3: Goldin and Lewis (1975) p. 324. Columns 4–7: Ransom and Sutch, *One Kind of Freedom*, pp. 257–258, Table F.2. Three-year averages are centered on given date except for 1859, which is not a three year average. Per capita refers to rural population.

[a] Alabama, Georgia, Louisiana, Mississippi, and South Carolina.

[b] Figures in parentheses are 1859 per capita income without scale efficiencies and with a reduced labor supply. See text and footnote 8.

These data, given in columns 4 through 7, also exhibit a substantial decline in per capita income from 1859 to 1869, ranging from 6.9 to 5.9% averaged annually. But instead of rising rapidly in the following decade, per capita income in the five-state cotton South increased slowly; the average annual rates of growth in columns 5 and 7 are 0.9 and 2.0%. Growth in per capita terms was smaller for crop output in these five cotton states than for commodity output in the entire South. It is no wonder that migration out of this five-state region dominated labor mobility in the South for many decades after 1870. As Table 1.2 demonstrates, net out-migration from the five-state cotton South exceeded that from all other Southern states. Indeed, many of the migrants from these five states remained in the South, having moved to higher income states.[9]

There is disagreement as well over Ransom and Sutch's contention that the 1860 cotton crop was abnormally high and that it must be adjusted to facilitate comparisons with postbellum crop figures. The cotton crop may have been abnormally high in 1860, but this does not necessarily indicate an atypically high agricultural productivity. At the same time as the output of cotton was high, the production of grains and the number of livestock were low, indicating movement along the agricultural production possibility frontier and not necessarily a movement out.[10]

Even if 1860 had been an atypical year for cotton in terms of productivity, the adjustment of income per capita would depend on the elasticity of demand for cotton. Obviously the more elastic the demand for cotton, the more incomes could have fallen, not risen with a high yield. If Wright's estimate of a unitary elasticity of demand is correct, incomes would in fact be invariant to a high yield. Of course, if, as Wright claims, the demand for cotton increased rapidly in the 1850s and then slowed down, a different conclusion would emerge. At this point, the most one can say is that there is no hard evidence that 1860 witnessed "spectacularly high productivity" (p. 6), and even if it had, per capita incomes may not have been augmented. A comparison between 1860 and 1880 may not be impaired under any circumstances, insofar as Ransom and Sutch claim that incomes in 1880 were abnormally high as well (p. 255).

There was, however, another change concurrent with emancipation that can account for much of the decline in postbellum per capita income. The plantation system, with its gang labor force and coordinated activities, was dissolved not long after the war, and with it went the economies of scale in the production of staple crops that were to be reaped from such organization. Conjectures about scale economies are neither new to the literature (Metzer, 1975; Fogel and Engerman, 1974), nor are they com-

[9] The Ransom and Sutch migration data (p. 196) are also from Vickrey (1969) but are for *gross* out-migration to *non-Southern* states. The exclusion of migrants within the South might be justified, although migration to any state seems most interesting here. The use of gross and not net migration is puzzling.

[10] See Fogel and Engerman (1977, pp. 281–282) on the issue of the 1860 cotton crop.

TABLE 1.2

Net Out-Migration of Black Population from Five Cotton States and the Entire South, 1870 to 1940

	1870–1880	1880–1890	1890–1900	1900–1910	1910–1920	1920–1930	1930–1940
				In thousands			
Alabama	−24.8	−15.9	−23.8	−31.6	−90.8	− 85.9	−79.3
Georgia	−24.4	+ 0.2	−33.1	−39.5	−71.9	−242.6	−88.1
Louisiana	− 3.9	+ 2.1	− 2.7	−19.2	−36.2	− 64.2	−25.2
Mississippi	+20.2	−11.6	− 8.1	−23.8	−13.9	−101.6	−84.0
South Carolina	− 4.6	−28.1	−50.2	−57.2	−73.7	−193.2	−88.2
Total five states	−37.5	−53.3	−117.9	−171.3	−286.5	−687.5	−364.8
Total South	−63.7	−99.5	−170.6	−188.2	−390.7	−865.9	−458.2
			As a percentage of decade average population				
Total five states	1.4	1.6	3.1	3.9	6.2	14.9	7.8
Total South	1.3	1.7	2.4	2.3	4.6	9.6	4.8

Source: Vickrey (1969), Table 41, p. 172, and Table 32, p. 157.

pletely ignored by Ransom and Sutch, who express considerable ambiva-
lence about their existence. Their argument that "there is reason to doubt
the premise that substantial scale-related economies existed in cotton
agriculture before the war" (p. 73), is contradicted just one page later by
their statement that "there was [clearly] some advantage to large-scale
operations" (p. 74). The presence of economies of scale in the antebellum
South is confirmed by much information about plantations (Metzer, 1975)
and is also consistent with the decline in postbellum land values and
measured income. (For an opposing view see Wright, 1978.)

Although Ransom and Sutch have chosen not to use existing estimates
on the relative efficiency of large slave plantations (Fogel and Engerman,
1977), one can employ such data to see "whether the decline in farm size
that accompanied the disappearance of the plantation had a significant
impact on agricultural efficiency" (p. 73). Estimates of the relative efficiency of large farming units indicate that had the distribution of farms in
1859 either by improved acreage, full-hand-equivalents, or total product
been altered to that in 1879, there would have been a drop of about 18% in
product per capita.[11] If there was, in addition, a decrease of 33% in the
slave labor input, per capita income would have fallen by about 27%,

---

[11] One version of an average efficiency index for Southern agriculture is the weighted
harmonic mean of the efficiency indexes (A_i), where the weights are the shares in the total
product (P_i).

$$A_{w_p} = 1/\sum_{i=1}^{4} (P_i(1/A_i)).$$

Such an index implies that in 1860, all the A_i's in each size class were equal to 100 or that
there were no efficiency advantages to larger scale even if farm size did not change. If all
farms have identical land-to-labor ratios one can weight by labor (L_i), or land (I_i),

$$A_{w_L} = \sum_{i=1}^{4} A_i L_i$$

or

$$A_{w_I} = \sum_{i=1}^{4} A_i I_i,$$

and produce results identical to the harmonic index weighted by shares in total product. If
the factor ratios are not identical across farm sizes, these weighted indexes will differ. The
actual differences for the case of Southern agriculture are small because the land-to-labor
ratio did not vary significantly by farm size, although farms with no slaves had fewer
improved acres per full-hand-equivalent than did the other size classes. The results for the
three weighted indexes are:

$$A_{w_p} = 1.215,$$
$$A_{w_L} = 1.202,$$

and

$$A_{w_I} = 1.213,$$

assuming a Cobb–Douglas production function and a decrease in labor constant across farm sizes.[12]

The loss of scale economies and the decline in labor supply reduce the 1859 per capita income figures given in Table 1 to the numbers in parentheses. Even though per capita commodity output in 1879 did not return to its 1859 level, it had indeed exceeded the 1859 level that would have existed with lower labor supply and no scale effects. Emancipation, in causing the reduced scale of farms and the decline in labor supply, produced a substantial "once-and-for-all" decline in per capita incomes. The South, unlike the North, could not easily "catch-up" to its prewar income. Although these losses were not to be regained again in income accounting terms, they were more than recouped by those who chose more leisure and life on a family farm. There was, as Ransom and Sutch note, a "host of other simultaneously occurring phenomena that accompanied emancipation, reconstruction, and the rise of tenancy" (p. 73), but these simple calculations do demonstrate why the South could have lost 27% of measured product.

Even though unraveling the history of Southern income per capita is of fundamental importance, the main point of this volume does not stand or fall on such a resolution. The authors' stated goal is to analyze the "flawed institutions erected in the wake of Confederate defeat" (p. 2.), tenancy and merchandising. Land tenure arrangements have been prominent in both the history and development literature, and a

which have been calculated from the following data:

	A_i	P_i	L_i	I_i
Number of slaves per farm	Efficiency index after correction	Total product (%)	Labor, in full-hand equivalents (%)	Land, in Improved acres (%)
(1) 0	100.0	12.7	19.6	16.0
(2) 1–15	100.8	24.3	29.2	29.5
(3) 16–50	133.1	37.4	31.1	34.6
(4) ≥ 51	147.7	25.7	20.1	20.0

Source: Fogel and Engerman (1977) and data on the distribution of factors and product by farm size from Robert W. Fogel and Stanley L. Engerman.

[12] The 33% figure for the decline in the slave labor supply is the mean of Ransom and Sutch's upper and lower bounds, 28 and 37%. The percentage decline in product resulting from this decrease in slave labor supply is given by

$$\Delta Q/Q = (\Delta L_s/L_s)\,\alpha_1(L_s L_t),$$

where $\Delta L_s/L_s = -33\%$; $\alpha_1 = $ labor's share $= 0.58$; and $L_s/L_t = $ slave labor as a percent of total labor in 1860 $= 0.556$. Therefore, $\Delta Q/Q = -0.106$. Note that a fixed proportion production function would result in $\Delta Q/Q = -0.183$.

thorough evaluation of their economic impact involves examining, among other variables, aspects of risk, the provisions of the actual contracts, changes over time in contractural arrangements, and productivity measures.

For the authors at least, tenancy by itself would not have been as severe an encumbrance for freedmen had it not been for the credit monopoly held by the country store. The merchant is truly the crucial element in Ransom and Sutch's analysis. As they emphasized, monopolistic merchants charged high implicit interest rates on supplies and dictated crop production in cotton, thus assuring themselves a continued and large business. Not only are the merchants accused of maintaining freedmen in a position of subsistence, even more importantly they are given primary responsibility for the economic ills of the South. Nevertheless, careful reflection indicates that the merchants may not have been monopolists, that their high interest rates may have been justifiable on the basis of costs, that if they dictated a crop mix it was, coincidentally, the social optimum, and that they could have played but a minor role in hampering the Southern economy. The discussion will cover, in order, the structure of the merchandising industry, evidence on interest rates from prior studies, the interest rate, and other data in the Georgia Department of Agriculture and the North Carolina Bureau of Labor Statistics documents—materials which form the basis of the merchant thesis, the relationship between the merchant and the landlord, and the issues of "cotton overproduction" and the "lock-in" mechanism (detailed more fully in Ransom and Suth, 1972, 1975b).

The ability of the merchants to charge high implicit interest rates and to manipulate the farmers' choice of crops derived, according to Ransom and Sutch, from their monopolistic positions. Each merchant had a territorial monopoly caused by the consumers' high costs of "shopping around." Even though the costs of information were high for the farmers, the cost for firms to enter the merchandising business were small. The equilibrium firm size was between $5,000 and $10,000, in terms of the pecuniary strength of the owner (p.138), and stores both entered and exited frequently. The growth in the number of stores in the cotton South was quite rapid, with an 18.5% average annual rate of increase between 1870 and 1875, 4.9% between 1875 and 1880, and 7.8% between 1880 and 1885. But, according to the authors, the entrants did not place themselves "in a location that would bring them into strong direct competition with existing firms" (p. 140). Ransom and Sutch thus imply that there were large numbers of farmers who had virtually no access to a merchant prior to the appearance of one of these new entrants. Despite evidence arguing for a highly competitive industry, Ransom and Sutch contend that merchants had virtual territorial monopolies.

Evidence gathered from the Dun Mercantile Agency credit ledgers on the structure of the merchandising business forms by itself an important chapter in Southern economic history. Although the authors have creatively employed these records, these documents give no direct support for the monopolistic position ascribed to the firms. Entry into the merchandising business was far too rapid, failure too great, and the authors' hypothetical distances between the firms may overstate the case against competition. Even though the evidence on industrial structure is not entirely convincing, it is the data on implicit interest rates that forms the corpus of their argument. "A strong prima facie case that southern merchants held a territorial monopoly can be pressed simply on the evidence that merchants charged rates of interest for credit that were far in excess of the opportunity cost of capital" (p. 144).

Inefficiency and monopoly is hard to detect from industrial structure alone, but as long as price is above marginal cost, monopoly is present in some guise. The existence of excessive rates of implicit interest on credit is therefore the key issue in evaluating Ransom and Sutch's main thesis. The primary sources drawn upon by the authors are the Georgia and Louisiana Department of Agriculture Reports (cited as well in M. B. Hammond, 1897), although other records have been used by previous researchers. The implicit interest rate data from the Georgia and Louisiana reports must be interpreted in conjunction with additional information contained in these records but not used extensively by Ransom and Sutch. This evidence includes the riskiness of loans, the fraction of farmers buying on credit, the percentage of yearly supplies purchased from merchants, the role of the landlord in furnishing tenants, the trend in tenant indebtedness, and the existence of racial differences.

Rates of interest charged by country stores have been collected haphazardly by various researchers who unsystematically searched extant store records for such information. (For example, Clark, 1944, took little interest in the price of credit.) The Georgia and Louisiana data are possibly the most complete and reliable sources for such data, but certain rates of interest reported in other studies are at variance with those contained in the state reports. Sisk (1955) found interest rates from store accounts ranging from 8 to 15% per annum in Dallas County and 10 to 25% in Shorters, Alabama. Although his sample is meager, his data provide a strong contrast to the 60% implicit interest rate calculated from the Georgia reports. The interest rates reported by Bull (1952) also do not conform entirely to those from the state reports, but the length of the loans and the existence of other fees are not made clear in her work.

The data on cash and credit prices from the Georgia and Louisiana Departments of Agriculture are, for the present, the most accessible information on implicit interest rates. All costs, including commissions, fees, and interest are included in the reported credit prices, and the length of the loans was usually six months. (Note that the Georgia Department of Agriculture Supplemental Crop Report for 1880 explicitly stated that "it is assumed that the average time for which advances are made is six months" (p. 6).)

Even though the cash and credit prices in the state reports imply an annual interest rate in excess of 60%, much more information is required before such data can be used to indict the merchant for the economic condition of the South.[13] The economic impact of these prices can only be determined with information on the percentage of total supplies consumed that were purchased on time. The Georgia Department of Agriculture also recognized the importance of this auxiliary information and asked several pertinent questions at the time the cash and credit prices for crops and supplies were collected. Although these questions varied somewhat from year to year and were often expressed in terms of annual changes, not in the more convenient form of absolute amounts, these data must be used in conjunction with those on prices. These additional facts, presented below, demonstrate that during this time period less than 20% of all supplies consumed were purchased on credit.

Ransom and Sutch contend on the contrary that "[f]armers rarely paid cash for the goods they bought" (p. 123). Their calculation of the material income of black tenant-farm operatives deflates the entire food budget, that is, 60% of the family's total consumption, by the computed cash or credit indexes (pp. 169 and 218). Such a computation implicitly assumes that *all* farmers purchased *all* of their required corn and bacon. But the 1878 and 1879 Georgia Department of Agriculture April Crop Reports showed that 56 and 60%, respectively, of the supplies purchased by farmers, were purchased on time, and the 1881 April Crop Report stated that 66, 60, and 84% of all farmers bought some bacon, corn, and hay, respectively.[14] Furthermore, many farmers in the state had sufficient supplies on hand at the beginning of the season to last them for the following year; on average about two-thirds to three-quarters of all the Georgia counties' supplies were home produced, see Table 1.3, line 1. (Note that M. B. Hammond, 1897, included much of this information in his presentation of the cash and credit prices.)

[13] Ransom and Sutch arrive at their 60% (actually 59.4%) figure by taking the average credit price of a bushel of corn, dividing it by the average cash price of a bushel of corn and then multiplying that number by 2. They doubled the rate under the assumption that the loan was paid back in at least six months time. (See their Appendix D and Tables 7.1 and 7.2).

[14] These figures from the April Crop Reports are not given in Table 3. They are somewhat scattered numbers which did not appear, as did the others, in an organized fashion from year to year. The first two figures can be found on p. 4 of the 1878 and 1879 April Crop Report and the three numbers for 1881 are from Table 1 on an unnumbered page. The 1878 April Crop Report specifically stated that these percentages applied to all supplies purchased, not to all supplies consumed (p. 4).

TABLE 1.3

Information from the Georgia Department of Agriculture Crop Reports, 1878 to 1890, State Averages

Source	1878	1879	1880	1881	1882	1883	1884	1885	1886	1887	1888	1889	1890
1. Percentage of full supply of provisions for year (t + 1) as reported in year (t)													
MCR[a]									74[b] 75[d]	66[b] 77[d]	71[b] 74[d]	65[b] 69[d]	75[b] 79[d]
SCR	83[a]	75[a]	71[a]	n.a.	98[b] 59[c]	82[b] 68[c]	66[c]	60[c]	62[c]	62[c]	61[c]	63[c]	63[c]
2. Indebtedness in winter of year (t) compared to winter of year (t-1)													
SCR	n.a.	0.82	0.82	n.a.	0.76	0.88	0.98	0.88	0.98	0.85	0.84	0.77	0.80
3. Supplies purchased in year (t) as a percent of those purchased in (t-1)													
ACR	75[f]	78[f]	n.a.	n.a.	84[b] 55[d]	36[b] 28[d]							
SCR						76[g]	94[g]	89[g]	88[g]	85[g]	88[g]	77[g]	78[g]

Source: Georgia (1878–1891), where ACR = April Crop Report for year given, MCR = May Crop Report for year given (replaced April Crop Report), SCR = Supplemental Crop Report, an end of season report written in December. n.a. = not available for that year.

[a] All supplies.
[b] Corn.
[c] Pork.
[d] Hay.
[e] "Supplies on hand May 1."
[f] Corn and bacon.
[g] "Supplies." Note that the difference between the 1883 ACR and the 1883 SCR figures probably indicates that farmers purchased supplies after April of that year. The SCR figures are end-of-year tallies.

Therefore, the high implicit interest rates reported in these documents could only have been paid by the 70% of all farmers who bought some fraction of their supplies.[15] Farmers purchased only supplies that were not home produced, that is, only about 30% of the total supplies they used per year. Furthermore, farmers who purchased supplies, bought, perhaps at a maximum, 60% of these on time. A farmer in Georgia could have expected, therefore, to purchase only 18% of his total supplies on time.[16] These data directly contradict the contention that credit was universally the rule in the South. These figures err perhaps by not illuminating the many inequities of the merchandising system. Those whose crops failed and whose hogs died of cholera were forced to purchase supplies and, most likely, were required by financial circumstances to buy on time. The farmers' dependence on purchased supplies appears from Table 1.3, line 3. to have declined steadily over the period, a fact that was commented upon extensively by the Commissioner and his correspondents. According to these data, farmers in 1890 actually purchased only 25% of what they had in 1882.[17] These data from the Georgia reports do not indicate the general lack of supplies and widespread use of credit that Ransom and Sutch have claimed. In fact, this information sheds additional light on the high interest rates computed from reports. Farmers heavily dependent on the merchant for supplies may have been riskier than others who had succeeded in growing their own supplies. The high implicit interest rates may have applied only to those farmers whose risk could not be reduced. Furthermore, as Temin aptly notes, the seasonality of the credit business meant that much of the merchant's capital was idle for about six months, and the yearly interest rate of 30% might be the more appropriate implicit price of credit.

The Georgia Department of Agriculture also published data on the indebtedness of farmers in the winter of a particular year as compared to the previous winter; see Table 1.3, line 2. Although it is not clear whether this index refers to the number of farmers in debt or the amount of debt they accumulated, it clearly and continuously declined over the years contained in Table 1.3.[18] The fact that farmers were in debt in the winter

[15] The 70% figure is an average of the three numbers in the 1881 April Crop Report, 66, 60, and 84%.

[16] If 70% of the farmers purchased some supplies and if 30% of the total supplies used by all were purchased, then, assuming equal consumption by all farmers, the 70% who bought goods purchased on average 43% of their wares. About 60% of these goods were purchased on time. Therefore, farmers who bought supplies purchased (0.43) (0.60) = 25.8% of them on time. The average farmer could expect ex ante, to purchase 18% of his supplies on time, (0.60) (0.30).

[17] This calculation uses only the Supplemental Crop Report (SCR) figures in Table 3, line 3, and is the product of the percentages from 1883 to 1890.

[18] Note that the trends in the aggregate figures for indebtedness in Georgia do not change if regions are used. Therefore, it is not the case that the absence of a weighting procedure for

raises another question in interpreting the high implicit interest rates. Merchants may have charged high credit prices because it was risky to hold debts into the following year and beyond. Although the normal time period for the loans was six months, some remained unpaid until the following year with no apparent change in rates.

The role of risk did not escape the Commissioner of Agriculture in Georgia, who reported in the 1887 Supplemental Crop Report that: "It is not altogether the merchants fault that such prices are demanded. In many instances the farmer could make arrangements to pay *cash,* if he would. The risk on such sales is exceptionally hazardous, and the seller must charge such a percentage on time sales as will save him from loss at the hands of those who fail to pay, or pay at the end of expensive litigation" (p. 141). The Bureau of Labor Statistics in North Carolina was also concerned with credit and risk and, in 1887, published a report on crops and labor conditions. Those who designed this survey recognized even more clearly than those in Georgia the problem of risk, and they ascertained that fully 25% of tenants did not "pay out."[19] This high percentage of defaults or extensions of credit can explain large differences between the credit and cash prices for supplies.[20]

The reports of both the Georgia Commissioner of Agriculture and the North Carolina Bureau of Labor Statistics frequently urged farmers to raise their own supplies. But the primary reason given by Ransom and Sutch for this advice, the avoidance of credit prices, was only one of many stressed in the reports. The Georgia Commissioner, for example, frowned on importing corn and bacon from the West, invoking a version of the multiplier hypothesis with his exhortation in 1886 that corn and

county data has distorted the indebted picture. The regional data for Georgia are as follows.

Indebtedness (D_t) in Winter of Year (t) Compared to Winter of Year $(t-1)$

Region	1879	1880	1881	1882	1883	1884	1885	1886	1887	1888	1889	1890	$\Pi_t D_t$
N. Georgia	0.82	0.71	n.a.	0.80	0.95	1.04	0.98	1.01	0.85	0.82	0.90	0.78	0.223
S. W. Georgia	0.88	0.96	n.a.	0.68	0.92	0.91	0.92	0.88	0.92	1.01	0.73	0.84	0.222
E. Georgia	0.69	0.78	n.a.	0.74	0.94	0.79	1.02	1.02	0.86	0.85	0.72	0.90	0.146
S.E. Georgia	0.81	0.65	n.a.	0.65	0.78	0.83	0.84	1.03	0.87	0.98	0.77	0.80	0.101
Mid Georgia	0.85	0.85	n.a.	0.81	0.83	0.90	0.66	0.96	0.77	0.52	0.71	0.68	0.054

Source: See Table 1.3.

Note: Computation of $\Pi_t D_t$ has assumed 1881 = 1.00 for all regions and gives the cumulative indebtedness by region.

[19] This number is an unweighted county average from W. N. Jones, North Carolina Bureau of Labor Statistics (1887, pp. 82–85). The report did not note whether "paying out" referred to the merchants or the landlords or both.

[20] Although Ransom and Sutch discuss the issue of risk in Appendix D and in Chapter 7, their only evidence on the default rate is a survey of general stores in Louisiana made in 1926 (footnote 10, p. 344). They have no direct information on the number of failures to repay, the length of the payment period, and the administrative costs when there was default.

bacon "may be profitably produced at home, and that the money . . . expended for such supplies outside the State, is an unnecessary and damaging drain on our resources" (Supplemental Crop Report, 1886, p. 435). In 1890 the same commissioner advised farmers not to plant cotton because the consequence of a large cotton crop was "ruinously low prices for this staple . . ." (Supplemental Crop Report, 1890, p. 18).[21]

The cash and time prices for corn and bacon taken from the Georgia reports by Ransom and Sutch appear, at first, to be rather compelling evidence for a merchant monopoly in credit. But when viewed together with other information in these documents, their interpretation becomes somewhat different. The percentage of farmers and farm income on which these prices actually prevailed is far less than suggested by Ransom and Sutch, and the condition of farmers with regard to debt and dependence on purchases was improving not deteriorating. The reasons for these high time prices given in the reports are at variance with Ransom and Sutch's statements. Risk, and not monopoly, was constantly stressed by those living at the time and observing the different prices. Most importantly, the statements of farm correspondents directly quoted in these documents never mentioned differences in interest rates or in quantities purchased on time with regard to race or tenure, although several explicitly racist remarks were made about "improvident" black farmers. The North Carolina report specifically inquired as to differential economic treatment by race, and only a very small percentage of the correspondents reported any. It seems that little evidence is contained in the Georgia Department of Agriculture reports substantiating a merchant monopoly and support- ing Ransom and Sutch's bold conclusions about the role of the merchan- dising business in the economic history of the South.

Numerous authors have written about the interest rates charged by merchants, and they have almost uniformly attributed high prices to problems in ascertaining risk. The South was merely an underdeveloped country within a more developed universe, and the real cost of capital far exceeded Ransom and Sutch's basis, "short-term interest rates in New York City" (p. 130). M. B. Hammond, whose book provided the original reference to the Georgia and Louisiana reports, rationalized the high implicit interest rates in those records on grounds of excessive risk. "[I]t is questionable whether the business of merchandising . . . presents such great possibilities of becoming speedily wealthy as the above price quota- tions would seem to indicate . . . The danger of losses . . . has been the prime cause of the great difference between cash and 'time' prices" (M. B. Hammond, 1897, p. 156). H. Hammond, agreed, "a mortgage given in January or February, on a crop not to be planted until April, is not taken

---

[21] See Wright and Kunreuther (1975) and DeCanio (1973, 1974) on this interpretation of "cotton overproduction," which DeCanio rejects as a valid explanation of contemporary statements.

as a first-class commercial security, and consequently the charges on the advances are heavy'' (H. Hammond, 1883, p. 82). Thomas Janes, the Georgia Commissioner of Agriculture in 1878, remarked on his own June Crop Report that "the percent charged on credit sales is largely the measure of the risk incurred" (Georgia, 1878, p. 11). Even Otken (1894, pp. 18–29), who condemned the Southern credit system, placed the blame for exhorbitant interest rates on risk not monopoly. Numerous other references concurring with these judgments of the credit system are given in Higgs (1977, pp. 56–57).

It is also useful to consider what portion of the rate charged for credit was ascribable to the riskless cost of short-term capital in the South, claimed by Ransom and Sutch to be, at a maximum, 10% (p. 130). Interest rate ceilings in various Southern states encouraged the charging of fees and commissions, and, in the case of merchants, the use of credit prices, not explicit interest rates.[22] M. B. Hammond (1897, pp. 164–165) reported various pricing schemes used by Georgia banks and loan agencies which charged commissions and fees or discounted the principal and interest. These policies resulted in rates ranging from 15 to 18%, with the lower rate applying to longer-term loans secured with real estate. The short-term borrowing rate from banks on secured capital appeared to be about 18% in the postbellum South. Land prices, even in the 1880s, were often no more than four or five times their rental values. Although there are many factors which might account for the depressed price of land, the high cost of capital could have been a prime cause.[23]

The apparently large differences between the cash and credit prices for supplies can be explained by several factors, none of which is predicated on a local merchant monopoly in credit. The actual opportunity cost of merchant capital may have been closer to 30 than 60%, depending upon the seasonality of credit and the length of the loans. The risks entailed appear to have been great with a significant fraction of borrowers not paying out, and even the riskless cost of capital in the South was quite high.

Even if one assumes that merchants had territorial monopolies, it is difficult to imagine landowners allowing them to extract most of the labor surplus from black tenant farmers. There were times when landowners were in a precarious financial position and were forced into relinquishing liens to the merchants. But, as M. B. Hammond noted (1897, p. 147), liens were signed over by landlords "during the era of low prices," and this

[22] According to M. B. Hammond (1897), "usury laws in all the states prohibit the taking of interest in excess of fixed maximum rates, but everyone familiar with legislation regarding usury knows how easily these laws are evaded" (p. 164).

[23] Note that a high interest rate in the South is consistent with Davis (1965), and with Swierenga's (1976) finding of short term credit rates of 3 to 5% per month in late nineteenth century Iowa (p. 7).

was considered an unusual practice reserved for unusually bad times. Jonathan Wiener's (1975) study of planters and merchants in Alabama clearly shows the rivalry between these two groups and points to the eventual success of the black belt landlords in altering crop lien laws to their advantage. Most importantly, merchants were not the only source of credit in the postbellum South. Landlords as well performed the function of advancing funds, even though this fact has not received much attention by Ransom and Sutch.[24] Landlords in North Carolina in 1887 charged, on average, 19% above the cash price, at the same time the merchants were reported to have charged 35% (Jones, 1887, pp. 82–85). Wiener and Sisk, both writing on Alabama, underscored the landlords' role as a credit source, and the latter author stated that the "tenant might look to his landlord for advances necessary to keep him going from one harvest to the next. . . . A very common practice was for the landlord to make arrangements at a store for 'advancing' all his tenants" (Sick, 1955, p. 706).

According to Ransom and Sutch, the merchants played a dual role in the elaborate scenario of maintaining blacks in poverty. Not only did they presumably charge exorbitant prices for supplies, but they have also been portrayed as the cause of "cotton overproduction" and economic inefficiency. There is no doubt that the South produced relatively more cotton than corn in 1880 than it did in 1860. It is less clear why this change occurred, whether it was merely a continuation of an antebellum trend, the result of transport changes and of Midwestern developments, or the product of postbellum "cotton overproduction."

The term "cotton overproduction" has been used in a variety of ways by contemporaries of the postbellum period and by many latter-day authors, and there seems to be much confusion about its meaning. DeCanio (1973, 1974a) and Wright and Kunreuther (1975) discuss rationalizing contemporary statements about cotton overproduction by noting that with a low short-run price elasticity of demand, total revenues would rise with a reduced crop. Wright and Kunreuther (1975), (for an opposing view see McGuire and Higgs, 1977, to which Wright and Kunreuther have replied, 1977) appeal to the emergence of a group of "gambler-farmers" who purchased the chance to escape tenancy by accepting the greater risk of a nondiversified crop. Some contemporary authors seem to be using the term "overproduction" to describe the relative production of cotton and corn evaluated at the credit price ratio for both. If farmers purchased at the credit price ratio but sold at the cash price ratio, they might have wanted to produce relatively more corn but were forced to produce a crop mix consistent with the cash price ratio.

---

[24] Ransom and Sutch do note that planters furnished their tenants supplies during especially bad times (pp. 146–148).

Ransom and Sutch define cotton "overproduction" in two ways and their position on both is most clearly stated in Ransom and Sutch (1975). They contend that some merchants coerced farmers to produce more cotton relative to corn than had these farmers been free agents, faced with the unconstrained or cash price ratios for the two crops. But they also state that "cotton overproduction" resulted at times from the merchant dictating production consistent with the cash price ratio. The latter definition of "cotton overproduction" implies that merchants coerced farmers to produce a socially optimum mix, and I shall, therefore, focus on the former definition which implies that merchants caused farmers to produce a product mix that differed from the social optimum.

Neither Ransom and Sutch nor Bull (1952) has found crop liens which specified that cotton be planted in preference to corn. The North Carolina Bureau of Labor Statistics Report for 1887 indicated that merchants did demand cotton but not for the reasons given by Ransom and Sutch. Merchants insisted on cotton because of the lower transaction costs of dealing in it. "Cotton is as easily handled almost as money, and therefore the merchant wants cotton for his supplies. He does not want hay, clover, grain, potatoes, etc., they are too much trouble to handle, and when a farmer proposes to raise these articles, it is impossible to get supplies from a merchant" (Jones, 1887, p. 76).

The crucial issue is not only what merchants actually did, but also whether even monopolistic merchants would have wanted to force tenants into overproducing cotton, in the absence of transactions costs differences between cotton and other crops. To prove that a "lock-in" mechanism existed, forcing farmers first into cotton and then into debt peonage, Ransom and Sutch (1975) develop a model which rests on one critical assumption. They assume the monopolistic merchants faced a "limit" corn-to-cotton price ratio that they could charge. Any price above this limit would be unprofitable, either because of merchant entry or because farmers would find it paid to "shop around." The actual corn-to-cotton price ratio was monopolistically set somewhere between the competitive ratio and this upper bound. The other, less crucial, constraints in their model are that farmers are required to have a specified amount of corn at the beginning of each season and that merchants must always leave farmers with some, subsistence, income at the end of the trade. These last two assumptions are innocuous, The first is not, however, for it allows Ransom and Sutch to prove that merchants have an incentive to force farmers into producing relatively more cotton than the farmers would otherwise have produced, given the competitive or cash price ratio. The merchant gets more business at the constrained price by selling more corn monopolistically and is, therefore, better off by having the farmers "overproduce" cotton.

Dong (1976) has demonstrated that merchants can always do better by having the farmers produce where the competitive price ratio is tangent to their corn–cotton production possibility frontier and by charging them a higher corn-to-cotton price ratio than that given by the limit one assumed by Ransom and Sutch. To assume that this limit price ratio exists but that merchants have the power to force cotton production at the expense of corn, is to imply that farmers and/or potential entrants into the merchandising business experience price illusion. A potential entrant not only observes prices but also the quantities sold, to arrive at the complete profit picture in deciding whether or not to enter. Farmers not only notice prices but are also aware of production restrictions, in computing the implicit prices they are paying for supplies. The two constraints Ransom and Sutch claim merchants employed would not maximize profits in the absence of price illusion. Only production at the competitive equilibrium point would, unless that point involved the production of the minimum corn requirements. Merchants who had some monopoly power, derived from their locational advantage, could exercise it best by letting farmers produce the optimal mix of cotton and corn, given the free market price ratio. But since the farmers' purchase or credit price ratio of corn to cotton was above that which dictated production decisions, it logically appeared to some contemporary observers that there was "cotton overproduction."

Note that the argument raised earlier about the presence of higher transactions costs for selling crops other than cotton implies that the price ratio of cotton-to-corn *net* of these costs was made steeper. Even a competitive merchant would, under these circumstances, demand that tenants produce relatively more cotton than these farmers might otherwise desire. Such a situation might appear from the farmers' point of view to be coercive, resulting in "overproduction" of cotton, even though it was the logical outcome of higher costs for the merchant.

The role of the merchant both in exploiting farmers and in rearranging production decisions is not at all clear. There were obviously many varieties of merchants with regard to honesty, competitiveness, and landholdings; their only common bond being the wares they sold. Perhaps an investigation of the extant general store records and the liens filed in the county courthouses will discover more of the facts concerning the merchant.

There are two related economic consequences of monopoly. A monopolist can redistribute factor payments and can, as well, allocate economic resources inefficiently. There is no a priori reason for both of these effects to be large, and even though the redistribution of income could seriously harm some individuals, the impact on per capita income and growth could be small. Ransom and Sutch contend that monopolistic merchants caused both redistributive harm and allocative inefficiencies. It is possible that a merchant monopoly could have resulted in a redistribution of income, although the material presented here argues otherwise. But there is no basis for the claim that the dead weight social loss of a merchant monopoly was large and was growing over time. The quantity of foodstuffs demanded was relatively insensitive to price but high in the aggregate, and the supply of labor was probably not very wage elastic.

Nevertheless, the postbellum South did experience substantial economic change: There was growth in real per capita income, even for blacks, there were educational advancements for the children of freedmen, there were changes in the forms of tenancy, there were class struggles between landlords and merchants, and finally there was disfranchisement, which curtailed many of the positive economic changes preceding it.

Although Ransom and Sutch focus on the increase in the freedman's economic well-being over that of a slave, they do not ascertain the growth in the standard of living of blacks beyond that initial transition. Robert Higgs (1977, p. 102) has attempted to estimate this change from 1868 to 1900 and concludes that income per capita of all Southern blacks increased by about 2.7% average annually, a figure in excess of that for whites. Whether this is a large or small number depends on one's reference point, and studies of the economic mobility of propertyless immigrants in Northern cities may provide some basis for comparison. Still, Higgs' figures demonstrate that change was possible, even in what was undeniably an environment filled with constraints.

Surely the greatest hope for black advancement was in education, and disfranchisement at the turn of the twentieth century reversed the initial progress (Kousser, 1974). Prior to this governmental repression, blacks in many states received positive monetary transfers from whites. Their schooling may have been of a lower quality, but blacks, at least in North Carolina, received more schooling per tax dollar contribution than did whites (Kousser, 1977). These positive transfers, in Kousser's terminology "black balance of payments," ended with disfranchisement and, at times, even became negative. The state, not the merchant, was the racist strong-arm of the people.

Many of the issues omitted in Ransom and Sutch's book have been argued elsewhere by Higgs, DeCanio, and Kousser, writers who have stressed the role of the market in providing competition and the state in enabling coercion. Ransom and Sutch take an opposing position and view the individual as having the power to coerce and the market as failing miserably. One would like to have more of a blending of these two positions, for emancipation was not one kind of freedom; it was many.

CHAPTER 2

Freedom and Coercion:

Notes on the Analysis of Debt Peonage in *One Kind of Freedom*

PETER TEMIN

The history of the American South is in large part a history of coercion, whether overtly and legally through slavery, Black Codes, and Jim Crow laws, or through less open and legal means. The attempt by Americans to look at this coercion has proven difficult. Authors are concerned alternately to minimize and justify or exaggerate and condemn it; a balanced view appears to require an elusive aloofness.

The trend in Southern history writings since the Second World War has been to emphasize the coercive nature of Southern institutions. Opposing a long-standing tradition that emphasized the paternalistic, even pedagogical, nature of slavery, Stampp (1956) and Elkins (1959) concentrated their attention and the attention of scholars who followed them on the conflicts in slavery. Interpreting observed characteristics of slave behavior as resistance to the owners authority, Stampp sought to describe and Elkins to explain the nature and origin of the conflict. Woodward (1951) set a similar tone in the study of the postbellum South, emphasizing the continuance of coercion after the demise of slavery by both legal and nonlegal means.

One Kind of Freedom continues in this recent tradition. Ransom and Sutch have concentrated on the coercive aspects of the postbellum agricultural economy. Their thesis, as reflected in their title, is that the freedom conferred upon American slaves by the Emancipation Proclamation was of a peculiarly limited kind. The abolition of Southern slavery reduced, but hardly eliminated the exploitation of blacks by whites, according to Ransom and Sutch.

Nevertheless, they have overestimated the extent of coercion in postbellum Southern agriculture. I do not wish to assert that coercion was

25

MARKET INSTITUTIONS AND ECONOMIC PROGRESS
IN THE NEW SOUTH 1865–1900

absent or unimportant; it clearly was not. I want instead to show that the evidence presented by Ransom and Sutch is compatible with historical stories which do not involve the degree of coercion Ransom and Sutch say was present. My disagreement therefore is one of degree not of kind. It concerns Ransom and Sutch's measurement of the degree of coercion present in the postbellum South. Specifically, I will argue that the "overproduction" of cotton noted prominently in Chap. 8, as Ransom and Sutch implicitly acknowledge in passing (pp. 167–68), may not have been present.

The argument will start from generalities and get more and more specific and technical. A subsidiary theme of this chapter is that even the most technical choices made by historical investigators reflect their underlying point of view. (To avoid confusion, let me emphasize that I do not say this is bad; rather, it is inevitable.) Concluding comments will return to the original level of generality to recast the technical conclusions in more accessible form.

Ransom and Sutch summarize their argument on overproduction clearly (p. 165):

> The paradox of why free farmers in the New South ignored the widely publicized incentives to turn to self-sufficiency is easily resolved by an explanation that argues farmers were not, in fact, "free." Farmers grew cotton rather than food because the will of the merchant prevailed over the interests of the farmer.

The language used by Ransom and Sutch reveals their underlying construction of the postbellum economy. They assume that the interests of the merchants and the farmers differed and conflicted. Given the existence of this conflict, the actual pattern of behavior could not have been in the interests of both farmer and merchant. It had to be in at most one group's interest. The paradox then is why farmers were not acting in their own interests, with the implication that they were acting in the merchants'. The paradox is resolved by asserting that freedmen were not "free."

Ransom and Sutch do not mean that emancipation was a nonevent or a cruel joke. They wish to say that it only partially redressed the balance between whites and blacks. At this level of abstraction, no one can disagree. But when we come to delimit the extent of the postbellum farmer's "unfreedom," room for disagreement is created.

How did the interests of the farmers and merchants conflict? For any given level and pattern of production, there was conflict over the distribution of income. Higher prices for merchandise bought by the farmers and for credit with which to buy it meant more income for the merchants and less for the farmers. Ransom and Sutch argue that merchants earned 60% on credit advanced to farmers (p. 130), increasing their income and decreasing the farmers'.

Ransom and Sutch do not stop here. They also argue, as shown in the quotation, that the merchants prevailed upon the farmers to grow too much cotton. This is the overproduction of cotton mentioned above and frequently in the text of *One Kind of Freedom*. It is unlike distribution, for a misallocation of resources—planting too much cotton—implies a loss in efficiency and a decline in the aggregate income of merchants and farmers. On the assumption that a greater aggregate income meant a larger income for merchants, the argument must be that the merchants were willing to forego income "to thwart the farmer's quest for independence" (p. 163). The foregone production provides an index of the extent of the coercion described in *One Kind Of Freedom*.

This is a strong conclusion. Ransom and Sutch assert that the desire for dominance was not solely for economic gain, since the merchants sacrificed part of their economic gains to maintain dominance. The argument brings to mind all sorts of questions about the merchants' motivations, their knowledge, and their ability to enforce their will through postbellum institutions.

But before proceeding to speculate about the answers to these questions, we need to examine the evidence for cotton overproduction in order to connect these questions with the historical events. And here we must begin our descent into the technical depths. In the choice between two products, productive efficiency is achieved when the ratio at which the two products can be "transformed" into each other by reducing the production of one and allocating the freed resources to the production of the other equals the rate at which they can be exchanged for one another in the market. In any other circumstance, greater income can be gained by changing the proportions of each product produced.

Ransom and Sutch argue that the rate at which cotton and corn could be transformed into each other by reallocating farm land and labor differed from the rate at which they could be exchanged in the market. They infer from this finding that there was a clear incentive for the farmers to reallocate their land and labor from the production of cotton to the production of corn.

Ransom and Sutch calculate the "physical trade-off between crops" from data on farm outputs (pp. 166–67). In making this calculation, Ransom and Sutch assume that the scarce factor in a farm's production was labor, not land. Wright and Kunreuther (1975), however, argue that land was scarce to the individual sharecropper. This is an important difference because both sets of authors agree that the labor needed to grow one acre of cotton could grow two acres of corn. Lack of agricultural expertise precludes an exploration of this line of argument here. Let us accept Ransom and Sutch's calculation of the physical trade-off between cotton and corn for the purposes of this discussion with the comment that if Wright and Kunreuther are right, this change would strengthen the argument made here.

The rate of exchange of corn and cotton poses more problems. The price of cotton is clear, but the price of corn is not. Ransom and Sutch have a choice of the cash price or the credit price of corn. They use the credit price, and conclude that the farmer who paid credit prices for corn could have increased his income (at the margin) by approximately 30% by shifting his production out of cotton into corn (p. 167). They note elsewhere that the two prices for corn differ by approximately 30% as well (p. 129). It follows that if *cash* prices for corn are used, the incentive for the farmer to reduce his production of cotton in favor of growing more corn vanishes. As Ransom and Sutch themselves state (p. 167):

> As one would expect, the retail prices of corn and cotton reflected the relative productivity of labor in producing these two crops.

Equivalently, the ability of farmers to transform cotton into corn through reallocation of their own labor and land reflected the retail prices of these two products.

In short, by using credit prices, Ransom and Sutch have found cotton overproduction. This overproduction provides evidence of coercion, since farmers would not have chosen to overproduce cotton on their own. Going further, it provides evidence of heavy coercion, since the power of the merchants was pitted against the power of the market. But if cash prices are used, Ransom and Sutch's evidence of overproduction and merchant coercion disappears. Clearly, the choice of which corn price to use is critical to the argument.

One Kind of Freedom does not contain an explicit argument for using the credit price rather than the cash price. The discussion of overproduction in the book is based on an article by Ransom and Sutch (1975), and the argument is made there. After calculating the quantity of corn that could be grown with labor released from cotton cultivation, Ransom and Sutch say (p. 424):

> Since this added corn output would free the farmer from the necessity of purchasing that amount of corn from the merchant, we value it at the merchant's credit price.

The alternative to growing corn was buying it on credit, and the opportunity cost of homegrown corn therefore was the credit price.

This argument appears to confuse two kinds of corn. When the farmer decided what to plant, he was choosing between having cotton and corn at the *end* of the growing season. But when he bought corn on credit while awaiting the harvest, it was because he had inadequate supplies at the *beginning* of the growing season. For his production decision, he considered this year's corn; for his consumption decision, last year's.

Ransom and Sutch use a static model, in which the distinction between this year's and last year's harvest is not made. And this type of model obscures the actual choice made by the farmer at the time of planting. The amount that the farmer would have to borrow to get through the growing season was already determined at the time he made his choice of crops. He would have no income before the harvest, so he had to borrow to finance any consumption greater than his existing liquid wealth, that is, his holdings of cash and corn. The cost of borrowing, therefore, was a sunk cost at the time of planting. Irrespective of what he planted, he would have to pay interest to the merchant to get through the year. But this interest should not have been a factor in his decision of what to plant.

When deciding what to plant, the farmer should have chosen a crop mix that would maximize his income in terms of corn. He did not consume cotton; he grew it only to acquire the income used to buy corn. (He consumed other products as well, of course, but I follow Ransom and Sutch's practice of letting corn stand for a composite bundle of goods.) And the corn bought after the harvest with the proceeds from his cotton crop could be bought for cash. The relevant price ratio for deciding what crops to plant therefore was the ratio of the cotton price to the cash price of corn. With these prices, as Ransom and Sutch admit, there was no incentive for the farmer to alter his behavior.

Ransom and Sutch's static model has led them into confusion on this point, as can be seen in this example from their text. In the course of describing the impact of crop liens on farmers, they say (p. 162):

> Presumably, a comparison of the farmgate price of cotton with a cash farmgate selling price for corn had led them to prefer a crop mix that concentrated upon cotton and that therefore necessitated the purchase of food. It was this food deficit that produced a need for credit.

The second sentence errs. The food deficit produced a need to purchase corn. Only a wealth deficit produces a need to borrow. If the farmer produced enough cotton to buy a year's supply of corn, he would have no need to borrow, even if he produced not a single ear of corn. Ransom and Sutch talk of the farmers' need to borrow if they were not self-sufficient in corn. But lack of self-sufficiency in corn means only that the farmers needed to buy corn, not that they needed to borrow to do so. The alternative to buying on credit was not autarky; it was buying with cash, produced (presumably) by income-maximizing agriculture. *which cotton was*

Separating the production and consumption decision for a given growing season destroys the evidence for cotton overproduction. It therefore forces a reexamination of the extent of coercion perceived by Ransom and Sutch. If the farmer understood the difference between fixed and variable costs, then he would have reached the production decision he did on his own. But if this difference continues to confuse modern scholars, we may suspect that it eluded the illiterate freedmen Ransom and Sutch described so vividly in their book as well. As the authors of *One Kind of Freedom* correctly assume throughout the book, freedmen in the postbellum years were not the omniscient market analysts of current economics textbooks.

How then was the crop-mix decision made? Two possible hypotheses may be advanced. The sharecropper may have had some indication of what was involved without being able to carry through the analysis himself. He therefore was guided to the proper decision by his local storekeeper. Coercion was absent, but direction from the merchant was not. Alternatively, the sharecropper may have followed the contemporary press cited by Ransom and Sutch and wanted to reduce his dependence on cotton. The merchant opposed this tendency toward inefficiency by insisting that the farmer grow cotton. In this story, the merchant coerced the farmer for their joint benefit. Neither hypothesis implies that the merchants enforced inefficient overproduction of cotton.

The altered story of cotton production has implications for Ransom and Sutch's tale of the merchant's local credit monopolies as well. Under reasonable assumptions about transport costs, any retail outlets will spread themselves out over the available market. The dispersion of country stores across the South therefore can be taken as evidence of competition as easily as of monopoly. But perfect competition is incompatible with significant transport and information costs. We would find spatial competition of the sort analyzed by Hotelling (1929) and Lösch (1954) instead.

According to the spatial competition model, each merchant faced a downward sloping demand curve, but his market power was constrained by the presence of surrounding, competing stores. While there was a definite boundary between his customers and his neighbors', as Ransom and Sutch assert (p. 137), the location of this boundary was a function of the relative prices of the merchant and his neighbors. Each merchant's market power therefore was limited by competition from his neighbors. The modern analogy is the neighborhood pharmacy, not the electric company.

Now the point here is partly a matter of terminology. Local storekeepers did have some market power. It is a matter of taste whether this power is described as a local monopoly or as the result of spatial competition. But the words have different connotations about the degree of coercion involved; monopoly implies a greater degree of coercion and control than spatial competition. And the issue is not simply one of terminology; the extent of local market power needs to be evaluated.

The spatial competition model is consistent with the evidence of small scale that Ransom and Sutch present. It is consistent as well with the apparent lack of accumulated wealth among local merchants (pp. 137–46).

It is not consistent, however, with the finding that merchants earned 60% on capital invested in loans to farmers (p. 130). This is evidence of substantial monopoly power.

The 60% figure is derived from the 30% markup of credit prices over cash prices by noting that the credit price involved a loan of six months, from May to the fall harvest. Thirty percent for half a year is 60% for a whole year (Appendix D). The argument seems so simple that the implicit assumption that the merchants' funds were invested in loans to farmers throughout the year seems unimportant.

But this implicit assumption is critical. Ransom and Sutch have used the same static model they used to analyze crop choices and ignored the yearly cycle of agricultural production. Farmers borrowed during the year to finance consumption and repaid their loans after the harvest. On average, their outstanding balance could only have been half their maximum balance. And if they had a little left over after they repaid their debts at harvest time, their average balance over the year was even smaller. The merchants earned 60% on the funds actually loaned, not on their total loanable assets. And since all their agricultural debtors were subject to the same agricultural timetable, we may infer that the merchants earned 60% on average something less than half the time, or equivalently, on somewhat less than half their assets.

The merchants' funds would be invested at market rates for the other half the time, bringing in an additional 5%. The gross return from lending then was 30 or 35%, not 60%. As Ransom and Sutch correctly note, a variety of costs must be deducted from the gross return to get a net return. They assume that the risk of default is measured by the records of actual defaults (p. 131). But as they note in several places, the common practice was for merchants to extend the terms of loans when farmers could not pay (e.g., p. 163). The gross rate of return earned by merchants on their loanable portfolio therefore was smaller than Ransom and Sutch assert, while the deductions from it needed to arrive at a net figure are larger than they assert. The true net figure was far smaller than their 60%. And even this revised figure still overestimates the merchant's overall rate of return, since lending was only one of his activities, and the one in which he had the largest market power.

The evidence of monopoly returns, like the evidence of cotton overproduction, is derived from models in which the agricultural timetable is inadequately represented. The static model underlying these parts of *One Kind of Freedom* is not appropriate for these problems. And when a more realistic model is used, it emerges that there may not have been any overproduction of cotton and that the profits of merchants may have been only slightly above competitive levels.

What then does that tell us about coercion in the postbellum South? Ransom and Sutch clearly are right to emphasize this part of their history, as the other parts of their book demonstrate, but they appear to have overestimated its extent. There is no evidence that the white concern for dominance over blacks forced Southern agriculture into an inefficient pattern of production. Nor is there evidence that the local storekeepers were growing rich on the labor of their customers. The brief comments given here do not allow an assessment of the extent of coercion; they only suggest that the picture in *One Kind of Freedom* may be somewhat exaggerated. The failure of the federal government to supply each freedman with ''40 acres and a mule'' may have been enough to determine the relative economic positions of whites and blacks after the Civil War. The appropriate economic analogy to the postbellum South may be a current less-developed country (LDC), not antebellum slavery.

CHAPTER 3

White Land, Black Labor, and Agricultural Stagnation

The Causes and Effects of Sharecropping in the Postbellum South

JOSEPH D. REID, JR.

The postbellum South is the great enigma of American history. During the nineteenth century, non-Southerners persistently changed locations, techniques, and occupations: They moved west or into cities, shifted from human to nonhuman sources of effort (animals in agriculture, water and steam in industry), and left farms for factories and stores. These changes propelled higher material living standards. Measured in dollars of 1840, non-Southerners' per capita income rose steadily at 1.5% per annum, from $114 in 1840 to $282 in 1900.[1] Schooling and other indicators of life's betterment rose as well.

Southerners, in contrast, persisted in agriculture: While the percentage of non-Southerners in urban areas rose from 14 in 1840 to 85 in 1900, the percentage of Southerners in urban areas went only from 7 to 18.[2] Over the same period, Southerners' real per capita income rose unsteadily from $76 to $118, so that the real income gap (measured in 1840 dollars) between Southerners and non-Southerners increased from $38 in 1840 to $164 in 1900. Furthermore, the gap increased by twice as much between 1880 and 1900 as it did between 1840 and 1860 ($37 vs $19). In sum, outside the South, changes of location and activity accompanied steadily rising prosperity; within the South, persistence at old tasks accompanied slow and unsteady improvement.

Financial assistance of National Science Foundation Grant SOC 75-19084 and research assistance of John Bender and Seung Dong Lee made this work possible. Comments by Richard Bean, Martin Bronfenbrenner, Claudia Goldin, and participants at the Duke University Symposium on *One Kind of Freedom* have improved this paper.

[1] The statistics reported in this and the following paragraph are calculated from data in Tables 2.2, p. 34; 2.16, p. 52; and 2.20 p. 55, of Davis *et al.* (1972). Many other evidences of non-Southerners' life's betterment are presented in Chaps. 2 and 3 of that text, in particular.

[2] Calculated from Series A 172, 178, 179 in U.S. Bureau of the Census (1975), p. 22.

33

MARKET INSTITUTIONS AND ECONOMIC PROGRESS
IN THE NEW SOUTH 1865–1900

The question, then, is why. Was improvement outside the South secured by change of jobs, and was relative impoverishment within the South guaranteed by persistence at old jobs? If so, what blocked Southerners' migration from old tasks to new? The ever-increasing shortfall of Southerners' per capita income should have accelerated change of jobs or locations, if change were possible and mattered (Sjaastad, 1962). Clearly, the tasks of the historians of southern economic development are to determine if change mattered and, if it did, why change was so slow in the South.[3] Because Southerners so persisted in staple agriculture, it seems likely that the wanted answers require the close study of southern farming. Because cotton was the most pervasive staple, it seems best to begin in the cotton South.[4]

Not only were Southerners slower than other Americans to abandon farms for factories, so too were they more likely to farm leased land. Indeed, the standard picture of the postbellum Cotton South (Ransom and Sutch, *One Kind of Freedom,* 1977; Wright and Kunreuther, 1975) emphasizes that over one-third of Southern farms were leased in 1880, while only one-fifth of farms outside the South were. In 1910, the gap was greater: Then half of Southern farms and a quarter of other farms were leased (Reid, in press, Table 2). Southern farmers, especially tenant farmers, were more commercial than other farmers: Half of the tilled acres in the Cotton South were inedible cotton in 1880 (*One Kind of Freedom,* Table 8.2, p. 157). Although four-fifths of the remaining acres were planted to corn, purchased food was needed and, perversely, became more needed as its price rose relative to that of cotton. Dependence upon purchased food (because of more mouths per acre) was most prevalent among tenants, especially among sharecroppers who gave labor for a share of the crop (colloquially but inaccurately put at one-half), seed, workstock and implements, and "furnish" provisions at credit prices.[5] At cotton, earnings of hired laborers were less than earnings of sharecrop-

---

[3] These are, of course, the tasks of all students of economic development, current, as well as past. The close resemblance of the postbellum south to many contemporary regions (such as northeast Brazil) where seemingly unrewarding cash crops are cultivated by impoverished tenant farmers makes the economic history of the South of exceptionally fruitful interest.

[4] Ransom and Sutch (1977) define and sample data from the "Cotton South" of "more than 200,000 square miles, ranging from the Carolinas through Georgia, Alabama, Mississippi, and westward into the prairies of Texas" (p. xii) that raised cotton disproportionately. More generally, I will follow them and analyze data from "five cotton-producing states: South Carolina, Georgia, Alabama, Mississippi, and Louisiana" (p. xii) when manuscript census sample data are not at hand.

[5] Ransom and Sutch (Chap. 8) report the requirements and productions of food crops. Reid (1973) and DeCanio (1974a, Appendix B) describe the variety of farming arrangements in the postbellum South.

pers (who supplied labor, primarily), and earnings of sharecroppers were less than earnings of share-tenants (who furnished some capital, some work-stock, and more knowhow, in addition to labor) or renters (who furnished all inputs but land).[6] At cotton, the low earners disproportionately were blacks: in 1880, for example, half of black and one-quarter of white farm operators leased on shares in the Cotton South (Table 5.1 p. 84).

As the gap between Southerners' and non-Southerners' per capita income widened, share tenancy increased (Reid, in press, Table 2). Such continued poverty and lack or perversity of response to changing prices and incomes are a puzzle, for Southerners previously showed no lack of motivation. Before the Civil War, Southerners moved readily to new lands and quickly took up more profitable crops (Fogel and Enger-man, 1974). Many have attributed postbellum southern poverty to the labor intensity of southern agriculture. This, in turn, is attributed to the destruction of Southern farm and transportation capital in the Civil War. Ransom and Sutch argue, however, that wartime destruction of farm capital was more than offset by the withdrawal of labor by freedmen (Chap. 3). Railroads were soon repaired and, in fact, extended (Stover, 1955). In short, neither a flaw in Southern character nor a lack of physical capital explain Southern poverty after the war.

Ransom and Sutch propose a traditional resolution of the puzzle of Southern poverty, a resolution composed of the staples of postbellum history—cotton, sharecropping, and country stores. Their explanation is especially relevant for blacks, for blacks interacted disproportionately with all three. "The root of the problem [of Southerners' slow economic progress is] . . . that the institutions established after the war effectively prevented the blacks from progressing . . ." (p. 12). Sharecropping hindered tenants' accumulation of human capital and retarded land im-provement, they argue, while excessive furnish at usurious rates lowered tenants' income.

That Southerners, especially black Southerners, *chose* these im-poverishing institutions Ransom and Sutch attribute to the legacy of slavery and the war. "[S]lavery proved a poor preparation for freedom" (p. 15) for blacks, Ransom and Sutch contend. The freedmen were illiterate, poor, and consequently unfit for any employment except as field hands. In particular, slaves "had never negotiated a contract, borrowed on credit, determined the crop mix, marketed a cotton crop, or read an agricultural journal" (p. 15). Almost as ill-prepared were the so-called poor whites. Before the Civil War they had practiced subsistence farming or frontier clearing. The backward shift of the supply of black labor at

---

[6] At sugar, gang laborers earned more than did tenant farmers right after the war (Sea-grave, 1971).

emancipation, however, enticed many poor whites into cotton farming on shares and into country-store furnish—just as it did blacks. For unprepared blacks and whites, the share landlord promised needed direction, wanted risk absorption, and required tools. Country stores offered feed and seed until harvest. High-priced cotton promised profits.

Documentation for these facts is sketchy or controversial. For instance, Fogel and Engerman (1974) suggest that blacks took into freedom sufficient *skills* for prosperous farming, but lacked the cooperating physical resources of land and capital. I, however, believe with Ransom and Sutch that freedmen were woefully unprepared to farm on their own. The specialization and continuous direction of slaves' work, documented by Fogel and Engerman (1974), argue that slaves did not learn many managerial and marketing skills. Moreover, it seems likely that slaves' specialized work skills were not competitive after the war. A slave carpenter built quarters for slaves, a slave blacksmith made tools for slaves. But slaves' comfort was undervalued by masters, so it is plausible that specialized skills employed to house, clothe, and feed other slaves were rough and crude, indeed. Furthermore, slaves needed to be watched, lest they shirk or escape, and there is evidence that slaves' work habits and tools aided watching as much as crop raising (Reid, 1979). Freedmen were their own masters, so plausibly they wanted more skillful skills, as well as work habits and tools designed solely for crop production and not at all for chattel protection. As unprepared as freedmen for profitable farming in the cotton areas were poor whites, who before the war practiced subsistence farming on lands marginal in location and productivity. The offer to landlords of shares of the crops by these new black and white tenants promised to secure landlords' assistance and attention, and thereby to make tenants' prosperity quick and sure (Reid, 1973, 1976b).[7]

The shifts to store furnish and to cotton were motivated by want for profits, just as plausibly. The deflated price (1880 dollars) of cotton was 45 cents per pound in 1865, four times its 1860 level, for example.[8] Although it fell rapidly as production rose thereafter, the real price of cotton did not fall below the level of the booming late 1850s until 1875. With such high prices, to shift from agricultural periphery to center and from food crops to cotton understandably seemed the way to success.

Was it immiserizing? Ransom and Sutch speculate that it was: Landlords' control of sharecroppers was too close and landlords' decision-making was too extensive for freedmen and new white cotton farmers to learn much from their tenancies (pp. 89–105). Although too close for learning by doing, landlords' control of tenants was not close enough to prevent progressive deterioration of lands or to permit better crop selec-

---

[7] I elaborate these points below.
[8] Calculated from U.S. Bureau of the Census, 1960, p. 115, series E 1; p. 124, series E 104.

tion. Cotton, cotton, and more cotton wasted the present and the future of the Cotton South.

Their speculations rest primarily on the neoclassical economic analysis of tenant farming. In that analysis (Marshall, 1920, pp. 535–536), the tenant farmer will supply effort at the rate at which his reward is equal to his foregone reward from an alternative occupation (the local wage, most generally). The share tenant, for instance, will labor so that *his* reward from share tenancy is equal to his foregone wage. The share tenant's reward, however, is but a fraction (his share) of his marginal product. Hence, the unsupervised share tenant will apply too little effort for overall efficiency. The fixed rent tenant, in contrast, will apply effort at the efficient rate, for he receives all of his marginal product. In sum, the neoclassical analysis of share tenancy implies that the share tenant will shirk (Reid, 1976b).

But Ransom and Sutch conclude that share tenants did not stint their labor at crops. In their 1880 sample of small tenant farms, Ransom and Sutch find differences between share and rent tenants too slight to support the existence of significant shirking. For example, they find that black share tenants farmed eight acres and raised $13.30 worth of crops per acre, while black renters farmed seven and one-fourth acres and raised $14.26 per acre (p. 100). If the Cobb–Douglass production function

$$\text{Output} = (\text{Labor})^{\frac{1}{2}} (\text{Land})^{\frac{1}{2}}$$

described southern agricultural production, then the Marshallian predictions would be that the labor-to-land ratio of renters would be four times that of sharecroppers, not 1.10. Similarly, the value per acre of output on rented land would be twice that on sharecropped land, not 1.07. Finally, the total product of renters would be one-half that of sharecroppers (one-fourth as much land times twice as much product per acre), not the sample 0.97.[9] Sampling errors more likely than Marshallian inefficiencies explain these slight actual differences.[10]

Both share and rent tenants have an incentive to stint maintenance and improvements of land, however, for tenants' who are subject to dismissal have uncertain claim to future yields from present efforts. Share tenants,

[9] That share tenants who furnished their own mules and feed received two-thirds of the corn and three-fourths of the cotton crops (Reid, 1973) suggests that the Cobb–Douglas production function

$$\text{Output} = (\text{Labor})^{\frac{1}{2}} (\text{Land})^{\frac{3}{8}} (\text{Capital})^{\frac{1}{8}}$$

better describes cotton farming. If so, an unrestrained Marshallian sharecropper would farm eight times as much land as a renter, other things equal.

[10] Some of the sample statistics deviate substantially from census statistics. See *One Kind of Freedom*, Table G. 11, p. 293.

applying Marshall's logic, have a greater incentive to mine the land, for their future yield from present effort is a fraction of renters'. Fearing that tenants will waste land, landlords will stint maintenance, and improvement of land, as well.

Because they find insignificant differences between acreages and yields of comparable sharecroppers and renters, Ransom and Sutch infer correctly (Reid, 1973) that share landlords policed their croppers and tenants closely. They conjecture, however, that although landlords' supervision of tenants was too close for tenants to learn farming by tenanting, supervision was too loose to prevent waste of land. For evidence of support Ransom and Sutch exhibit many laments of contemporaries that tenants required more than farmers' pay to ditch, fence, or drain lands—that is, to do more than farm (p. 101). This waste of land, in the interpretation of Ransom and Sutch, was masked by "prodigious" (p. 102) and inefficiently expensive use of commercial fertilizers.[11] But no substitute was found for owners' blunted incentive to tinker, worry, and otherwise increase agricultural productivity. This need not have been so, Ransom and Sutch concede: Longer tenures and varied terms to tenants for varied work might have prompted good farming practices, and even progress. But "the fact is that the Southern landlord typically did not establish fixity of tenure, make side payments to sharecroppers to install improvements, or offer superior land on different terms than inferior land. The result was a lack of agricultural progress . . ." (p. 103).

Although stated authoritatively, these are *not* the facts. To be sure, the vast majority of tenant leases were for one year. But the vast majority were renewed (often with changes in terms or location). In 1872, for instance, landlord Charles H. Rice of St. Paul's Parish, South Carolina, renewed an improvement contract with his share tenant B. Kelley. Their old contract gave Kelley all the crops for two years from land he cleared new, and three-quarters of the crops from lands cleared previously. This was renewed, with the amendment that Kelley plant all the old cleared land, as well as the new. In the same year, Rice converted J. Smith's part-money, part-shares contract into an all-shares contract and renewed Henry Daniels' one-fourth share lease, but Rice reduced from twenty-five to twenty-three the acres allotted to Daniels. The tenants of Rice, as those of other Southern landlords, could expect renewal of leases upon satisfactory performance.[12]

---

[11] One closer to the facts thought contemporaries' laments exaggerated. Hilgard's (1884, II, p. 522) South Carolina reporter observed that "[e]ight out of nine correspondents report that under the present system the lands are not improving but deteriorating, especially those rented and worked on shares. . . . Though there may be much sad reality in these statements, . . . within the last decade the two leading crops in this region have increased, one by 172, and the other by 139 percent."

[12] Tenants' contracts with Rice and other postbellum southern landlords are described

Tenants were encouraged to maintain or improve land, as well as to farm, by sidepayments. North Carolina landlord Alonzo T. Mial in 1877 gave J. Phipps and T. Earp horse feed, thirty dollars, and use of a field, in return for use of their horse, half of their crop, and their promises to ditch and to build a twelve-rail fence. In 1886, Mial's share tenant Pool was required to build a tobacco barn. Landlord Thomas Lenoir secured share tenant James Cody's promise not to cut timber and to maintain fences and ditches (Reid, 1976a, pp. 82–83). Sidepayments reported by Taylor (1943) to three South Carolina sharecroppers varied net shares by 9%.

Finally, local scarcities or qualities of resources prompted varied shares. H. Hammond (Hilgard, 1884, II, p. 522) reported that South Carolina sharecroppers typically received half of their crops, except in Greenville and portions of Fairfield and Spartenburgh counties. Wharton (1965, pp. 69–70) found that Mississippi croppers' shares were lower on lands of higher quality.

Southern tenant leases, in sum, varied in ways that enhanced efficiency. Although sharecroppers on halves, share tenants on thirds and fourths, and renters on 1,000 pounds of cotton for a one-mule farm are general summaries of postbellum southern leases, they are incomplete summaries. Since inflexibility of lease terms is the keystone of Ransom and Sutch's "proof" of the inefficiency of southern tenancy, the factual flexibility of lease terms requires a different evaluation of why tenancy, especially sharecropping, was chosen by so many, and what tenancy did accomplish in the postbellum South.

Ransom and Sutch are correct that the demise of slavery markedly shifted back the supply of farm labor (Chap. 4 and Appendix C). Emancipation redirected blacks' efforts, as well. The source of profits under slavery was the relative cheapness of coercion. Coercion was cheapest on the staples—cotton, rice, sugar, and tobacco. For one thing, these crops wanted labor fairly stably over the year: Indeed, average daily labor on cotton prior to harvest equaled that at harvest.[13] The short growing time of corn relative to the long Southern growing season meant that work at corn could be scheduled to mesh with the fluctuating wants of commercial staples: For example, on one plantation which raised corn and cotton, Metzer (1975) calculated that between 11 and 87% of available man-days of labor were employed at cotton, but that between 80 and 100% of available man-days were employed in cotton and corn. This

---

more fully in Reid (1973), upon which this and the following paragraph are based. Ironically, the sharecrop contracts of tenant Fenner Powell with landlord Alonzo Mial which Ransom and Sutch reproduce (p. 91) is a renewal.

[13] Calculated from U.S. Bureau of Census, 1960, series K 94–95, p. 281.

seasonal complementarity meant that little complexity, just two crops, were required to keep slave labor (and its management) employed day by day. Cost of coercion was reduced further by the labor of the Southern crops. Thus, day in and day out, one overseer could direct and coerce the employment of many slaves. Such seasonal complementarity and physical closeness of slaves employments were not gained without cost. In the Cotton South, for example, first corn was planted too early to escape fully the winter cold and second corn too late to escape the drought and bugs of late summer; livestock was raised without labor, but on less fattening mast during the summer; and land clearing and maintenance were pushed into the winter.

In sum, coercing labor from unwilling slaves was the slave manager's major task. The possibilities of keeping many slaves close together (offered by labor intensive crops, such as cotton) constantly (as made possible by alternation between staple and corn over the seasons) made coercion pay. To economize on the supervisory cost of coercion, however, too much labor sometimes was applied at suboptimal times: Corn, for example, was cultivated too early and too late with too few tools, because the labor was cheaply available and (for managers' safety) wanted employment. Such use of slaves' labor secured corn enough, and kept slaves docile, too.

The slaves' legacy, therefore, was training at efficient cultivation of the staple and at too labor-intensive cultivation at inappropriate times of the complementary food crops. The techniques of cultivating food crops learned by slaves were most inefficient where food was cheapest—along the Mississippi where imports were cheap or on more rural plantations that lacked vents for labor not used in raising the staple crops (nearby towns, for example). On alluvial plantations, foodstuffs were bought and cotton labor was stretched. On isolated plantations, out-of-staple labor was substituted for machinery to achieve self-sufficiency but no more.[14] At emancipation, in consequence, the freedmen were better farmers of cotton than of corn, especially in the more rural lower south.

Cotton prices were high and free black labor was scarce after the war. In response, poor whites were attracted out of subsistence agriculture on fringe lands into a new crop, cotton. Recent immigrants facing new crops and new conditions, needed help, just as did the freedmen: risk absorption, guaranteed instruction, ready tools. Somewhat conjectured (but not crucial) is that the supply of talented farm managers was disproportionately reduced by the war: In addition to these losses from disproportionate war deaths, planter-managers' attempts to regain political hegemony meant that the survivors' time could be devoted less constantly to agricul-

---

[14] This analysis of slavery is elaborated in Reid (1979).

ture. With demand for farm management raised (more unknowledgeable farmers wanted more knowledge) and supply reduced by death and distraction, the rapid rise of share tenancies is not surprising. Equally unsurprising is the variety of other tenures, from wage labor through owner-cultivation, which flourished in the postbellum South.

As discussed above, the traditional (Marshallian) analysis of sharecropping stresses the tenant's *dis*incentive to labor because he gets but a share of his product. But the unsupervised wage laborer has even greater disincentive to labor, and the unwatched renter should mine the land most rapidly for maximum profit. Only the owner-cultivator can be trusted to farm and maintain his lands properly, for only he receives with certainty the full marginal product of his efforts. Every tenure but owner-cultivation, therefore, requires supervision of the laborer to offset his incentive to shirk. To the extent that supervision of farm workers and tenants is costly, it follows that other tenures are less profitable than is owner-cultivation.

The variety of tenures (see Table 3.1) in postbellum Southern agriculture is prima facie evidence, then, that tenant agriculture was practiced for reasons other than profit, or that supervisory costs were low, or that the benefits of supervision exceeded the costs. The traditional argument accompanied the first reason. Ransom and Sutch, for example, argue that whites refused to sell or to rent land to freedmen, for to do so would admit equality with blacks (p. 86). Trapped into sharecropping, blacks learned little and landowners recognized no advance in sharecroppers skills, so that blacks too long remained tenants (pp. 180–181). To me, however, the large proportion of white sharecroppers and the extent of blacks in other tenures suggest that low supervisory costs and high benefits from supervision explain better than does racism the incidence of different tenures within the South.

The raw inputs of postbellum agriculture in the Cotton South were: freedmen better trained to raise cotton than corn; poor whites poorly trained to raise either in *new* surroundings, but better trained to raise corn; yeomen whites well trained to raise cotton and corn; and plantation masters in need of a way to instruct and manage heterogeneous laborers. The chosen means, as we have seen, to restart production was a variety of tenures: directed labor paid set wages, closely supervised sharecropper labor paid an incentive-share, less closely supervised share tenants paid a bigger share, renters not directed but restrained from certain practices, and completely unrestrained owners. A variety of tenures was used because the cooperating farm inputs—labor, land and implements, and know-how or management—were owned in differing proportions. At emancipation, the Cotton South freedman owned much labor and cotton know-how, less corn know-how, and no stock, tools, or land. His

TABLE 3.1
Percentage Distribution of Farm Operators by Tenures and Race
within and without the South, 1880–1910

Region and race	Tenure	1880	1890	1900	1910
United States—All	Owners[a]	74.4	71.6	64.7	63.0
	Tenants	25.6	28.4	35.3	37.0
	Rent[b]	8.0	10.0	13.1	11.2
	Share[c]	17.5	18.4	22.2	24.8
Non-South—All	Owners[a]	81.0	78.4	74.5	74.9
	Tenants	19.0	21.6	25.5	25.1
	Rent[b]	5.7	7.6	9.4	9.6
	Share[c]	13.3	14.0	16.1	15.5
South—All	Owners[a]	63.8	61.5	53.0	50.4
	Tenants	36.2	38.5	47.0	49.6
	Rent[b]	11.8	13.5	17.5	14.6
	Share[c]	24.4	25.0	29.5	33.0
South—White	Owners[a]	65.9[d]	NA[e]	63.9	60.8
	Tenants	34.3[d]	NA	36.1	39.2
	Rent[b]	7.7[d]	NA	10.0	10.4
	Share[c]	26.5[d]	NA	26.1	28.9
South—Nonwhite	Owners[a]	19.6[d]	NA	25.4	29.7
	Tenants	80.2[d]	NA	74.6	75.3
	Rent[b]	25.7[d]	NA	36.7	32.1
	Share[c]	54.4[d]	NA	37.9	43.2

Source: Reid, Table 2, forthcoming b.
[a] Includes full owners, part owners, and managers.
[b] Other and unspecified tenants included with rent tenants.
[c] Includes sharecroppers, share tenants, and livestock share.
[d] Calculated for "Cotton South" sample (One Kind of Freedom, Table 5.1, p. 84).
[e] NA—Not available.

neighbor-yeoman, in contrast, owned his labor, equal know-how about cotton and corn, as well as stock, tools, and land. The newly arrived poor white perhaps had some stock and some tools (if he had not sold them in the move), and likely had more corn than cotton know-how (although his know-how about each pertained to different soils). The plantation owner had his labor, his land [cut up into a large section of woods, another large section of meadows, and a large section of cotton or corn lands (Prunty, 1955)], his knowledge about crop growing and marketing, and his knowledge about managing free labor. Of course, he yet possessed his know-how at directing gang tasks, but emancipation made that valueless, except on the richest alluvial lands, principally at sugar (Roark, 1977; Seagrave, 1971; Shlomowitz, 1975).

At the beginning of the crop year of, say, 1879, each owner of an unbalanced bundle of different resources went to market to buy, rent, or promise for the help of sufficient cooperating resources to farm with profit. The prices of the conventional farm inputs, land, labor, and implements were set in the marketplace. To any particular Southerner, the value of each reflected the imbalance of his resources' bundle, and in the market he got or gave use of resources to achieve balance, that is, until the marginal value of each resource remaining under his direction just equaled its market price. Balance of conventional resources could have been achieved under any tenure. Share tenures, as noted above, differed greatly in the amounts and proportions of conventional inputs supplied by landowners and laborers. But positive supervisory costs imply that owner cultivation (often with mortgaged land and tools) would have been the only tenure observed, if land, labor, and implements were the only inputs to farming. If lenders' risk required sufficient supervision of mortgagors, renting of land and tools might have been observed. Certainly, however, neither farming for wages nor for shares would have been used if only balance of conventional inputs were wanted. Imbalances of know-how prompted these tenures.

The price of farming know-how was set in the marketplace, just as were the prices of land, labor, and capital. The value of know-how to a particular Southerner depended on the length, certainty, and amount of its yield. Length of yield from know-how rose as its age of acquisition fell. Certainty of yield was doubtlessly greater for whites than for blacks in the Cotton South, for know-how was complementary with other inputs whose supply perhaps was discriminatory or imperfect (*One Kind of Freedom*, pp. 179–181). Diminishing marginal productivity assures that know-how's marginal yield rose with lack of knowledge. Thus, young and immigrant Southerners plausibly most wanted to gain farm know-how. Because of greater certainty of yield, at each price whites wanted more know-how than did blacks. Older, more successful farmers wanted to sell know-how.

These considerations set the demand and supply of tenures in farming. The capable manager with strength and time for farming—reflecting lacks of alternative employments, or very locale-specific farm knowledge, or the real or imagined importance of prompt execution of appropriately timed decisions (that is, reflecting the characteristics of sugar and alluvial cotton culture in the postbellum South)—sought to direct wage laborers continuously (Schlomowitz, 1975). The very youngest or strangest (hence, with the most to learn) and the dullest (least capable of learning) sought wage work. Those laborers with sufficient knowledge to get safely from day to day, but with ambition to learn more, sharecropped and, later, furnishing more of the tools and other inputs, share tenanted. The share laborer's landlord relished the reward for his passed-on expertise *and* his ability to pass his knowledge to many intermittently; trusting the incentive of the share to keep his tenants industrious, often he moved to town or opened another business. Grown older or busier elsewhere, or perhaps new to the area and therefore unknowledgeable, the landowner rented and made only sufficient visits to guard against waste. Grown more feeble or more busy elsewhere, the landowner sold out. The share tenant, for his part, if sufficiently wealthy to bear the risk of a bad year and sufficiently knowledgeable to face alone an unknown year, sought to rent or own (and thus reap the rewards of knowledge and of risk bearing). Share tenures, to emphasize, attract the younger and less knowledgeable laborers and the more knowledgeable landlords with broader interests.

The above paragraph is an idealized portrait of the agricultural ladder, the ladder climbed rung by rung in the folklore of American agriculture (Reid, in press). With allowance made for the risks and transaction costs of different combinations of land, labor, know-how, and other farm inputs, the agricultural ladder seems to well depict postbellum agriculture in the Cotton South. Southern farm laborers were younger than farm operators. Although life-cycle progression from share tenant to rent tenant to owner need not be revealed well in a cross-section, for what it is worth their average ages in 1880 in the Cotton South were, respectively, 35.2, 37.4, and 43.6 for whites and 40.5, 41.4, and 45.5 for blacks (*One Kind of Freedom,* table 9.4, p. 181). The same story—that sharecroppers were younger than renters, who were younger than owners, but that blacks were more persistent on the lower rungs of the agricultural ladder seems revealed in Table 3.2 for 1910.

The meaning of blacks' persistence on the lower rungs of the agricultural ladder is ambiguous. On the one side is the argument by Ransom and Sutch that whites' reluctance to recognize above-average capabilities in blacks or discrimination stopped blacks progression up the agricultural ladder (p. 180). Discrimination might well prompt a black to farm for wages or shares longer than a white, so that the black could prolong his landlord's incentive to champion him. Arithmetically, discriminatory restriction of blacks' access to owned land will inflate the proportions of black farmers renting and on shares. If renters are more ready to be

TABLE 3.2

Percentage of Farmers Who Are Share Tenants S, Renters R, Tenants T, or Owners O, in Different Age Classes by Races for the South, 1910

Region—Race	Tenure	Age class						
		All	−25	25–34	35–44	45–54	55–64	65+
South—White	S	28.9	60.6	40.6	26.9	9.9	15.5	10.2
	R	10.4	16.0	13.6	10.3	8.4	7.1	5.4
	T	39.2	76.5	54.2	37.2	28.3	22.6	15.6
	O	60.1	22.8	45.1	62.0	71.0	76.9	84.0
South—Black	S	43.2	64.7	52.5	43.1	34.7	31.2	26.8
	R	32.1	28.2	32.8	34.1	33.0	30.7	28.5
	T	75.3	92.9	85.3	77.1	67.8	61.9	55.3
	O	24.6	77.0	14.6	22.7	32.1	38.0	44.6

Source: U. S. Bureau of the Census (1922, Table 5, p. 353).

owners than are share tenants, such discrimination will inflate the proportion renting more than the proportion sharing. In fact, 80% of black farm operators in the Cotton South versus 66% of white farm operators were tenants, but only 68% of black tenants versus 77% of white tenants were on shares. That is, black tenants disproportionately rented (p. 84, or see Table 3.3). In the Georgia cotton belt, Higgs (1974) too found that black tenants rented more frequently than did white tenants. Within each county, that is, in like farming conditions, however, Higgs (1974, pp. 478–479) calculated that black tenants paid shares slightly more often than did white tenants. The proportion of Georgia tenants that farmed for a fixed rent varied directly with the extent of wage labor on large farms, that is, varied directly with the absorption of management elsewhere and, after allowance for the availability of farm management, not with race. In short, the distribution of conventional and unconventional inputs seems, on a balance, to explain the distribution of tenures and races.

The different distributions of blacks and whites within the South are hinted at by the different percentages of blacks in the populations of the Confederate South, 40%, and of the Cotton South, 52%, in 1880 (U.S. Bureau of Census, 1975, series A199–200, pp. 24–35). Between 1860 and 1880, the white population increased 2.08% per year in the Confederate South and 1.41% per year in the Cotton South. Twenty-year average annual growth rates within Cotton South states of the white population varied from 1.16% in Alabama to 1.62% in Georgia. The black population annually increased 1.96% in the Confederate South and 1.90% in the Cotton South. Within the Cotton South, the black population's average annual growth rate varied from a low of 1.59% in Alabama (also the low state for whites, 1.16%) to a high of 2.235% in Georgia (also the high state for whites). Within the states of the Cotton South, whites and blacks migrated to the better cotton producing counties. The result was tenancy and cotton. To farm after the war, other institutions had to change, as well. With the antebellum cotton factors gone, bankrupted by the war or by the failed attempt to resurrect plantation agriculture immediately after the war, cotton needed a new outlet. Country stores spread throughout the Cotton South.[15] The stores *lowered* the prices of northern machinery and foodstuffs to the yeomen, as well as marketed their cotton. The reason is that where antebellum distribution was through planters and factors, the low cost of out-of-cotton labor made plantation production up to self-sufficiency cheap, and thereby made the delivery cost high of Northern products wanted by scattered yeomen farmers. So the expansion of country stores raised the profitability of cotton to yeomen farmers and they responded by contributing to the increase in the ratio of cotton to corn.

---

[15] See Woodman (1967) for an account of replacement of cotton factors by country stores as agents of marketing and financing of cotton.

The poor whites did, too, for that is what they came to do. And the freedmen did, for added leisure cost less if gotten from corn grown inefficiently than from cotton grown efficiently.

How postbellum farmers produced more cotton is consistent with my above assessment of their needs and of the payoffs of different tenures. In the Cotton South, the yeomen were interspersed among antebellum plantations, on soils of about equal quality. Some blacks still labored as hired hands, or in gangs where the return to constant white management was enough to pay the gang labor surcharge (Shlomowitz, 1975). Where white management was too thin, blacks and "poor whites" tenanted the old plantations. Consistent with this map, DeCanio (1974a, Chap. 5) concluded that whites were more productive than blacks at cotton, but equally productive at other crops. DeCanio reasoned from county-aggregate data: value of crops, white population, black population, and so forth. The link between his productivity measures and the cotton-belt data is that more cotton whites and more cotton meant more constant managers. Accordingly, more cotton went with more blacks less talented at other crops. Where less white management was available, blacks *and* poor whites sharecropped dissected plantations. The latter grew cotton less successfully, however, so they disproportionately went to lands and farm situations of more balanced potential. The end result: In the richest cotton areas, tenancy was less and likely was for fixed rents, for white management was concentrated on gangs; elsewhere, whites and share tenancy were more prevalent.[16]

My emphasized *cause* of tenure choice, to best balance owned resources (land, labor, and know-how) with unowned resources in order to produce most profitably, differs from others' explanations. Ransom and Sutch offer a sociological explanation that emphasizes a psychic status ladder, rather than a functional tenure ladder: "[w]hites discouraged any sign of black independence that might have suggested a move [by blacks] toward social or economic equality" (p. 86), and therefore discouraged blacks from owning or renting farm land; blacks wanted land to own and would not continue the emasculating gang labor of slavery; for whites, black sharecropping was of sufficiently low status to be tolerated; for blacks, sharecropping was of sufficiently high independence to be accepted.

Their contentions are that whites' concern for status shifted back and made less elastic the supply of land for rent or sale to blacks, while blacks' concern for status shifted back and made less elastic the supply of gang

---

[16] This interpretation is supported by data in Higgs (1974). This is *not* the interpretation of DeCanio (1974a, pp. 220–221), who finds support for a "Land Occupancy and Ownership Hypothesis" that different population groups (blacks, yeomen, and poor whites) remained in their prewar places—a conjecture that seems to be incorrect—and that whites got the best lands on subdivided plantations.

labor. Given that whites' racist distaste for blacks was more evenly spread across the South than was good cotton land or blacks, their hypothesis implies that share tenancy rates of blacks should be higher than for whites and should be less affected by changed economic conditions, such as by the importance of cotton, the distribution of knowledge and of different soils, climates, or distances to market. The few and scattered investigations, however, have not found blacks confined to the bottom rungs of the tenure ladder uniformly across the South. As noted previously, Higgs (1974) found the majority of difference between blacks and whites in rates of sharecropping stemmed from the different distribution of the races across counties. Dowell (1977) found that for counties in 1930 Mississippi (more overtly racist than in 1880), opportunities for off-farm employments more strongly and surely affected the ratio of renters to share tenants than did the ratio of blacks to whites in agriculture. All told, there is yet little evidence that racism played more than a small part in the story of tenure choice in Southern agriculture.

Admittedly, to identify economic interests, rather than racial prejudices, as the impetus to sharecropping, renting, and other employments in the postbellum South is not the same as identifying exactly which economic interests dictated tenure choices in the postbellum South. Above, I emphasized the costs and risks in getting owners of profitably cooperative resources to, in fact, cooperate as dictating tenure choice. It follows that knowledgeable landlords will want share tenants and somewhat unknowledgeable but ambitious farm workers will be share tenants. Furthermore, I expect tenants and landlords to increase their preferences for sharecropping where cooperative response to changed conditions will raise farm profitability. Cheung (1969), in contrast, recently resurrected an alternative economic explanation of tenure choice; he argued that sharecropping would be most preferred where crops were most risky, that is, where yields were most uncertain. Elsewhere I quarreled with his logic and his facts: I argued that the ease of risk dispersal through a variety of jobs or of crops destroys any relation between tenure choice and simple crop risk (Reid, 1976b). Recently, however, Wright and Kunreuther (1975) extended Cheung's approach and argued that more willingness to bear real income risk prompted more cotton on postbellum Southern farms. From regressions of aggregate data for 386 counties of the 1880 Cotton South, Wright and Kunreuther (1975, p. 543) conclude that the extent of risk borne (proportionate to the share of tilled acres planted to cotton) increased with the extent of tenancy (share and rent), wealth (proportionate to average farm size), and poverty (proportionate to the proportion of farms smaller than fifty acres).

They interpreted the regressions as showing that the postbellum South was, indeed, locked into cotton by the lures of country-store creditors (proxied by tenancy) and by the lure of gambling when there is nothing to

lose (proxied by poverty). Elsewhere, Wright (1974, pp. 632–633) estimated that growth of demand for Southern cotton was retarded after the
Civil War, so that gambles on cotton had less and less chance of paying
off.

However, these results are unproved. The aggregated logic is faulty: To
be enticed or locked into cotton and then exploited by a merchant may
redistribute income, but it will raise measured income as long as cotton is
the most profitable crop, on average. But sharecropping, cotton, and
country stores originally were indicted because, somehow, they held
income down. Clearly, this puzzle requires that the rising acreage of
cotton and the simultaneously rising price of corn be faced squarely.

Cotton prices were high right after the war, as we have seen, absolutely
and (surprising in a starving South) relative to corn (*One Kind of Freedom*, p. 155). Both the absolute and the relative-to-corn price of cotton
fell rapidly, however. By the mid-1870s the prewar relative price was
regained, and it stayed there (with annual fluctuations up or down) until
1890. Cotton acreage relative to corn acreage steadily rose while, less
certainly, corn yields rose (*One Kind of Freedom*, pp. 155–156), which to
Ransom and Sutch and Wright and Kunreuther was further evidence of the
lure and the lock-in. Not only did farmers raise more cotton relative to
corn in 1890 than they did in 1875, but the tenancy rate rose, too.

There is another explanation, however, which has been overlooked by
Ransom and Sutch. This explanation has several ingredients. First, there
is food: Between 1860 and 1870, per capita cows, pigs, and other inter-
mediaries between corn and people in the South fell by about one-half
(*One Kind of Freedom*, p. 152). One reason might have been impoverishment. Another might have been the capital costs of rebuilding livestock
overdepleted during the war. A third might have been the improved terms
of trade for northern foodstuffs after the war; the expansion of railroads in
the North and in the South surely affected the price of foods. Surely the
fall in Southern rail costs and the discoveries of fertilizers in South
Carolina lowered the cost of cotton, especially on the farmed-over lands
of the old South (Stover, 1955, p. 277). A falling net price of fertilizer is
consistent with the rise in the relative yield of corn; for the worst corn
land would be the first returned to cotton.

The progressive cutting up of plantations into small farms probably
contributed, too. Antebellum plantations were not a bunch of small farms
just joined; they consisted of several very large areas, one at cotton,
another at corn, a third at fallow or meadow, and a last at woods (Prunty,
1955). After the war, tenants leased in the crop lands. Although tenant
leases granted access to the woods for fuel, none granted tenants' animals
rights to landlords' woods or meadows. If tenants did not wish to risk loss
of grazing stock to bandits or predators, and if there are imperfections in

TABLE 3.3
Regression Coefficients: Cotton South, 1880

Independent variables	Dependent variable[a]			
	Total (11)	Tilled (1)	Total (13)	Tilled (2)
Constant	0.297	−0.185	0.279	−0.304
Cotton yield/corn yield	2.59	2.84	2.60	2.66
	(4.63)	(5.64)	(4.64)	(5.18)
Population/improved acres	−0.072	0.586	−0.008	0.719
	(1.23)	(5.50)	(0.13)	(6.12)
Average farm size	0.0013	.00047	0.0014	.00048
	(5.63)	(4.92)	(6.21)	(4.70)
Tenancy rate	0.390	0.604		
	(6.76)	(11.6)		
Percentage of farms:				
Less than 50 acres	0.50	−0.149	0.070	0.139
	(2.70)	(2.11)	(4.45)	(2.36)
50 to 100 acres	−0.160	0.165	−0.190	0.243
	(6.76)	(1.13)	(4.54)	(1.52)
Tenancy rate on farms:				
Less than 50 acres			0.067	0.178
			(1.27)	(3.93)
50 to 100 acres			0.259	0.268
			(3.60)	(7.27)
Simple R^2	0.401	0.437	0.405	0.424

Sources: Hilgard (1884) and Wright and Kunreuther (1975, p. 543).

[a] Dependent variable: cotton acreage/total acreage (total), or cotton acreage/tilled acreage (tilled). $N = 386$ counties. t = ratios in parentheses. All variables as defined in text.

having landlords specialize in livestock production, then the plantations' demise played a role in the growing importance of cotton.[17]

The fact that plantation tenants got all cropland further explains the positive association between tenantry and cotton, especially when the dependent variable is changed from the ratio of cotton acres to total acres ("Total," the variable used by Wright and Kunreuther) to the ratio of cotton acres to tilled acres ("Tilled").[18] Table 3.3 contrasts Wright and Kunreuther (1975, p. 543) regressions 11 and 13 using Total with re-

[17] McGuire and Higgs (1977) note this point, too, in their critical discussion of Wright and Kunreuther (1975).

[18] The independent variable Population/Improved Acres is calculated as (Population − Farm Operators)/Improved Acres in the Tilled regressions. The Tilled results were computed by John Bender.

gressions on the more appropriate dependent variable Tilled. Substitution of tilled for total acres changes the role and the significance of dependents per acre. Wright and Kunreuther (1975, pp. 534–535), anticipated a negative sign, reasoning that more mouths to feed meant more corn. The positive sign suggests that dependents were workers, too, and were better working at cotton than at corn (because cotton grew lower to the ground, was easier for children to cultivate, and so forth?). The tilled regressions also imply that large farms put less land into cotton. Large farms doubtless were the uncut parts of plantations, farmed often by the landowner and several hired hands (Reid, 1973). Finally, the tilled results invert the relation between gambling (cotton) and size argued by Wright and Kunreuther. Other things equal, farmers cultivating 50 to 100 acres planted cotton most heavily; the poor (farmers on less than 50 acres) and the rich (farmers on more than 100 acres) raised other crops.

County-aggregate data are not truly appropriate for analyzing decisions of individual farmers, of course: Five dependents per acre, on average, for example, may be 10 per acre on half the farms as well as five per acre on all the farms. Hence, for more insight a small sample of 710 farms growing cotton and corn was drawn from the Ransom and Sutch sample of the 1880 manuscript census (*One Kind of Freedom*, pp. 283–294). This permitted an 1880 regression more comparable to Wright and Kunreuther's (1975, pp. 534–535) 1860 regressions on observations of plantations, for here dependents were distinguished from workers. To control for dependents' ages, the father's age and the square of the father's age were entered as dependent variables in some of the regressions. Other variables in Table 3.4 are self-explanatory. As in 1860 (Wright and Kunreuther, 1975, pp. 534–535), workers at home raise the importance of cotton, while dependents per acre reduce the importance of cotton. Further, rental and share tenancy raise the importance of cotton equally. Finally, no U-shaped relation between farm size and importance of cotton appears. An inverted-U relationship does appear between the age of the father and the importance of cotton, however; this is consistent with younger children being relatively more productive at cotton.

In the main, it seems that the regressions in Tables 3.3 and 3.4 reflect that cotton was a labor intensive crop, that child labor was a better substitute for adult labor at cotton than at corn, and that tenants on cut-up cotton plantations largely raised cotton. There is no earth-shattering news, there, and of course, no evidence of coercion, either. Rather, the evidence is that people with relatively more labor more suitable for cotton got on better cotton land and productively applied their labor. In the process, they produced correlations between race, tenure, foodstuffs raised per worker, and so forth, in which some interpret as coercion rather than choice at the margin.

TABLE 3.4

Regression Coefficient for 710 Farms, 1880[a] Dependent variable: cotton acreage/tilled acreage

	1	2	3	4	5	6
Constant	0.218	0.275	0.075	0.0812	0.294	0.268
Race dummy	0.115[b]	0.150[b]	0.121[b]	0.117[b]	0.146[b]	0.151[b]
	(4.75)[c]	(6.33)	(5.04)	(4.89)	(6.12)	(6.33)
Illiteracy dummy × 10^{-3}	-0.12	8.6	0.87	2.38	6.71	6.67
	(0.0054)	(0.381)	(0.038)	(0.105)	(0.295)	(0.295)
Fixed rental dummy	0.0764[b]	0.0928[b]	0.0851[b]	0.0811[b]	0.0852[b]	0.0929[b]
	(2.86)	(3.47)	(3.16)	(3.04)	(3.19)	(3.45)
Share rental dummy	0.0785[b]	0.0852[b]	0.0809[b]	0.0767[b]	0.0773[b]	0.0863[b]
	(3.60)	(3.87)	(3.63)	(3.48)	(3.55)	(3.91)
Dependents/tilled acreage		-0.176[b]			0.197[b]	-0.167[b]
		(3.65)			(4.30)	(3.45)
Number of workers/number at home	0.161[a]		0.173[b]	0.171[b]		
	(4.21)		(4.49)	(4.43)		
Tilled acreage × 10^{-3}		0.0079	0.45[d]			0.29
		(0.324)	(2.02)			(1.23)
Tilled acreage squared × 10^{-6}		0.672	-0.0664			0.110
		(0.201)	(0.195)			(0.327)
Amount paid in wages × 10^{-3}		0.0587[b]		0.0658[b]		
		(2.79)		(3.84)		
Age of head of house × 10^{-3}			6.46[d]	6.97[d]		
			(2.00)	(2.17)		
Age of head squared × 10^{-3}			-0.0813	-0.0848		
			(2.37)	(2.49)		
R^2	0.160	0.181	0.186	0.189	0.161	0.171
F	26.9	19.3	17.8	20.4	27.1	20.7
Standard error	0.2279	0.2256	0.2250	0.2244	0.2278	0.2267

Source: Sample from Ransom and Sutch 1880 Manuscript Census Sample, as described in text.

[a] Dependent variable: cotton acreage/tilled acreage.

[b] Significant at 1% for two-tailed test.

[c] The t statistic is in parentheses.

[d] Significant at 5% for two-tailed test.

An old story, almost as old as the one about the waste of sharecropping, is the one about the grasping monopoly of the country stores. Ransom and Sutch retell it. But at least they recognize a problem in turning an industry in which suppliers increased at 10% per year, and separate locations grew at 8.5% per year into a monopoly (p. 141). They conclude that calling the stores local monopolies and noting high credit prices and contemporaries' complaints about store profits resolves it adequately (Chap. 7).

As the rapid growth of country stores suggests, they filled needs. One was to provision farmers at less cost than, say, the cost of the leisure foregone by the now-freedmen when, as slaves, they busied idle hands inefficently. Another was to market the crops. A third was to distribute inputs to many and collect outputs from many, a task accomplished on the plantation in antebellum days. The last was to finance the crop so that purchased inputs and consumption could be gotten before the crop was sold; before the war, finance was arranged by the factors.

Contemporaries who decried the merchants' high credit charges faulted the scarcity of alternative bank credit (M. B. Hammond, 1909). Ransom and Sutch concur, building on Sylla's (1969) argument that the high capital requirements of national banks and their prohibition against holding mortgages of longer than five years duration stifled national banking in the South, while the tax on state bank notes stifled state banking in rural

TABLE 3.5
Advent of Free State Banking in South

State	Year	Minimum capital (dollars) required for cities of less than 3,000	
Tennessee[a]	1870	none	
Arkansas	1868	none	
West Virginia	1861–1863	25,000	
Texas	1876	10,000	(cities less than 2,500)
Mississippi[a]	1890	10,000	(cities less than 500)
Kentucky	1891	15,000	
Virginia	1902	10,000	
Florida	1900	15,000	
Alabama	1900	15,000	(cities less than 2,500)
Georgia	1891	15,000	
South Carolina	1905	none	
North Carolina	1903	5,000	(cities less than 1,500)
National Bank		50,000	until 1900
		25,000	thereafter

Source: Barnett, G. E., (1911), *State Banks and Trust Companies since the Passage of the National-Bank Act*. Pp. 31–32, 43.

[a] No restrictions on amount of loan to one borrower.

areas. Table 3.5 shows that free banking came relatively late to the South, but that state banks in rural areas were permitted with much less capital than national banks. Barnett (1911) indicates that the state banks chartered prior to free banking generally were not more constrained than their free banking successors. Barnett reports no Southern state bank had required reserves before 1887, that most could establish branches, that there were generally no restrictions against real estate loans, and that state banks were much less constrained than national banks in the proportion of assets they could lend to a single individual. Yet the Cotton South had few banks (*One Kind of Freedom*, p. 112). Since state banks were not legally constrained, this suggests the nature of Southern credit demand restrained banks relative to country stores.

As were other Southern institutions, so was Southern credit influenced by its support of staple agriculture. First, the staple secured Southern credit, so that the "goodness of credit" was set by the goodness of the staple crop. In other words, Southern credit was risky, and its risk could not be diversified locally.[19] Second, the staple was agricultural, so that the population was geographically dispersed. This raised the transaction costs of issuing, monitoring, and recouping credit. In response, wholesale credit suppliers hired local merchants and planters to guide local lending.

Because of risk and, more importantly high transaction costs of administering many small loans secured by one crop, credit prices were high. High prices are not unambiguous evidence of monopoly, however, and there are several reasons to suspect that competition, not monopoly, better characterized southern country stores. For one thing, there were a lot of stores: 8000 in the Cotton South, 5½ to 9 miles apart, on average (*One Kind of Freedom*, p. 136). To be sure, 5½ to 9 miles was a long way to travel on horse or foot in order to comparison shop. That is why trips by tenants to compare lease and furnish conditions were taken during the month-long break around Christmas, rather than during the crop year (Vance, 1929). By postponing their trips to a time when they were free, tenants minimized their costs of searching for the best deal.

Tenants found, it seems, many offers to choose among. Vance (1929) reported how landlords bargained for new tenants. In less explicit, but no less clear, testimony to the extent of competition in the merchant supply business, Robert Somers reported that "[o]ne receives at every step [through the South in 1870] a lively impression of the great power residing somewhere in the United States of filling the most distant and surprising places with wares and traffickers of all kinds" (Clark, 1943, p. 39). Clark (1943) observed that Northern manufacturers kept Southern trading potential under review constantly and responded quickly to indications by

---

[19] I am indebted to Hugh Rockoff for emphasizing this point to me.

their drummers that this-or-that location could sustain a store. The link of the Southern merchant supply system of rural credit to the national credit market is evident in the correlation between the credit charges of Georgia and Louisiana merchants (*One Kind of Freedom*, pp. 240–241). That credit prices measured the costs of credit, rather than the extent of debt peonage, is supported further by the convergence of credit prices to cash prices over the crop year (M. B. Hammond, 1897, pp. 154–155).

That Southern tenants had the time to shop and that Northern suppliers sought new purchasers for their wares suggest that the high prices of the Southern furnish system reflected high costs of doing business, rather than high rates of monopolistic exploitation. Additional evidence that competition, not monopoly, characterized the Southern furnish system, is the readiness with which landlords reassigned to their tenants the right to mortgage crops. Because Southern farmlands were such unsuitable securities after the war, southern legislators quickly passed laws that (generally) permitted landlords to give liens upon their tenants' crops (M. B. Hammond, 1909; Woodman, 1968, pp. 287–301). Alternatively, landlords could assign the power to grant crop liens to their tenants. Under the crop lien laws, a lien holder (a country store, most often) held a lien on any and all of a tenant's crops up to the amount of the credit advanced. Typical lien terms stipulated sales of crops at negotiated prices (written into the terms) or, at the debtor's option, the market price prevailing at time of payment. If a tenant's crops were insufficient to repay the credit extended, the lien was continued automatically to future crops. A landlord was prevented from discharging a tenant in arrears. Liens were satisfied, however, by payment of cash in lieu of crops, so that a landlord or another storeowner could rescue a tenant from the clutch of some particular store by payment of the tenant's debt. Surely, if crop liens were the engine of exploitation, then landlords would not have reassigned them to tenants so freely. Perhaps merchants' greed would have sustained a market in reassigned liens, as well. Neither evidence of high profits in furnish is to be found, however (except perhaps in Wiener, 1975).

By and large, it seems that country stores were the most efficient purveyors of market goods, of crop finance, and of market information to the dispersed aggregations of small demands characteristic of the rural South.

It was a new era in the South after the war: blacks free, factors gone, and planters damaged. Many institutions—sharecropping, country stores, voting—expanded rapidly. Devotion to cotton remained, as did racism. The triumph of racism resulted in the rural enclosure of blacks in the late 1880s. Devotion to cotton perhaps immiserized the South, although no one yet has shown how. In fact, no one has yet shown if the South grew remarkably fast or remarkably slow after the war. The fact that Southern per capita income grew as rapidly as Northern, while the share of prime workers fell in the Southern population and rose in the Northern suggests that those three pillars of the postbellum economy—cotton, tenancy, and country stores—proved worthy.

Why has *One Kind of Freedom* increased our understanding of the postbellum South and of blacks' new freedom so little? I think it is because Ransom and Sutch had preconceptions, that Southerners, especially black Southerners, never had a chance and were kept cleaned out continuously while whites sought institutions to facilitate such constant impoverishment. Declining crop values, deteriorating lands, and monopolistic credit were chosen, it seems, a priori, as the engines to drive such impoverishment. That cotton's value declined, however, does not imply that its relative profitability declined: cheap fertilizer and cheap land plausibly kept cotton the best crop. In the South, just as in the North, tenancy plausibly speeded enrichment. That credit was costly in the South did not mean that credit was unprofitable.

Ransom and Sutch missed the true story. That story was of Negro enclosure, which grew from 1875 to 1890 (Woodward, 1951; Wharton, 1947), and mired the post-1900 South in the racism and stagnation so *un*characteristic of the postbellum South. In that time (post-1900), racism and poverty were not dictated continuously by cotton, tenancy, and country stores. Racism and poverty came immediately and directly to blacks from the discontinuous manipulation of the law by the sheriff (so well described in Rosengarten, 1975), and less directly to all by the compelled stagnation of southern thought. In sum, because Ransom and Sutch misconstrued the postbellum South as stagnant, they missed its remarkable and deplorable evolution from new hope in 1865 to no hope in 1900.

CHAPTER 4

Credit Merchandising in the Post-Emancipation South: Structure, Conduct, and Performance

ROGER L. RANSOM

AND

RICHARD SUTCH

The last three decades of the nineteenth century witnessed only a minuscule growth in the agricultural output of the Cotton South.[1] By the beginning of the twentieth century, all dreams of a "New South" had been dashed and the region would be characterized by any reasonable criterion as economically backward. In *One Kind of Freedom* (Ransom and Sutch, 1977) we argued that this inability of the Southern economy to expand at the same pace as the rest of the nation stemmed from institutional flaws which stymied economic growth and development. We identified such flaws in the South's educational institutions, in its patterns and practices of land ownership and farm tenure, in the banking and capital markets, and in the rural merchandising system.

In preparing our remarks for publication we have benefited from the advice and comments of Claudia Goldin, Stanley Engerman, Peter Temin, Gavin Wright, and Joseph Reid, Jr. As will be clear to our readers, these individuals do not always agree with our interpretation and should not be held responsible for whatever misunderstandings remain.

[1] The Cotton South is defined in *One Kind of Freedom* as an area of over 200,000 square miles, incorporating 337 counties from the eleven former states of the Confederacy (pp. 273–283 and map on p. xx). Whenever data limitations force reliance upon statewide aggregates, we refer to the five states of South Carolina, Georgia, Alabama, Mississippi, and Louisiana. A discussion of the rate of growth of agricultural output in the Cotton South can be found in *One Kind of Freedom* (pp. 9–12 and Appendix F), as well as in Chapter 7, of this volume.

The institutional problems we pointed to have been discussed before, and indeed our attention to these issues did not represent a significant departure from the conventional historical interpretation of the period.[2] Despite its long heritage, our analysis of the role of the rural merchant has become the focus of considerable controversy among our colleagues in economics. Our characterization of the merchant's credit business as a "territorial monopoly" which produced a system of "debt peonage" has been challenged as logically flawed and misleading. The debate has continued for several years now, with only limited progress towards a concensus.[3] Since the symposium at Duke University extended the analysis of rural merchandising and produced a new round of critical discussion, this seems an appropriate place to expand on and hopefully to clarify our own position on the issues.[4] In *One Kind of Freedom* our concern was not (as is the fashion in some quarters) to demostrate that the standard theory of competitive market behavior could be applied to yet another historical situation. Rather, we hoped to better understand the performance of the South's agricultural economy by examining the structure and conduct of an important industry with which it interacted: rural merchandising. The outcome of this approach was an economic model specifically tailored to reflect the peculiar features of the time and industry under study.[5] We presented that model in an earlier article in *Agricultural History* (Ransom and Sutch, 1975), and we relied heavily upon it in preparing our description of "territorial monopoly" for *One Kind of Freedom*. The *Agricultural History* model incorporates a number of features of the Southern credit merchandising business which we thought were of fundamental historical importance, particularly the crop lien and the dual price structure.

Our economist critics object, claiming that there is no need for a "new" theory, since the existing competitive models employed by economists to study a wide range of problems explain the situation in the postbellum South "well enough." Claudia Goldin, Peter Temin, and Joseph Reid

---

[2] C. Vann Woodward's *Origins of the New South* (1951) is a highly regarded history of the period. The bibliography by Charles Dew (1971) and the review by Harold Woodman (1977) are also useful guides to the historical literature.

[3] The basic elements of our debt peonage argument, together with supporting evidence, appeared in Ranson and Sutch (1972, 1975). Our conclusions were challenged by Brown and Reynolds (1973), DeCanio (1973; 1974a, pp. 111–113), and Higgs (1977, pp. 56–57, 184).

[4] We do not intend to suggest that the other elements of our discussion in *One Kind of Freedom* were accepted without question or criticism. Some of the other issues raised by the other authors here are dealt with in Chapter 7. Our original arguments on sharecropping and racism have been extended in Ransom and Sutch (1978a).

[5] This methodological procedure has been standard in the field of industrial organization at least since the appearance in 1959 of Joe S. Bain's *Industrial Organization* (Bain, 1968). We employ the term "industry" in Bain's sense of that word. The output which defines this particular industry is seasonal agricultural credit secured by a crop lien.

each raise this argument in the present volume, as did Stanley Engerman during a symposium held at Duke University in 1978.[6] They differ, however, in their choice of the competitive model offered as an alternative. Temin seems to favor models of "spatial competition of the sort analyzed by Hotelling and Lösch" (Temin, Chapter 2). Engerman spoke of "imperfect competition" and "monopolistic competitors"; terms which are commonly used to describe models associated with E. H. Chamberlin and Joan Robinson. Reid made the even bolder claim that credit was supplied "competitively" and "efficiently," suggesting that he was thinking of the model of pure competition developed by Smith and Marshall (Reid, Chapter 3). Goldin offered no explicit competitive model, but took pains to argue that "merchants may not have been monopolists" (Chapter 1).[7] As a consequence, a considerable portion of the debate has been directed toward the demonstration that some competitive model or another is an adequate framework within which to examine the issue of economic growth in the postbellum South.

The first point that needs to be made is that neither our approach nor that of any one of our critics can be said to be "incorrect." Each offers an "explanation" of the economic behavior of merchants and farmers in the South after 1865, and they all focus attention on the role which market forces played in shaping that behavior. Our interpretation concludes that competitive forces in the credit markets were stifled by certain institutional features; our critics tend to stress that powerful competitive pressures were nonetheless present and affected the economic outcome. We claim that the credit charges of merchants were higher than they would otherwise have been because of the merchant's exploitive monopolylike position; our critics insist that the magnitude of these charges can be justified by legitimate costs incurred in providing the credit services. We insist that farmers in the South, confronted by monopolistic prices, would have preferred to grow less cotton and more corn, but were forced to do otherwise; our critics insist that Southern farmers concentrated on growing cotton because they perceived the advantages of that crop in the South.

[6] Brown and Reynolds (1973), DeCanio (1973, 1974b), and Higgs (1973, 1977) have made similar points elsewhere. For a more complete exposition of our views on the methodological issues at stake, see Ransom and Sutch (1978b).

[7] Elsewhere, DeCanio has suggested the applicability of a model of "monopolistic competition" in which the "rate of profit is driven down to normal levels" (DeCanio, 1979). Though Higgs stresses the force of competitive pressures, he comes the closest of our critics to our own position by asserting that monopoly power played a role in explaining merchant behavior (Higgs, 1977, pp. 57–58). Brown and Reynolds do not offer an alternative model "derived from competitive theory," and they even agree with us when they say "it may be useful to describe the merchant-creditors as possessing some degree of monopoly power" (Brown and Reynolds, 1973, pp. 862, 866). Their tone, however, remains skeptical.

To some observers this dispute may appear as merely a metaphysical dialogue on the part of economists, each concerned to show that his or her abstract model of "competition" or "monopoly" best fits the "reality" of the postbellum South. However, we believe that there is more at stake than the theoretical elegance of economic models. The methodological issues which lie at the center of this debate are of importance to historians as well as economists, and the question of whether or not Southern farmers earned lower incomes than they might have in a different institutional environment is of considerable historical interest.

From the beginning our thinking about the role of the Southern merchant was influenced by the historical evidence (subsequently summarized in *One Kind of Freedom*, pp. 149–164), that farmers vociferously and repeatedly complained that merchants would not allow them to farm as they wished. The farmers explained that their need for seasonal credit and the absence of an alternative supplier of such credit compelled them to accede to the merchants' wishes. Since this description was consistent with other evidence, we accepted it as accurate, and intentionally constructed a model of the mercantile business to incorporate a form of monopolistic power and to offer an explanation for the farmers' complaints of exploitation. Throughout the debate, our critics have placed little weight on this historical evidence. Some of them ignored it outright; others dismissed the farmers' complaints with a non sequitur that "historically, 'middlemen' have not been held in high repute."[8]

In this situation, one might at first be inclined to believe that our interpretation might best be defended by gathering even more evidence that the farmers' complaints were real, and that they accurately reflected the situation. Since no alternative model has adequately explained the farmers' outcry, such additional support might settle the issue. On the other hand, we recognize that conventional theories of economics do not admit the possibility that exploitation by a credit monopoly and the forced overproduction of cotton could have happened in the market economy of the postbellum South. Therefore, we concluded that what is needed is not more historical evidence that these phenomena were real, but rather a reasonable theoretical mechanism which explains how such things could happen.[9]

[8] Brown and Reynolds (1973, p. 866). DeCanio devotes a chapter of his book to an argument which suggests that contemporary literary evidence ought to be ignored as inherently unreliable by quantitative historians (1974a, Chap. 2). An analysis and rejection of DeCanio's argument can be found in Sutch (1975, pp. 402–406).

[9] In this regard, consider Claudia Goldin's comment that "the crucial issue is not what merchants actually did, but whether [they] would have wanted to force tenants into overproducing cotton . . . ." (Chapter 1). We believe that what merchants actually did is indeed the crucial issue, but we recognize the need to provide an explanation of their actions which is consistent with the basic principles of economic analysis.

We originally proposed such a mechanism in the *Agricultural History* article already mentioned (Ransom and Sutch, 1975), but our critics remained skeptical. As we understand it, their skepticism is based on a feeling that the theoretical model which we employ to describe the workings of the post–Civil War credit monopoly system is not applicable to the historical situation in the sense that it has implications which are inconsistent with evidence presented in *One Kind of Freedom*. Therefore, rather than offering new evidence, we shall try to respond to the specific questions directed to the theoretical issues involved in our arguments. To order our remarks, we have organized them under three traditional headings: Structure, Conduct, and Performance.

STRUCTURE

The issues raised with respect to our description of the industrial structure of credit merchandising are captured in the rhetorical question: "How can an industry with thousands of small firms, each located only a few miles from its nearest counterpart, an industry frequently experiencing both new entry and failures of existing firms, and exhibiting rapid growth be characterized as "monopolistic?" Since none of the critics took issue with the quantitative data we presented to describe the structure of merchandising (*One Kind of Freedom*, pp. 132–146), the dispute must involve the way in which we and our critics interpret the evidence. As we see it, there are at least three substantive issues involved. One regards the size of the firm, the second regards barriers to competition, and the third involves the frequent entry of new firms and the growth of the industry.

Size

It is true that the typical country store in the postbellum South was small. It served fewer than seventy farms, and probably did less than $6,000 of business annually (*One Kind of Freedom*, p. 137). But we maintain that small size is not incompatible with monopoly power. In the South stores were isolated from direct competition with each other by the high costs of transportation and information. In our view, this isolation gave each merchant a monopoly within his own limited market area. We characterized this type of geographically constrained monopoly as a "territorial monopoly." Small size, of course, makes entry easier for potential competitors. However, this point should not be exaggerated. The "optimal-sized" firm seemed to require a net worth of between $5,000 and $10,000; a sum well beyond the means of most southerners (*One Kind of Freedom*, p. 138). In any case, there were substantial barriers to competition.

Barriers to Competition

According to our argument in *One Kind of Freedom*, the localized monopoly of the rural merchant was protected from direct competition by various barriers to successful entry. We believe that the most important of these barriers were: (1) the particularistic nature of Southern society that excluded most outsiders from participation in the social life of the community and thus made economic life there less attractive (*One Kind of Freedom*, pp. 117, 120); (2) a coincidence of interest between landlords and merchants that made it difficult to shift tenant farmers away from their established merchant without the landlord's cooperation (*One Kind of Freedom*, pp. 127–128, 146–148); (3) the political and social power of established merchants that made it unwise (and even dangerous) for customers to shift their patronage elsewhere (*One Kind of Freedom*, pp. 126–127, 147–148); and. (4) economies of scale which made firms capitalized at less than approximately $5,000 poor risks (*One Kind of Freedom*, pp. 137–140). Of these four arguments, only one—the coincidence of interest between landlord and merchant—has been questioned by our critics.

Goldin and Reid both ask why the landlord would not have had an incentive to prevent the exploitation of tenants by the merchants.[10] Although these authors presented neither evidence nor an argument suggesting that landowners actually did have an economic interest in protecting their tenants, one possible argument along these lines was offered by Stanley Engerman. He suggested that exploitation of tenants by merchants might have lowered the land rent which could be charged by landowners. Such an argument presumes a significant elasticity in the demand for rented land, so that lower expected incomes for tenants would lead to lower demand for tenant farms. Engerman's conjecture also presumes that landlords perceived their class interest in making tenant farming more attractive, and acted in concert against merchants to achieve this end. We think there is a good reason to reject both of these presumptions.

It is misleading to think of Southern farmers as freely choosing to pursue an agrarian life from some number of other alternatives. Most farmers, particularly the newly emancipated blacks, were trapped into agricultural occupations by their poverty, ignorance, and immobility. To suggest that the level of income which they expected to earn from farming had much impact on the aggregate demand for land rentals strains the

---

[10] Goldin (Chapter 1) draws on the work of Jonathan Wiener (1975) for evidence of planter–merchant conflict. However, we interpret the conflict which Wiener focuses on as being political and social rather than economic in nature (*One Kind of Freedom*, p. 346, footnote 34). In *One Kind of Freedom* we discussed merchant–landlord relations on pp. 146–148.

historical evidence. If the demand for land was elastic, why did it take over a generation for a sizable outmigration from Southern agriculture to develop?[11]

Even though the aggregate demand for tenant farms—and therefore rents—was unlikely to be very responsive to the level of expected income, it might still have been possible for an individual landlord to charge higher rents than were generally prevailing if he could promise a less exploitive merchandizing arrangement. The farmer would be indifferent to the choice, however. In one case he would be exploited by the merchant charging an exhorbitant price for credit, in the other he would be exploited by the landowner charging an exhorbitant rent for land. While the possibility of increasing rents might have an obvious appeal to landlords, the problem they faced was finding a way to successfully force the merchant to provide better terms to the farmer. In principle, one can imagine the use of political or physical force; or the effective use of moral suasion to accomplish this end. However, there is no evidence that such attempts were common. Apparently landlords who were not themselves merchants did not typically have the power to countervail the merchant's monopoly over the supply of credit.[12]

The most obvious way for a landlord to divert any potential monopoly profits into his own pocket was to become a merchant himself. It is obvious that in any case where the roles of landlord and merchant were combined, no conflict of interest would exist to protect the tenant borrower. In some regions of the South, the planter class actually did take over the merchandising business, and in other parts the merchants took over the land, displacing the previous landowners (Wiener, 1975, 1976, 1978; *One Kind of Freedom,* pp. 146–148). We have not estimated what fraction of tenant farmers rented land from an individual who was both landlord and merchant, although we believe that such situations were common.[13]

[11] Incidentally, this point about elasticity appears to be relevant to the argument that Goldin attributes to Fred Dong that tenants would refuse to enter a business in which they would be victimized by merchants. According to our way of thinking, the tenant farmers had little choice.

[12] We do not believe that the political disagreements or the hostility between merchant and landowning classes were prompted by attempts on the part of landlords to improve the lot of their tenants. To cite these conflicts as evidence that landlords protected tenants ignores the many other sources of conflict between groups. Moreover, the fact that tenants would not, in any case, escape exploitation makes such counterfactual speculations irrelevant to our major point.

[13] In *One Kind of Freedom* we reproduced a contract between Fenner Powell, a sharecropper, and A. T. Mial, his landlord (Fig. 5.1, p. 91). Interestingly, Mr. Mial was also a credit merchant (Fig. 6.2, p. 124). Our conjecture that such situations were common should perhaps be tested by a detailed study of merchant landholdings.

Entry and Growth

Our identification of the barriers to successful entry into rural merchandising is fundamental to our argument since entry is generally regarded to be the nemesis of monopoly power. Some critics, however, see a contradiction between our claim that barriers to competition protected the monopoly of the general store and our quantitative evidence that attempts to enter were nevertheless common. Thus, it is equally important to our argument to maintain that effective barriers to competition are not necessarily incompatible with frequent *attempts* to enter the industry, nor with growth in the number of firms. Many of the new ventures into merchandising would be doomed to an early failure, of course, if the barriers were truly in place. That, at least, is the interpretation we put forward in *One Kind of Freedom* to explain the high rates of entry and failure observed (pp. 140–146). Our critics apparently question this explanation on the grounds that prospective competitors would be foolish to even attempt entry if it were clear that barriers to success were insurmountable. In a static environment this argument would carry some force. However, during the period over which we measured entry into and exit out of Southern merchandising (1870–1885), the industry was experiencing rapid growth. In a 27-county sample, the number of general stores increased over fourfold (Table 7.6, p. 141). We believe this growth was in response to four factors which served to expand the demand for the merchants' services. First, there was the growth of agricultural output, which we estimated expanded 45.7% between the two dates (Table F.3, p. 259). Second, there was the spread of tenancy as the old plantation system broke down (pp. 68–71, 87–88). Third, there was the consolidation of the furnishing business into the hands of general merchants and away from the planter elite and the cotton factors (pp. 107–109, 117–125). And finally, there was the rapid growth of general stores located in towns and cities (pp. 141–142).

The increased demand for merchants' services in rural areas could not be met by an expansion in the scale of existing stores much beyond a capitalization in the neighborhood of $10,000. We conjectured that the information and supervison costs became excessive beyond that size (*One Kind of Freedom,* pp. 137–139). With a limit on the size of an individual store, expansion of the tenant system and the expansion of agricultural production meant that there was room for some new entrants to successfully establish themselves. Although the threat of failure was very real (approximately one-third of all new entrants between 1870 and 1885 failed within five years), the lure of monopoly power and the chance to establish a new business in a growing industry apparently attracted a continuous stream of potential store operators into the furnishing business (*One Kind of Freedom,* Table 7.8, p. 143).

The expansion of the market for merchants' services meant that the geographical size of the existing merchants' territory could shrink as entry took place without reducing the volume of business or weakening the effective control which established merchants held over the farmers still within their territories. An examination of the location of successful entrants demonstrated that for the most part they located on the boundary between two or more existing markets (*One Kind of Freedom,* p. 140). Thus, the successful new entrant was able to carve out a market of his own that was geographically distinct from those of nearby stores. However, from the perspective of the farmer, such new entry would rarely bring effective competition.[14]

CONDUCT

The most significant issue concerning the conduct of the rural merchant's business which our critics raise is whether or not the rate of interest charged for seasonal credit was exhorbitant. We believe that three aspects of this question must be kept distinct: (1) Was the credit price for supplies exhorbitant in the sense that it exceeded marginal cost? (2) Did we correctly calculate the implicit rate of interest which farmers who bought on credit had to pay? (3) What does the interest rate paid by the farmer imply for the rate of return on the merchant's capital?

Credit Prices

There is no question that the differential between cash and credit prices was substantial.[15] Data reported by the Georgia Department of Agriculture between 1881 and 1889 showed that credit prices averaged 29.7% higher than cash prices. The high markup for credit does not, of course, represent a prima facie case for exploitation. Temin, Goldin, Reid, Engerman, DeCanio, Brown and Reynolds, and Higgs have all suggested that these high credit prices may have merely reflected the high risks of lending to tenant farmers during this less-than-prosperous era.[16] While

---

[14] The inference drawn by Goldin that "there were large numbers of farmers who had virtually no access to a merchant prior to the appearance of one of [the] new entrants" is, we believe, unwarranted. Despite the rapid growth in the number of rural store locations, the average distance between a farmer and his geographically nearest merchant was only modestly reduced. The increase by 2.4 times in the number of store locations in 27 representative counties between 1870 and 1880 (Table 7.6, p. 141) implies that the average geographical area covered by a merchant contracted from 169.4 to 70.3 square miles, with an accompanying fall in the radius of the merchant's territory (the distance x in *One Kind of Freedom,* Fig. 7.1, p. 136) from 8 to 5.2 miles. We believe that 8 miles would not make the store location so remote as to be beyond the range of a typical farmer.

[15] Claudia Goldin, who has made an extensive review of available data on credit prices, has accepted the reliability of the Georgia data which we employed.

[16] Our calculations are given in *One Kind of Freedom*, Tables 7.1 and 7.2 pp. 129–130. See

this is a plausible argument, these writers do not provide evidence relating to the actual levels of either the costs or risks in the 1880s.

In *One Kind of Freedom* we constructed an example to illustrate what a "reasonable" markup for credit sales might be, making what we argued were generous assumptions about the costs of lending and assuming a 5% rate of default on loans outstanding. In order for the merchant to earn a 10% return on the capital invested, our example showed, the credit price would have to have been about 10% above cash prices—or only one-third the level of the observed credit/cash price differential in Georgia (*One Kind of Freedom*, Appendix D). No one has criticized our method of calculation or our cost estimates. The only point which appears to be at issue is the true magnitude of the default rate. We chose a level of 5% for our example on the basis of a 1929 study by Sherrod Morehead. We argued that twentieth century default rates would surely exceed those of the period before 1890, and we also built into our calculations a generous allowance for supervisory costs. Calculations reported in *One Kind of Freedom* indicated that the reported default rate would have to have equalled 38% per year to justify the markups actually charged (pp. 242–243).

The only additional evidence presented by our critics on this issue of default rates is Goldin's report that 25% of the tenants failed to fully meet their end-of-the-year obligations. This statistic was taken from a survey of landowners conducted by the North Carolina Bureau of Labor Statistics in 1887 which reported that approximately 75% of tenants were able to "pay out" that year (Jones, 1887, pp. 82–85). We believe that two points need to be made. First, while the proportion of farmers left in debt may have been as high as 25% such a figure can not be taken as evidence that one-fourth the mercantile debt was defaulted each year. The relevant statistic is not the proportion of farmers who failed to pay fully on time; but rather the proportion of all money lent out that was carried forward or lost. Since even those farmers who failed to "pay out" must have typically repaid a sizable fraction of their season's debt, a 5% overall default rate is a reasonable estimate in the context of our example. Second, the North Carolina Report is not inconsistent with our model of merchant behavior, which suggests that the storekeeper would attempt to expropriate as much as possible of the farmer's surplus income and leave the farm family with little or nothing after paying their end-of-the-season debts (Ransom and Sutch, 1975, pp. 413–415). In such a world, it would hardly be surprising if as many as 25% of the farmers fell below the line.

There is no doubt that more research is needed to improve our knowl-

---

Chapters 1, 2, and 3 as well as DeCanio (1979), Brown and Reynolds (1973, pp. 866–867), and Higgs (1977, pp. 56–57) for the views of these authors.

edge about the actual rate of default on nineteenth century merchant loans. Until such work is completed, however, we remain convinced that our earlier estimate of a 5% rate of default annually is likely to exaggerate the true figure, and it is virtually certain that the truth was nowhere near the 38% rate required to justify the credit charges actually observed.

The Rate of Interest

In *One Kind of Freedom*, we calculated that the rate of interest implicit in the cash-credit price differential was 59.4% per year (Table 7.2, p. 130, and Appendix D). Goldin and Temin both suggest that our method of computation exaggerates the rate of interest implied by the credit prices. For the purposes of our calculations, we assumed that all loans were repaid when due. They argue that the loans were frequently left unpaid in November and carried without charge into the subsequent calendar year. If that were the case, then the average length of the retail credit loan involved would exceed six months, and the effective interest rate paid would be correspondingly lower. We cannot accept this suggestion for several reasons. First, our model of the merchant's business suggests that he would have strong reasons to prevent the farmer from accumulating a debt which he could not pay off on time. As Robert Higgs has observed, "promoting a perpetual indebtedness would have meant giving away real resources."[17] Second, we have found no evidence that merchants actually did carry sizable accounts from one year to the next. On the contrary, our evidence suggested that merchants were likely to curtail the credit of someone who was in jeopardy of overextending his means of repayment. Third, when bad weather or miscalculation left a farmer unable to discharge his obligations, the typical practice seems to have been for the merchant to carry the debt at some explicit rate of interest. Jaqueline Bull reports that such a rate varied between the legal ceiling of 8% up to 25%. (Bull, 1952, p. 48). Our critics present no evidence that debts were generally carried from year to year without additional charge.[18] Finally, it is worth noting that if our critics were right and we were wrong on this point, it would only affect the rate of interest *received* by the merchant. Assuming that the debts were paid when due is the correct method of calculating the contractual rate of interest *charged* the farmer. If the farmer entered the agreement in good faith, then the contractual rate is the one which must have influenced his decisions at the beginning of the season. An adjustment of our interest rate figures would be justified only if it is shown that farmers expected at the outset that

[17] Higgs (1977, p. 58). Also see Ransom and Sutch (1975, pp. 413–414, and *One Kind of Freedom*, p. 163.

[18] Bull does mention this possibility in her account and cites one instance in which the books of a merchant appear to have recorded no interest charged on a debt carried forward (Bull, 1952, p. 48).

their debts would be carried without additional charge beyond the November date. We have encountered no evidence that suggests tenants held such expectations.

Rate of Return

Temin suggests that we may have exaggerated the rate of return earned by the merchant because the typical loan period was six months rather than one year. He argues that the merchant's financial capital could not have been loaned out at the exhorbitant rates for the entire year. Rather, the merchant dispensed credit only as the farmer requested it throughout the year, leaving much of the mercantile capital idle for long periods of time. In Temin's model, that capital which was not loaned to farmers would be invested at the "normal" rate of return, thus earning income for the merchant. Over the period of a year, therefore, only about one-half the merchant's money would be invested in "exploitive" loans; the remainder would earn only a normal return. As a consequence, concludes Temin, the correct order of magnitude for the return to capital for a merchant whose credit prices were 30% above cash prices, was only 30%—not the 60% which we estimated.[19]

This particular dispute is unnecessary. Since we made no attempt in *One Kind of Freedom* to calculate the rate of return on merchants' capital, we could not have miscalculated such a number.[20] Our attention was directed to assessing the impact of the high credit prices on the farmers who had contracted to pay them; the profitability of the credit merchandising business was of only incidental relevance to our discussion. The rate of interest charged on the principal (the figure we calculated) is not the same concept as the rate of return on the total capital invested (the figure Temin discusses).

In any case, Temin's line of argument is invalid because it is based on an inaccurate description of a typical merchant's operation. The storekeeper did not, as Temin argues, set aside a fixed sum of his capital upon which to draw when his clients needed credit; the typical merchant was himself a borrower of capital. He obtained goods on consignment and paid the prevailing rate of interest for the credit extended. We found no evidence in our examination of Southern merchandising that commission rates were substantially above the rate prevailing in the North or West. Nor did we find evidence that store owners had substantial capital tied up in inventories.

---

[19] Goldin accepts Temin's argument in her chapter of this volume.

[20] We did estimate that 51 out of 94 successful merchants increased their net worth at the rate of at least 15% per annum (*One Kind of Freedom*, pp. 144–145). We noted that in some instances these gains were accomplished by attracting outside capital, but in any case, the point remains that the rate of growth of capital is not the same as a rate of return.

PERFORMANCE

Four issues have been raised about the evidence we provided on the performance of the merchandising industry. Our critics doubt that merchants were able to redistribute income in their favor by making monopolistic profits. They question our finding that merchants were able to force farmers to produce more cotton than they wished. Goldin suggests that we exaggerated the extent of the merchant's impact on southern agriculture by overstating the number of farmers who borrowed on credit and overestimating the magnitude of their credit purchases. And, largely by implication, our critics seem to discount our argument that the merchandising system helped to stifle economic growth.

Merchant Monopoly Profits

We chose the term "monopoly" to characterize the rural merchandising industry because we wished to emphasize the control which merchants exercised over their farmer-clients. Their power to influence the farmer's activities was a consequence of the absence of alternative sources of credit, and the extent of that power was reflected in the magnitude of the credit prices charged. Although we did not stress the point, there is another implication of the monopolistic structure of the business which has attracted attention. While our model does not invariably predict that merchants would accumulate large personal fortunes, their monopoly power and the high prices charged do raise the possibility that successful merchants significantly increased their net worth. Such evidence as we were able to gather substantiated our claim that this process did occur with some regularity (One Kind of Freedom, pp. 144–146), and contradicts Peter Temin's claim that a model of "spatial competition" in which only normal profits are earned fits the evidence equally as well as our concept of "territorial monopoly." [21]

Overproduction

No aspect of the arguments presented in One Kind of Freedom provoked more controversy than our assertion that merchants compelled

---

[21] We would emphasize that our model does not imply that territorial monopolists would invariably reap substantial profits. In the first place, no model of monopoly—ours included—implies that price will inevitably exceed *average* cost by a substantial margin. Prices which exceed *marginal* cost are the hallmark of monopoly power. We do not wish to press this point, since our examination of the successful merchants in the Mercantile Agency records and our cost estimates both suggest that price did exceed average cost in the usual case. Our monopoly model does suggest, in contrast to classical models of monopoly, that the scale of the firm will be constrained by the limits to the territory which can be served. Failure of mercantile houses to grow much beyond the size represented by a "pecuniary strength" of $10,000 cannot, therefore, be used as evidence against the applicability of our model.

their customers to plant more cotton each season than the farmers desired.[22] So many different points have been raised in this discussion that perhaps the best starting point is from the common analytical ground which we share with our critics. All of the commentators seem to accept our underlying assumption that Southern farmers were market-oriented producers who responded to changes in relative prices.[23] An implication of that assumption which seems to be universally accepted is that, in the absence of distortions, Southern farmers would have chosen to devote some fraction of their acreage to cotton as a cash crop and would devote the remainder of their acreage to feed and food stuffs such as corn.[24] The proportions of cotton and corn would be adjusted each year at planting time in accord with the farmer's expectations about market prices which the two crops would command at harvest. A geometric portrayal of this market response is displayed in Fig. 4.1, where the curve CC reflects the production alternatives of a given farm. In the diagram, the expected market price ratio for the two crops is measured by the slope of the straight line PP. As in the traditional analysis, the Southern farmer would prefer to produce at point S, where PP is tangent to CC.

The main point at issue is how this simple analysis should be modified to reflect the presence of a dual price for corn: one price for corn purchased with cash; the other for corn purchased on credit. It was our argument that the two-price structure would give those farmers who anticipated ending the current season with an insufficient surplus (of either corn or cash) to meet the farm's corn requirements in the subsequent year a different perspective than that of other observers. The cash price of corn would be irrelevant to such a farmer. He would not anticipate having surplus corn to sell at the cash price. Moreover, he would be unable to purchase all of the corn needed at the postharvest cash prices and therefore would be forced to fill his corn deficit at the higher credit price. At the margin, corn grown this season will be worth more than its cash price to such a farmer. Anticipating that he will have to pay the credit price for purchased corn in the future, the farmer would wish to plant more corn this year (if he were allowed to) than would be the case

[22] Goldin, Reid, and Temin each raise questions or express doubts on this point in the previous chapters.

[23] DeCanio (1973) has taken some care to establish this point econometrically. Gavin Wright makes the point that an assumption of market orientation should not be accepted uncritically. Many small farms may have shunned the market in order to protect themselves from the uncertainty and from a dependency inherent in market activity. However, even Wright accepts the *assumption* that farms were influenced by market forces in the post Civil War environment (Wright, 1978, pp. 45–47; 164–176). Most of the other commentators accept the assumption of market orientation without question.

[24] As Temin makes clear, it is convenient to allow "corn" to represent a composite good which aggregates all of the feed and food crops on the farm, just as cotton could stand in the analysis for any of the other southern cash crops.

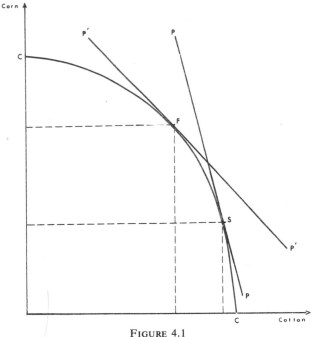

FIGURE 4.1

were there no difference between cash and credit prices. The higher the anticipated credit price, the more corn and less cotton would be desired at the outset of any year. Put in terms of Fig. 4.1, the introduction of a credit price for corn reduces the slope of the price ratio as viewed by such a farmer from PP to $P'P'$, and shifts the desired crop mix from S to F. [25]

Would Southern farmers have perceived their self-interest as our analysis presumes? If not, there was certainly no shortage of advice from those who urged farmers to consider the *credit* price for corn supplied and not the cash price when making their decisions at the outset of the season. The January 1880, report of the Georgia Department of Agriculture was explicit:

> Think of this farmers of Georgia who buy bacon at credit prices: Can you not raise bacon at less than twelve cents per pound?
>
> If farmers had the cash to purchase the year's supply early in the season when the price is low as it has been for several years past, from 4½ to 5½ cents, it might possibly be cheaper to them than raising a full supply; but how few avail themselves of these low prices. Do they not deceive themselves with the idea, however, that they cannot raise it at 4½ cents per pound, and yet buy at twelve cents?
>
> The fact that it sells during the winter at 4½ cents does not benefit him who

[25] See our earlier presentation of this argument in Ransom and Sutch (1975, pp. 407–411), and in *One Kind of Freedom*, pp. 161–162.

must purchase during the summer at twelve. The question for him to consider is not whether he can raise it at 4½ cents, but whether it is not cheaper for him to raise his bacon than to buy at 12 cents.[26]

Temin argues that our analysis of the dual price (and by implication the argument by the Georgia Department of Agriculture just quoted) contains a logical flaw. He explains his case as follows:

"The cost of borrowing . . . was a sunk cost at the time of planting. Irrespective of what [the farmer] planted, he would have to pay interest to the merchant to get through the year. But this interest should not have been a factor in his decision of what to plant. When deciding what to plant, the farmer should have chosen a crop mix that would maximize his income in terms of corn. He did not consume cotton; he grew it only to acquire the income used to buy corn. . . . And the corn bought after the harvest with the proceeds from his cotton crop could be bought for cash. The relevant price ratio for deciding what crops to plant therefore was the ratio of the cotton price to the cash price of corn.

We do not accept this argument. It is true that the cost of the current year's borrowing is sunk, it is the *anticipated* high cost of corn in the subsequent year which is relevant to our model; not the magnitude of the current year's debt or the current credit price of corn. (The line $P'P'$ is based on the selling price of cotton and the purchase price of corn which the farmer *expects* to face at the end of the season.) If the farmer changed the crop mix this season to favor corn, he would obviate the need to purchase so much exhorbitantly priced corn next year.

Temin objects, arguing that a farmer who did as we suggest would not be maximizing his income. This objection would only be correct if we assess the contribution of the current year's corn crop to income in terms of the cash price of corn. Our argument is that it should be assessed, not at that price, but at the expected credit price for corn in the subsequent season, since that is what it is worth to an indebted farmer. Temin counters that this part of our argument overlooks the possibility that the farmer could buy corn at cash prices after the harvest with the proceeds of the cotton crop. But there was a feature of the credit merchandising business which rules out this possibility. It must be remembered that the merchant was able to manipulate both the credit price and the amount of cotton to be grown in a way that the current year's corn requirements (at credit prices) would be such a large fraction of the farmer's total output that there would be no cotton left for the farmer to sell on his own account (Ransom and Sutch, 1975, p. 415).

Our basic argument comes down to a simple proposition: The cost of credit should not be irrelevant to a farmer's crop mix choice since he would reduce his future need for credit by adopting a more corn-intensive

---

[26] Georgia Department of Agriculture (1880, p. 6). The credit price of 12 cents a pound used by the GDA in this example exaggerates the typical situation. The average credit price for bacon in 1879 was 9.5 cents a pound; the average cash price was 7 cents per pound (*One Kind of Freedom*, Table D.1, p. 239).

crop mix this year and year-in year-out.[27] In the Appendix to this paper we reiterate this argument in a more rigorous fashion.

Temin observes that if farmers were actually producing at point F in Fig. 4.1, they would be operating inefficiently since, from any perspective other than the farmer's, PP represents the relevant price ratio, and S the efficient crop mix. The farmer is oblivious to this inefficiency, since from his perspective, corn is more valuable than its cash price would suggest.[28] Most other Southerners would have had no powerful interest in avoiding this inefficiency by intervening to prevent the farmer from choosing the more corn-intensive crop mix at F. However, the merchant would do less business with a customer producing at F than with a customer who produced at S. For this reason, the merchant would exercise whatever power he could bring to bear on the farmer in an attempt to compel a greater production of cotton than the farmer would prefer. In other words, the merchant would act to push the farmer away from F and back towards S.

The merchant offered the only credit that could be secured with a crop-lien, and the farmer who had no other colateral would have been unable to resist the merchant's insistence that sufficient cotton be planted before a credit line would be approved. Because the farmer was prevented from growing more corn in response to the merchant's credit prices, the efficiency loss commonly associated with the distortion of monopoly prices was largely avoided. The farmer was compelled to grow more cotton, and this reduced the "deadweight social loss" from allocative inefficiency. However, the social increment generated by the forced specialization was taken by the merchant in the form of exhorbitant credit charges.[29]

---

[27] In the course of his remarks, Temin suggests an alternative way to analyze the presence of a dual price for corn. Rather than think of two different prices for corn, think of two distinct goods —"cash-corn" and "credit-corn"— each with its own unique price. In principle, we have no objection to this approach. With three goods in the analysis there would be two relative price ratios, the cotton/cash-corn price ratio as before and now the credit-corn/cash-corn price ratio. Of course, this last relative price is a simple function of the rate of interest, and we discussed its magnitude at length in *One Kind of Freedom* (pp. 128–131 and Appendix D). Farmers faced with a high credit-corn/cash-corn ratio would choose, if free to do so, to produce more credit-corn than they would if the price ratio were lower. To increase the production of credit-corn (corn grown this year and stored until next year) would require that less cotton be grown. This is, as one would expect, the same result obtained in our analysis. Facing high prices for credit, the farmer would prefer to grow less cotton and more corn than he would otherwise.

[28] We have no quarrel with Temin's formal definition of economic efficiency in terms of market price ratios. We merely wish to point out that when there are more than one set of market prices, efficiency is not uniquely defined. In this case the indebted farmer's notion of efficiency is different from that of other observers.

[29] Claudia Goldin misrepresents our position when she sees both allocative inefficiency and redistributive harm as a consequence of our model. Redistribution of income in favor of the merchant is an implication of our model, but large static inefficiencies are not.

How great was this redistribution? In *One Kind of Freedom* we presented two measures of the effect. We calculated that a farmer who paid credit prices in 1880 could have increased his income at the margin by about 29% by shifting resources from cotton to corn had he been free to do so (pp. 166–167). A second measure considered the effect of credit prices on a black tenant family in 1879. We estimated that when the family purchased on credit rather than cash it lowered their real income by 13.5% (p. 169).

Extent of the Monopoly

How many farms were affected by the merchant's monopoly? We estimated that 44.2% of all farms in 1879–1880 might have *avoided* dealing with the credit merchant (Goldin, by the way, estimates that only 30% escaped purchasing supplies on time).[30] However, many (83.5%) of the farms that avoided dealing with the merchant did so by acheiving self-sufficiency in the production of corn and foodstuffs. We believe that roughly 60% of these self-sufficient farms escaped the merchant by ignoring relative prices and adopting a "safety first" strategy of producing their own supplies in sufficient quantity to insure continued self-sufficiency. Cotton is then grown only as a "surplus" crop.[31] These farms have escaped dealing with the merchant, but they have not remained unaffected by his power. In order to avoid the threat of falling into debt, they have accepted a lower income (at self-sufficient production) than they would have if they were able to maximize the value of output measured by cash prices (at S in Fig. 1). (See Ransom and Sutch, 1975, pp. 412–413.) Our final estimate of the proportion of farms that were affected by the merchant's monopoly is 78%. This estimate includes the 55.8% of farms which were locked in, plus the 22.0% indirectly affected. Of course, the locked-in farms did not purchase everything they required on credit. Most farms began the year with some cash reserves, which would typically be exhausted within a few months (Sisk, 1955, p. 707). We suggested that a

---

The historian would wish to stop short of lauding the merchants as benefactors of the South for two reasons: If it were not for the merchants' exhorbitant credit prices, farmers would not wish to farm "inefficiently" at F in the first place, and in the second place, it was the merchants and not the farmers who were the beneficiaries of the coercion.

[30] *One Kind of Freedom*, p. 164 and note 52, p. 351. This estimate is based upon the calculation that 28.7% of the small farmers were self-sufficient, and the assumption that all of the 21.8% of southern farms that were larger somehow avoided purchasing on credit (p. 164). Elsewhere we reported the results of a survey taken in Georgia in 1875 and 1876 that approximately 25% of the farmers avoided purchasing on credit (p. 123).

[31] The 60% figure is the fraction of the self-sufficient farms that were characterized as small family units *One Kind of Freedom*, Fig. 8.5 and Table 4.3; pp. 160, 169). This is admittedly a rough guess. The safety-first model has been discussed extensively by Wright and Kunreuther (1975) and Wright (1978, pp. 62–74).

typical end-of-the-year debt for a farm family would have been in the neighborhood of $80.00 (*One Kind of Freedom,* p. 123); about 42% of the farmer's annual income (p. 216).

Claudia Goldin appears to take issue with this picture of Southern farming. "The Georgia reports do not indicate the general lack of supplies and widespread use of credit that Ransom and Sutch have claimed." In her chapter, Goldin calculates that "farmers purchased only supplies that were not home produced, that is, only about 30% of the total supplies they used each year." "Furthermore," Goldin continues, "farmers who purchased supplies, bought, perhaps at a maximum, 60% of these on time. A farmer in Georgia could have expected, therefore, to purchase only 18% of his total supplies on time." Goldin's estimate that 30% of all supplies were not home-produced is based on figures reported in line 1 of Table 1.3. These estimates, however, refer to the extent to which local production met the needs of the entire county; they do not refer to the extent to which farmers who were locked-in and paying credit prices were forced to purchase supplies (Georgia Department of Agriculture, 1890, p.4). Our self-sufficiency estimates suggest that much of the supplies that small farms had to buy on credit was actually produced within the county on the larger farms.[32] Goldin's second proportion—that 60% of the supplies purchased were bought on time—actually refers to the "per cent. of [all] farm supplies purchased on time," not to the percentage of *purchased* supplies. It is also probable that this estimate refers to the entire county and not solely to those farms that were not self-sufficient (Georgia Department of Agriculture, 1879, p.8). If our interpretation of the Georgia reports is correct, then the proportion of all supplies bought on time was approximately 60% not 18%.

Goldin's further insistence that the credit problem diminished over time also fails to convince us. Her analysis rests on an interpretation of figures from the Georgia Department of Agriculture Reports. In Table 1.3, she presents summary statistics from the responses of agricultural correspondents in Georgia between 1878 and 1890 to the questions:

(1) "[Give the] indebtedness of farmers, compared to last year, per cent."

(2) "Give amount of farm supplies purchased in comparison with last year, per cent" (Georgia Department of Agriculture, 1890, p. 4).

Goldin calculated the statewide averages from the county data, and cumulated the figures from year to year to discover the total change over a number of years. Her conclusion is that there was a continuous decline in indebtedness, and a marked lessening in farmers' dependence upon pur-

---

[32] *One Kind of Freedom,* Table 8.3, p. 159. Incidentally, we believe Goldin also mistakenly projects our calculation of the impact of credit on small locked-in family farms operated by blacks in 1879 to all farms (cf. *One Kind of Freedom,* p. 169).

chased supplies over the years 1882 to 1890. The aggregate fall in these variables, if we accept Goldin's analysis, is dramatic. She claims that "farmers in 1890 actually purchased only 25% of what they had in 1882." The corresponding reduction implied by the indebtedness figures in Goldin's table suggests that farmers in 1890 owed only 32% of the debt they owed in 1882.[33] However, these statistics are very misleading.

We have closely examined the reported figures from each of Georgia's 137 counties for the question on indebtedness for 1884, 1885, 1886, and 1887.[34] Our review suggests at least three major problems with the interpretation which Goldin has presented:

(1) Each year, only a fraction (approximately 70%) of the counties reported answers to the question. Only 48 of the 137 counties reported for each of the four years noted. The state average used by Goldin refers to a continually changing geographical area. Since counties experienced very different patterns of changing indebtedness, Goldin's failure to adjust for the nonreporting of counties calls into question the meaningfulness of her numbers.

(2) Table 4.1 presents the distribution of the 389 separate observations reported on the question of indebtedness, along with several summary statistics describing this distribution. It is immediately apparent that a simple average is a misleading index of the general trends. Although the average for all observations was 93.3—suggesting that a 7% annual improvement was typical—there were considerably more observations above the mean (217) than below (176). Sixteen percent of the reports indicated "100," or no change, and 46.5% of all reports indicated either no change or an *increasing* indebtedness of farms. These figures hardly describe a situation of steady improvement which saw the indebtedness of farms decline by seven percent per year.

The simple mean across the counties which Goldin relies upon is a biased estimate of the figure she wants to report. When calculating the average across counties of these "percentage changes in the percentage reported," the appropriate procedure must take into account the percentage of farmers who were indebted in the base year. The following example, comparing two counties in which each experienced a decrease of indebtedness amounting to 10% of all farmers, illustrates the point. Suppose in one county 80% of the farmers were indebted in the previous year. The correct response to the Georgia questionaire would be 87.5%. Suppose in another county only 20% of the farmers had been indebted the previous

---

[33] Goldin does not present the second estimate in Chapter 1, in part because of the ambiguity in the meaning of this question.

[34] Only four years were examined because county-by-county figures are not available in published form for most other years.

year, which means the decline would have been reported as 50%. A simple average of the two reports would be 68.75; leaving the impression that, in the counties taken together, indebtedness had decreased by 31% when in fact, if the counties were of equal size, it had actually declined by only 20%.

(3) Taken at face value, Goldin's statistics on debt and the dependence of farmers on purchased supplies suggest a view of the trends totally at odds with that presented by contemporaries. Moreover, the implied trends in Goldin's table are inconsistent with other evidence in the GDA reports. For example, Goldin reports that the annual percentage of a full supply of provisions of pork and corn produced on farms remained stable at about 60 to 68% for pork and 75% for corn. These figures seem plausible, and agree with our own estimates of self-sufficiency presented in *One Kind of Freedom* (p.160). Yet the statistics Goldin reports on the amount of supplies purchased in one year compared to the previous year are uniformly below 100% and when cumulated over the entire period imply that by 1890 farmers had reduced their dependence on purchased

TABLE 4.1

Distribution of Responses to the Question Regarding Indebtedness, from 137 Georgia Counties, 1884–1887

Reported response (relative %)	Number of observations	Percentage of total number
Below 75	40	10.3
75–79	45	11.6
80–89	54	13.9
90–93	37	9.5
94–99	32	8.2
100	62	15.9
100–109	33	8.5
110–119	39	10.0
120–129	38	9.8
130 and above	9	2.3
Total responses	389	100.0
No response	159	
Total	548	

Mean = 93.3
Standard deviation about the mean = 22
Median = 95
Mode = 100

Source: Georgia Department of Agriculture (1884, 1885, 1886, and 1887).

supplies to only one-fourth the level at the outset. Such an implication is not only inconsistent with the GDA evidence that the deficit in pork and corn remained unchanged; it also conflicts with the data reported in the 1890 Census of Agriculture, which gives evidence of a decline in the per capita production of food crops and swine between 1880 and 1890 (*One Kind of Freedom*, Table 8.1, Fig. 8.1, pp. 152–153).[35]

The Dynamics of Monopoly and Growth

Our critics have focused their attention on the logical consistency of our theoretical model of credit merchandising. This is perhaps to be expected, since ours was not an orthodox theory, and it yielded conclusions which might, at first glance, appear counterintuitive to an economist. We hope that the discussion in this chapter has served to clarify our position and justify our methodology.

We are concerned, however, that all of our attention to the details and logical ramifications of our theory may have obscured our broader issues. In *One Kind of Freedom* we constructed a model of the merchant's business which incorporated what we viewed as the unique features of the industry: the dual price system and the crop-lien. We did this because we believed that only such a complete model would shed light on the dynamic aspects of southern economic history.[36] If our analysis is correct, the rural merchandising industry contributed to the lack of growth and development in the South in ways which are quite apart from the theoretical disputes over the structure and conduct of the industry. Succinctly put, the merchandising industry stifled economic *growth* in at least three ways:

(1) The high price of loanable funds supplied by the merchant discouraged investment while at the same time barriers to entry acted to discourage capital flows from outside the region.

(2) The net income of many farm families was reduced to such low levels that their ability to save was severely impaired, and as a consequence, direct investment by families in their farms was made more difficult.

(3) One of the effects of a perpetual cycle of seasonal indebtedness was to constrain the mobility of labor.

---

[35] In the Georgia reports answers to the request "[Estimate the] condition of farmers, compared with last year, per cent." averaged 94% for 1884, 96% for 1885, 92% in 1886, and 98% for 1887. These four averages cumulate to 81.4%. This report of worsening conditions contrasts sharply with Goldin's conclusions that indebtedness and dependence upon purchased supplies were declining. What this contradiction suggests to us is that the answers obtained to questions of this nature are not very reliable. It was for this reason that we did not report such information in *One Kind of Freedom*.

[36] In the context of the historical narrative offered in *One Kind of Freedom*, our economic model of the dual price and crop-lien system has the further advantage that it offers a ready explanation of the frequently repeated and very explicit complaints of farmers that they were compelled to grow more cotton than they wished (*One Kind of Freedom*, pp. 159–162). Our critics have provided no alternative explanation for this agrarian discontent.

Economic *development* was also hindered because:

(1) The merchandising system tied Southern agriculture more tightly to the declining fortunes of the international cotton market.

(2) The expansion of the manufacturing sector was impeded by the absence of a more effective financial system which could have served as an intermediary between agriculture and industry.

(3) There may also have been a negative effect on the demand for manufactured products produced by the redistribution of income inherent in the merchant's exploitation.

These, of course, are difficult issues to deal with, and we only began to explore them in *One Kind of Freedom*. With the analysis there, however, we hope to have established a firm foundation for further investigation. The criticism of *One Kind of Freedom* expressed here should prove helpful not only in sharpening the theoretical models which comprise this foundation, but in revealing broad areas of agreement among scholars on the importance of the issues and the direction of subsequent research.

APPENDIX

Diagramatic Presentation of the Impact of Credit Prices for Corn on the Crop Mix Decision

A farmer who anticipates the perpetual need for seasonal credit will prefer (if the merchant would allow) to produce at F rather than at S in the diagram presented in Fig. 4.1. This point can be demonstrated by adding to Fig. 4.1 the level of corn requirements needed for the coming year. Suppose that the required level of corn is equal to M. Fig. 4.2 reproduces the production alternatives frontier and the two price ratios from Fig. 4.1 and adds the horizontal line MM at the level of the assumed annual corn requirements. (By assumption, M is greater than the amount of corn grown at F.) Whether the farmer produces at F or S, he will have to finance a corn "deficit" for the following year. If he produces at F, the corn deficit is $M - C_f$. If he produces at S, the deficit is the larger amount $M - C_s$. In either case, these corn deficits will have to be financed at credit prices, since the farm can not produce sufficient cotton to both meet this year's debts and finance next year's corn deficit at cash prices.

At credit prices, the price ratio of corn to cotton is indicated by the slope of the line $P'P'$. The line $P''P''$ in Fig. 4.2 is drawn with that same slope. Thus, D_f is the cotton equivalent of the corn deficit for a farmer at F. And D_s is the cotton equivalent of the corn deficit for a farmer at S.

It is true that the farmer at S will produce more cotton (Y_s) than the farmer located at F (Y_f). Note, however (and this is our point), that the anticipated *net* cotton income in the subsequent year after financing the corn deficit at credit prices will be higher for a farmer who chooses to produce at F this year than for the farmer who stays at S. That is, the distance $Y_f - D_f$ is greater than the distance $Y_s - D_s$. This result does not

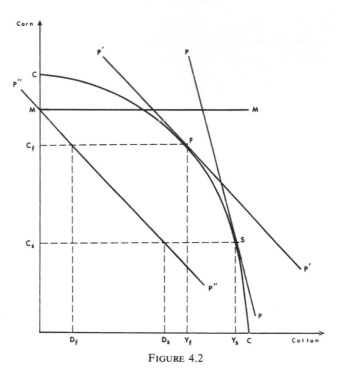

FIGURE 4.2

depend upon the shape of the production alternatives curve (as long as it remains bowed out), nor upon the magnitude of the credit–cash price differential. Recognizing the superiority of a sequence of years at F over a sequence of years at S, the farmer will be willing to make the move to F this year even though the current year's indebtedness is a sunk cost which can not be affected by the crop choice.

In terms of its cash value, total output at F is less than total output at S. (S is the production mix which maximizes the value of output evaluated at cash prices.) The farmer is willing to make this current sacrifice in order to reduce the necessary level of indebtedness (and increase *net* income) in future years. Indeed, the farmer does not even perceive that he would be making a current sacrifice, since he values corn not at cash prices, but at credit prices. (From that perspective, F is the production mix which maximizes the value of output.)

It would be the merchant who would perceive the loss of output entailed in a decision to move to F rather than to stay at S. For this reason, the merchant forces the farmer to produce at S by refusing to finance the current year's requirements unless the farmer agrees to plant Y_s cotton. In our terminology, the farmer is "locked-in" by the merchant to a continual sequence of years at S. While the merchant's action forces the farmer to be "efficient," the farmer would prefer to be at F (where he is better off), and he therefore continually complains not only about the high price of credit, but also of not being free to grow as much corn as he would like.

PART II

Economic Progress in the New South

CHAPTER 5

Freedom and the Southern Economy

GAVIN WRIGHT

Writing in 1857, Hinton Helper predicted that "three-quarters of a century hence, if slavery is abolished within the next ten years, as it ought to be, the South will, we believe, be as much greater than the North, as the North is now greater than the South" (p. 142). To a Northern observer of the 1970s generous enough to allow Mr. Helper the leeway of a half-century or so, his prognosis seems uncomfortably accurate. But in the nineteenth century, it was the poverty and disappointment of freedom which seemed most striking, the weakness and apparent perversity of the South's response to its own liberation. These are the central themes of *One Kind of Freedom*: the limited range of choices actually open to freedmen, the thwarted hopes for landownership, the stifling of progressive energies by exorbitant credit costs and racial barriers, the failure of the Southern economy to progress toward the national norm. As Helper's example attests, one could attempt to diminish the indictment by taking a longer view of the matter, by asking for a longer "time for adjustment" as it were, or by placing the South and the freedmen in a worldwide rather than merely a national comparative contest. Since historical conditions are seldom permanent, and since there are innumerable choices of comparative standards, this strategy can hardly fail; relativities like these are the historians' stock-in-trade.

This chapter proposes to examine *One Kind of Freedom* in a broader context, not to celebrate the long-run outcome of the developments deplored by Ransom and Sutch, but to show the elements of ambiguity and relativity in the economic issues under debate. Occasionally, we need to be reminded that the past contains multiple realities; a simplifying abstraction which successfully captures the essence of some historical situation for some purpose should not be confused with the history itself. Many of the analytical distinctions and working presuppositions which economists have brought to the study of the postbellum South

85

MARKET INSTITUTIONS AND ECONOMIC PROGRESS
IN THE NEW SOUTH 1865–1900

are not, in my view, well suited to unraveling important parts of that history.

My purpose, however, is not to preach a new nihilism but to identify some points of implicit consensus and to propose an alternative organizing framework which yields operational suggestions for research.

ECONOMISTS AND HISTORICAL THINKING

Two aspects of economists' thinking that are relevant for my purposes are (1) the treatment of static allocational efficiency in product and factor markets as a norm, and (2) the neglect or the unhistorical treatment of risk and uncertainty. Nonhistorical economists might well express astonishment at these two items, since economics journals are filled these days with proposed models of market failure, models of behavior in the presence of risk and uncertainty, models of imperfect information and transactions costs, models of altruistic behavior, malicious behavior, political behavior, and random behavior, models of dynamic disequilibrium behavior, models of Marxian economic relations, and many more. Economics is not as narrow as it is often depicted, but I believe these two phrases do aptly describe the economics that cliometricians have applied to history, and the explanation is not that cliometricians are poor economists. No one could possibly approach history or any empirical economic research with an infinity of theoretical possibilities in mind. Instead cliometricians do what all historians do, they come to history with a working conception of how an idealized economy works, which they commonly draw from the mainstream of conventional economics, and they examine the historical record either for confirmations or for deviations from that conception. In taking an efficient market resource allocation as a norm and then searching for deviations and exceptions, historical economists follow the format of economics teaching. Typically, students learn first the optimality properties of general competitive equilibrium in a world of profit-maximizing firms and utility-maximizing individuals; the instructor then moves through a conventional list of situations where these optimality rules are violated—external effects, monopoly power by firms or other organizations, consumer ignorance, racial discrimination, dynamic learning and technological developments, inequitable distributional results—and discusses the merits of government intervention in each case.

It is not necessarily true that this approach implies an antireform bias toward the status quo, nor a strong belief that markets do, by and large, work for the best. To prove this assertion with a counterexample, we need look no further than Ransom and Sutch, whose major research energies are devoted towards showing deviations from the competitive equilibrium: (1) in their treatment of slavery, they emphasize the exploitation which resulted from the fact that slaves were denied access to a free labor market; (2) their interpretations of debt peonage revolves crucially around the argument that merchants established territorial monopoly power in credit markets; (3) they define "overproduction" in terms of the relationship between the ratio of cotton and corn prices on the one hand, and the marginal rate-of-transformation in production on the other; (4) they fault sharecropping because it allowed land–labor ratios to differ inefficiently on farms of different tenure types; (5) and they view racial discrimination as resulting in large part from faulty beliefs by whites in innate racial inferiority. This list does not do justice to the many subtleties and insights in the connecting narrative, but these are the hypotheses which are formally developed and stressed. The purpose of the list is not to launch a refutation of these propositions, but to argue that Ransom and Sutch's definition of the important issues has largely been shaped by the focus on competitive equilibrium as a norm. And in common with many other economists, they tend to presume that the important factors in determining the rate of economic progress for blacks and for the South are closely related to the allocational efficiency of the Southern economy.

The organization of discussion around deviations from a competitive norm may be useful in many respects, but it is only one of many possible organizing principles, and it is highly abstract and simplified. Despite appearances, most of the issues which derive from this framework are not objective and well defined, because of the existence of risk and uncertainty in the real world. For example, "overproduction" in the Ransom–Sutch sense cannot be conclusively tested because cotton and corn yields were variable and uncertain, and the *interaction* between cotton and corn yields in a context of uncertainty is a complex, probabilistic phenomenon. Similarly, monopoly power is not sharply definable in a context of risky loans for risky purposes, spatial competition, and price discrimination. The spatial theorist Melvin Greenhut writes that "the inclusion of economic space requires recognition and acceptance of uncertainty as a basic property of the system. We also . . . find that economic space, uncertainty, and oligopoly go hand-in-hand" (Greenhut, 1970, p. 4). My point in making these observations is not to say that the Ransom–Sutch categories are meaningless or useless, but only to argue that we need to ask not so much whether these analyses are precisely true, but how well these abstractions really capture the most essential elements of the historical situation. On some of these points, it appears that the attempt to translate contemporary comments into this economic framework has led them into some conceptions which are narrower and weaker than they need to be.

Now cliometricians frequently do have to confront the reality of risk and uncertainty in the world, and when they do, they draw on a large economic literature. But the concept of uncertainty as it is used by nonhistorical economists is nonhistorical; by and large, uncertainty is treated as riskiness, which is an intrinsic attribute of an asset or an activity, and when cliometricians appropriate these theories, they merely broaden the notion of equilibrium to include premiums for riskiness. This approach to risk is a common dimension of the otherwise quite different analyses of sharecropping advanced by Robert Higgs (1973, 1977, pp. 50, 67–68) and Joseph D. Reid, Jr. (1973). Changes in these institutions over time are taken to be moving equilibria, responses to changes in riskiness or in the degree of risk-aversion in the population. In this way uncertainty is reduced to certainty equivalence, without any essential effect on the character of the analysis. This approach is useful in analyzing sophisticated financial markets, but it does violence to history and historical modes of thought. The record of Southern history from the Civil War until World War I is not fifty years of "riskiness" but is simply a recording of fifty years (*outcomes*) of activities carried out in a context of uncertainty. As historians we ought to entertain and indeed make the most of the notion that many of these outcomes were *unlikely*; and since in the historical mode of thought, these games of chance were not independent but serially connected, much of the whole history may have been improbable in some reasonable sense of that term.[1] From this vantage point, there is an essential indeterminacy to the debate over whether the merchant's credit charges were "justified" by risk, since we have only ex post measures of default and variance to go by. This is only one example of the widely demonstrated proposition that it is difficult and often impossible to infer behavioral or utility functions from observed market outcomes (Sanderson, 1974; Sonnenschein, 1973).

Let me propose a methodological strategy which might help us to escape the present impasse. First, in the hopes of focusing on objective and operational rather than subjective and unresolvable issues, I suggest that we reduce our attention to questions of motivation and tests of optimizing behavior, and concentrate instead on identifying the relevant constraints on choices, the set of options actually open at any time to tenants, landlords, merchants (and the economy as a whole), and how these changed over time. Second, I suggest that we focus on a magnitude which is objective, which constrains choice, and whose determination reflects a cumulative historical process, namely wealth. Third, I suggest that we not look for the "representative" tenancy or the typical credit market structure (monopoly or competition), but that we analyze explicitly the *distribution* of the relevant population in both the spatial and statistical

[1] For an analogous argument, see Crafts, 1977.

senses of that term. The following sections explore some of the disputed
issues with these precepts in view.

A major contribution of *One Kind of Freedom* is the finding that most of
the decline in output after the war is attributable to the reduction in
effective labor supply from the black population, a reduction which they
estimate to be between 28 and 37% per capita. Whether the labor-supply
effect accounts for the whole of the fall in per capita output between 1860
and 1880 (or whether there is significant room for an additional loss of
plantation scale economies) remains a bone of contention; but there
seems to be a consensus on the reality and significance of this voluntary
withdrawal of labor from the fields. In their text, Ransom and Sutch
demonstrate that mules were in ample supply after the war (p. 49); they
minimize the burden of replacing the farm capital physically destroyed by
the war (p. 50), and they give particularly short shrift to cultivable land as
a factor of production on the grounds that "the war did not, of course,
literally destroy the land. Therefore, with the decline in the labor supply it
is obvious that the land–labor ratio must have risen" (p. 48). They note
that the "improved acreage" reported in the 1870 census was actually
20% below the level of 1860, suggesting that "only limited scope existed
for increasing the land–labor ratio" (p. 48).

This all seems clear. But there is a surprise waiting if we actually
compute the ratio of acreage to effective workers on the slave plantations
of 1860 and black family farms of 1880. Using the information on p. 184 of
One Kind of Freedom, we find that the black family farms of 1880
averaged 7.5 acres of crops per worker, or 3.0 acres per family member.
Applying relatively generous adjustments for improved acreage other
than cropland, these figures translate into roughly 9.4 and 3.7 improved
acres, respectively. In the Parker–Gallman sample, plantations with more
than 50 slaves averaged 8.4 improved acres per capita, or more than 9
improved acres for each member of the black population. In other words,
far from attempting to *increase* the land–labor ratio with emancipation,
planters actually reduced the per capita allotment of improved acreage by
about 60%, a reduction roughly twice the size of the per capita withdrawal
of black labor. One may quarrel over precise measures and over the
representativeness of these two classes, but the conclusion that the labor
intensity of cotton cultivation actually increased is difficult to escape in
the aggregate. In the five-state area, the ratio of rural population to
improved acreage was more than 40% greater in 1880 than it had been in
1860, a good bit more than the black labor-supply effect can account for.
Ransom and Sutch have overlooked this development because their references to land are to the aggregate stock, whereas their analysis of labor
supply is in per capita terms.

These considerations do not, of course, falsify the Ransom–Sutch contention that the withdrawal of black labor was the dominant development of the postwar economy, but they lead me to wonder whether they have told the full story. Their estimates (pp. 232–236) are heavily weighted by observation in the late 1860s and early 1870s. Their description of a persistent "labor shortage" rings true for that period, and it is difficult to see how else to account for the useable acreage standing idle in 1870 "for the want of labor." But by 1880 improved acreage had returned to its 1860 level, and it is not evident that good cotton land was in surplus. There is reason to believe that labor markets were much softer in the late 1870s than they had been a decade before. This was partly a political development, as the federal government abandoned their efforts to police Southern labor relations, and freedmen reluctantly abandoned aspirations to independent farmownership. But the changed climate also reflected underlying trends in the Southern economy, particularly the continuing pressure of population and the steady deterioration of the cotton price between 1866 and 1879. The accelerated growth of the Southern textiles industry, which required an ample supply of cheap labor (but which employed few blacks) dates not from the 1860s but from the late 1870s.[2] The small black family farms of 1880 were cultivated so intensively (*One Kind of Freedom*, pp. 183–185) that one has to wonder whether the families could profitably have clocked more hours if they had wanted to.

The welfare interpretation of the hours of labor is thus fraught with ambiguities. It seems utterly reasonable that free black families would want to work less than slaves, but it is worth remembering the modern studies which indicate that the *self-employed* work much longer hours than wage laborers (Scitovsky, 1976, pp. 94–95). One man's leisure time may be another man's disguised unemployment, and what began as a new liberation may have been transformed over time into a new constraint. Gallman and Anderson have argued plausibly that "changes in the work proclivities of freedmen may not have been altogether a product of their choice . . . [because] labor no longer had the character of fixed capital to the planter" (1977, p. 41). They propose that the revolution in property rights changed the effective principles of resource allocation, and their argument directs our attention to the impact of wealth on the behavior of planters. The search for a summary measure of efficiency may have caused us to overlook a more fundamental development, but we would never see it if we insist upon a "long-run" framework where detached producers respond only to the relative prices of factors of production.

---

[2] The timing of the acceleration is documented in Griffin, 1964, pp. 48–49. Testimony on the labor-supply effects of the falling cotton price may be found in Griffin, p. 46; Smith, 1960, p. 6; Mitchell, 1921, p. 145.

Wealth is also critical in the labor-supply behavior of workers, as we may learn from a recent theoretical analysis of slavery by Yoram Barzel (1977). Barzel develops a model similar to Fogel and Engerman's, in which the profit-maximizing behavior of slave owners compels the slave to work longer and with greater intensity than an unconstrained freeman, producing more output and (because of the harder work) consuming more food. In a brief but significant section, Barzel goes on to show that exactly the same combination of work and output would be produced by a constrained freeman who is burdened by the need to repay a debt which is just equal to the net exploitation of a slave. Barzel observes that the comparison of free and slave equilibrium points "can be viewed as continuous and dependent on the level of wealth" (p. 91). My own view is that the higher apparent productivity of slave labor had more to do with specialization in market production than with the intensity of labor time. But the general message—that the constraints of debt can produce a self-coercion analogous to the outright coercion of slavery—ought to give us pause. No one would argue that the work patterns of slavery were restored, but liberally interpreted along crop-mix lines, Barzel's model fits the facts: When free farmers were impelled by indebtedness to move into production for the market, the cotton price settled at the same level as in the days of slavery.

This brings us to the question of why the resources of Southern agriculture in 1880 were so much more fully devoted to cotton than they had been in 1860. The real issue is explaining the dramatic decline of self-sufficiency in basic foodstuffs. The recent literature contains many hypotheses about the motives and behavior of farmers, landlords, and merchants in this connection. Ransom and Sutch point to the insistence by lenders that borrowing farmers plant a certain quantity of cotton as a precondition for credit; the behavior of the merchant is said to involve not merely a demand for collateral, but an effort to "drive the farmer into increased dependence upon purchased supplies" (p. 161); these requirements are said to have locked in debtor-farmers to overproduction of cotton (pp. 165–168).[3] Critics of this analysis have denied that merchants possessed monopoly power in credit markets, disputed the claim that merchants controlled planting decisions (or would have done so in a detrimental manner), and have doubted whether cotton was "overproduced" in any reasonable sense.[4]

There are obviously many different opinions here, but there is an

---

[3] A more detailed elaboration may be found in Ransom and Sutch, 1975b.

[4] Besides the chapters by Goldin and Temin, see DeCanio, 1974, pp. 111–118, 241–261; and Higgs, 1977, pp. 57–59, 71.

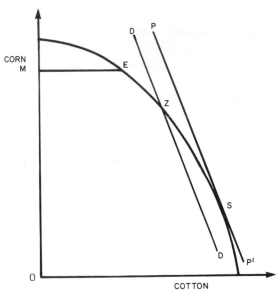

FIG. 5.1. The choice between cotton and corn.

essential core explanation to the main historical change which need not be
controversial if we focus on objective constraints rather than motives.
That is the proposition that self-sufficiency is not possible on very small
tenant farms, where the tenant has borrowed substantially to get through
the crop year. Refer to Fig. 5.1, adapted from Ransom and Sutch (1975b):
which illustrates the production possibility choices between cotton and
corn: line *OM* denotes the corn requirements of the farm; at point *S*
expected profits are maximized; and line *DD* (the slope of which reflects
the relative prices of cotton and corn) represents the level of indebtedness.

In 1860 small farms were self-sufficient at a point like *E*, despite the fact
that this choice did not maximize profits;[5] we may not agree on precisely
why they chose this point (whether it was risk, leisure preference, ignorance, or something else), but whatever their reasons, it is evident that that
choice was no longer open to a small farmer with indebtedness *DD*. If one
prefers to stress the labor–leisure trade-off, one could draw the analogous
diagram (following Barzel) with much the same implications. As Temin
notes, it is difficult to say but not really important whether the tenant
himself takes the initiative in expanding his cotton acreage in order to pay
back his loan, or whether (as it might appear to the tenant) the merchant's
insistence is the essential element. But Temin's phrasing illustrates the
importance of focusing on constraints:

[5] An extended review of the antebellum self-sufficiency literature which appeared in an
earlier draft has been omitted here to conserve space. A helpful survey may be found in
Gallman and Anderson, 1977, pp. 32–39.

The cost of borrowing, was a sunk cost at the time of planting. Irrespective of
what he planted he would have to pay interest to the merchant to get through the
year. *But this interest should not have been a factor in his decision of what to plant.*
(Emphasis added.)

The first point is valid and important—that the need to borrow is prior to
and independent of the subsequent planting. The second is the
economists' familiar slogan: Bygones are bygones, and sunk costs do not
matter. But that is only true if farmers intend to maximize profits at all
times: If they had intended to do something substantially different, as they
typically did in 1860, then the bygones of history did matter, because their
legacy (the debt) ruled out options, which, for one reason or another,
many farms had chosen in the less constrained situation of 1860. Furthermore, we need not agree on the theoretical reasons for the high interest
rates by merchants, in order to see that the higher the interest charges, the
heavier the burden of the debt will be, and the further the tenant will be
pushed into cotton. One need only glance at the differences in cotton—
intensity on owned and rented farms (*One Kind of Freedom*, p. 157) to see
how clear the association is between the rise of cash obligations and the
shift into cotton.

Some writers have characterized the difference between Ransom and
Sutch and their critics as a debate over whether "the market works" or
not. But this is an ambiguous criterion: One can reasonably argue that
Fig. 5.1 describes the way in which markets *do* work, not by magically
equilibrating marginal trade-offs at every instant, but by pushing producers towards an efficient crop mix (albeit, with the possible sacrifice of
some nonpecuniary goals). As the discussion at the 1978 Duke conference
made clear, there is no technical issue of substance over the notion of
"overproduction": No economist now defends the view that merchants
forced production of cotton to the right of point *S* in Fig. 5.1, at least in
normal years. The remaining differences revolve around more subjective
considerations: Can we understand contemporary use of that term sym-
pathetically, so as to enhance our understanding rather than demonstrate
our more rigorous terminology? "Overproduction" is a knee-jerk-
reaction word for economists: They hear it and they think "fallacy."
When they read contemporaries bemoaning food imports as a drain on
regional wealth, economists are sure they are dealing with utter economic
ignorance. But economists should not react so quickly: If the elasticity of
demand were unity, as it seems to have been for at least a substantial
range, the belief that food imports were a net drain on the South was
precisely correct. The South could have obtained the same cotton earnings producing less, and the homegrown food would be strictly gravy.
There was thus a resonance between the optimal regional allocation and
the traditional means of maintaining small-farm independence, which
should help us to appreciate the continuing temptation of intellectuals to

draw colorful parallels between the micro and macro developments. It didn't take an intellectual cotton farmer, however, to appreciate the fact that at the micro level, the loss of self-sufficiency involved a basic change in the character of social relations. With or without monopoly power, the debt was held by someone, and that creditor was bound to show a keen interest in the farmer's reliability, diligence, crop choice, spending habits, and so on; the farmer in the clear and self-sufficient at point E, in contrast, didn't have to take manure from anyone.

But Ransom and Sutch clearly describe a more involved calculation, in which the merchant did not merely try to ensure repayment of his exorbitant loans, but attempted to determine the wealth position of the farmer at the end of the year, so as to ensure his patronage in the following season. This is a difficult calculus to document, but it appears from their text (pp. 162–165) that Ransom and Sutch believe such a mechanism is needed to explain the *persistence* of indebted situations like Fig. 5.1. If self-sufficiency were attractive and credit expensive, why shouldn't small farmers have escaped from their dependent positions at the first opportunity? However, a reasonable simulation exercise might show that it just wasn't that easy to climb out of an initial indebted position with the earnings of a small family farm. For a family which begins without wealth, given the acreage on a typical tenancy, given plausible estimates of subsistence requirements and interest rates, is it in fact true that any crop mix between points Z and S would have allowed the accumulation of enough net worth to make possible a return to self-sufficiency—given the *actual* course of prices and yields over a particular span of time? This is, at any rate, an operational approach which might serve to reduce the bounds of disagreement. A farmer might say that he is trying to "escape the clutches of the merchant" in much the same sense that we all try to escape the clutches of the dentist or the undertaker—not so much because he is a monopolist but because he is providing a service we would rather not consume. The likelihood that the observed patterns of farm wealth, with the persistence of indebtedness and specialization in cotton, can be generated by the impersonal historical record in this way, is enhanced by the realization that the small-farm, low-wealth categories were constantly being replenished by the pressure of population. Ransom and Sutch's figures show (Table 8.3, p. 159) that a substantial majority of farms of medium scale or larger did in fact achieve self-sufficiency in foods.

Ransom and Sutch consider the analysis of the previous section incomplete. Figure 5.1 may characterize the position of an indebted landowner with a small holding, or a share tenant after his contract has specified the plot size; but to the landlord (and perhaps *ex ante* to the tenant), the size of the plot was open to determination. In their view, establishing the amount of land to be leased served as a supplement to supervision as an instrument of labor control, ensuring labor intensity in cultivation. Since "labor intensity" can be translated into "cotton intensity" with little loss of accuracy, we can view the crop mix as determined (implicitly or explicity) in the bargain over the plot size (pp. 97–99, 348).

The impulse to move towards labor intensity in comparison with antebellum practices is clearly explained by Gallman and Anderson. A slaveowner with limited or costly access to a rental market will try to fill in the work year as fully as possible; with his net investment dominated by the value of the slaves, he will try (approximately) to maximize the value of output per worker, assigning each hand as much acreage as possible. But when his property consists of the land alone, and labor is hired by the day or the month, the employer will cut out all labor activities which don't "pay for themselves" at the going wage. Alternatively, we can view him as now attempting to maximize the value of output per acre; since there is no disputing the superiority of cotton over food crops in terms of their yield per acre, this meant a shift toward cotton. As the Gallman–Anderson (1977) analysis would predict, emancipation transformed the planters' attitude toward regional inflows of labor.[6] And while economists frequently point to the spread of railroads and marketing channels and the rise of commercial fertilizer as alternative explanations for the shift into cotton, we can (with a certain license for hyperbole) view the favorable atmosphere for all of these developments as a manifestation of the planter's newly developed desire to augment the value of his land and maximize the value of output per acre.[7]

Returning to the micro level, the question becomes whether renting and sharecropping produce the same allocation pattern that landlords would have desired in dealing with wage labor. The answer seems to be that many landlords were able to use tenancies of both kinds to much the same effect by keeping plots small, encouraging and enforcing labor and cotton-intensity. As Joan Robinson and John Eatwell argue, describing a hypothetical sharecropping economy, "the landlord gains most when the holdings are small and the level of intensity of cultivation so high as to maximize output per acre. . . . From the landlord's point of view, the smaller the holding per tenant the better, provided that it is not so small that the tenant families are unable to live" (Robinson and Eatwell, 1973, p. 70).

Now the success of the planter in this endeavor is only possible if labor

---

[6] See Berthoff, 1951: "Plantation owners led the movement to bring in foreigners" (p. 328).

[7] The "penetration" of the South by railroads and Northern merchants is described, in somewhat conspiratorial terms, by Woolfolk (1958). On the spread of cotton processing facilities and Southern urbanization, see Weiher, 1977. On the fertilizer industry, see Taylor, 1953.

can be put in such a position, and it is in this connection that we will see
the matter most clearly if we focus directly on the distribution of the
tenant population in terms of geographic and economic alternatives (i.e.,
the elasticities of their labor supply to an individual landlord), rather than
trying to reach a summary characterization of the market as "competitive" or "coercive." A distinctive feature of *spatial* competition is that
even firms which are competitive in the usual sense will nonetheless
attempt to practice discrimination among their buyers.[8] My corner druggist may have some spatial market power, but if he cannot distinguish one
customer from another, I will capture the full benefits of competition on
the "fringe" even if I live next door. As soon as the druggist begins to give
credit, however, the situation changes: The lender's concern for the
identity of the borrower will have to carry over beyond the immediate
transaction. His desire for information and assurances is only reasonable,
but in the process of this negotiation, he is also acquiring the means of
discrimination. The fact that the druggist may be economically marginal
will not give his intramarginal customers much protection.

Ransom and Sutch have emphasized the merchant because it is easier
to build a case for monopoly pricing there, but when one remembers that
economic discrimination is an intimate aspect of spatial competition,
these considerations apply with equal force to the landlord. Even a
landlord who does not supply the "furnish" is engaged in a kind of
"credit" transaction, in that he is renting out durable assets and is
concerned for their treatment. Thus there is a difference between a wage
system and tenancy: And that is that when we move from a situation in
which one impersonal wage is obtainable to all comers to a world of
heterogeneous one-on-one bargains with detailed specifications (as
Reid emphasizes), discrimination in the economic sense is not only possible but inevitable.[9] And in a racist society, this economic discrimination
will be highly correlated with race. The protections of the market are
much weaker when economic discrimination is possible, because those
who can be exploited probably will be, even while the more mobile
tenants were able to drive hard bargains. The wide differences observed

[8] See Greenhut and Ohta, 1975: "A major difference—indeed the major difference—
between spaceless and spatial price theory lies . . . in the premise that in classical economic
theory competitors were conceived only to price nondiscriminatorily, while spatial competitors . . . generally discriminate in price" (p. xiii).

[9] It is not surprising that Higgs (1972) finds little discrimination in farm-labor wages, but
the scope of this result may be narrow. Ransom and Sutch (footnote 63, p. 339) assert that
share arrangements are different in these respects from fixed renting contracts, in which
"the rent per acre is the subject of negotiation, but once set the renter may in principle take
on as many acres as he wishes." But because of the heterogeneity and vulnerability of land,
I believe we will find that fixed rent agreements also specified a particular acreage as well as a
rental fee. If so, then the element of discrimination is present here too.

in land–labor ratios and in the fortunes of tenants are *prima facie* evidence that landlords were able to take advantage of limited geographic mobility on the part of tenants.[10]

Ransom and Sutch are quite right to insist that plot sizes are not demographically determined, but were objects of bargaining and strategy; but it is also true that the same trends were encouraged by the essentially demographic fact of the rise in rural population relative to improved acreage. On this count, it may be that the war itself was more costly than Ransom and Sutch allow, because the absolute level of improved acreage had barely reached its 1860 level by 1880 in the five-state area. In places, Ransom and Sutch seem to argue that landlords were actively holding back usable land (pp. 348, 351). Robinson and Eatwell, in the passage previously cited, also contemplate such a situation when they write:

> When there are not enough tenants to cultivate the whole area, the landlords will not let out such large holdings that output per acre falls very low; they prefer to keep a part of the land unlet . . . to prevent the peasants from becoming prosperous and independent.

Perhaps this is the Ransom–Sutch position, and perhaps it does describe 1870. But from the 1870s onward, it is difficult to understand an *economic* rationale for holding the major income-earning asset out of production as a regular matter. One suspects we need better evidence and a better argument to buttress the claim that land was macroeconomically in surplus in 1880.

Ransom and Sutch discuss the displacement of wage systems by sharecropping in detail (pp. 87–103), but as Engerman observed, they do not devote much attention to explaining temporal fluctuations and regional variations in tenure form; in general, our understanding of the coexistence of share and fixed-rent tenancies is limited. Robert Higgs views sharecropping as a risk-sharing arrangement, as contrasted with wage labor (where the planter bears the risk) and fixed-rent tenancy (where the tenant bears the risk). Higgs explains coexistence in terms of individual and local differences in risk aversion and the riskiness of crops; and changes over time (e.g., the rise of sharecropping after 1900) by changes in the riskiness of agriculture (caused by, e.g., the boll weevil).[11] Reid, on the other hand, denies that sharecropping served this kind of risk-sharing function, on the grounds that landlords and laborers could obtain equivalent risk–return combinations by mixing portfolios of fixed-wage and fixed-rent bargains. He develops an alternative model, in which sharecropping has many efficiency advantages when tenants are young or inexperienced, because of the mutual incentives to share advice,

---

[10] A geographic interpretation of racial differences appears in DeCanio, 1974, Chap. 6.
[11] Higgs, 1973, Higgs, 1977, pp. 67–68.

assistance, supervision, etc., throughout the crop year (Reid, 1973, 1976). Ransom and Sutch, in rebuttal, note that the life-cycle farm-ladder hypothesis fits the data much better for whites than for blacks (*One Kind of Freedom,* p. 181), an observation which would be consistent with Reid's analysis in conjunction with the Ransom–Sutch market signaling effect.

We cannot settle all these issues here, but the principle of Occam's razor suggests a simpler explanation, which emerges when one reflects on the fact that the wealthlessness of farm tenants imposes a constraint on the ability of landlords to avoid risk by fixing rents. No one can squeeze blood from a stone, and if the crop fails or the price of cotton falls out, the legal claim to a fixed rent is small consolation if the tenant is penniless. The constraints of wealth do not rigidly determine a set of tenure arrangements, but they clearly established bounds on the number of tenants who occupy the upper rungs of the ladder: farm ownership and fixed-rent tenancy. A wealthy man might choose to work on shares (and those who supplied mule and tools could and did work under the "thirds and fourths" system); but a poor man could not become a fixed-rent tenant until he raised the funds for his own mule and equipment. There are indications that this was the binding constraint in many cases: Nate Shaw tells of how he scraped together $100 for his own mule, borrowing the last $20 from his father-in-law, and he says: "Got me a mule and gived up working on halves. . . . Paid cash rent and made a profit from my farmin" (Rosengarten, 1975, pp. 117–118).

Hibbard's 1913 survey of Southern Tenancy describes "a well-defined caste system among the tenants" (p. 486):[12]

> The lowest class is represented by those who furnish little equipment and receive half, or less, of the crop; above this comes the group whose independence is measured by the possession of a mule and a plow and the means of subsistence till harvest time; the highest class consists of those who can be trusted to deliver a certain quantity of crop or possibly a sum of money, and who are by that fact emancipated in the main from the directing authority of the landlord.

Hibbard's criteria clearly encompass Reid's subjective elements, but they also indicate that asset-ownership and wealth were preconditions or entry-barriers into the renting class. Thus, the hypothesis suggests itself that the coexistence of tenure types and their relative change over time primarily reflect the success of farmers over time in accumulating and retaining assets, an accumulation which was constrained at any time by wealth.

It is difficult to test this hypothesis, because the last census to collect

---

[12] For other statements relating the move into renting to asset accumulation, see Brooks, 1912, pp. 60–65; Edwards, 1913, pp. 24–26. Compare Bell and Zusman, 1976, pp. 579–581.

household wealth data was 1870, and the first census to enquire into farm tenure was 1880. But I have carried out a limited test for Georgia in 1900, using county data on black wealth, collected by W. E. B. DuBois (1901) from tax records. This evidence indicates that the fraction of black farm tenants who are sharecroppers is negatively related to the average value of workstock and tools owned by blacks (or other measures of wealth), and with the fraction of black farmers in a county. The regression is

$$\frac{SHR}{TEN} = \underset{(2.85)}{1.30 - 8.45^*} \frac{WLTH}{TEN} \underset{(5.3)}{-0.010^* \%BL}, \qquad R^2 = 0.564,$$

where t ratios are in parenthesis. (The sample is 33 counties in the Georgia cotton belt for which data are available.)

Wealth is, of course, correlated with age and experience, and this argument is not advanced as a wholesale substitute for Reid's analysis. But the county data show much wider variations in levels of wealth than one would expect to see in age–experience structures, and the wealth hypothesis can readily account for the sharp differences in the age–tenure relationship for blacks and for whites. Finally, the analysis helps in understanding why the relative importance of sharecropping should have risen sharply after 1900 for both blacks and whites, at a time when the cotton economy was generally prosperous, and the percentage of black landowners was rising. It seems paradoxical, but there is a straightforward reason: namely, that the price of mules doubled between 1899 and 1905, and tripled between 1899 and 1918. Figure 5.2 depicts the dramatic developments. The same price pattern holds for mules of all ages and, because mules are transportable, for all parts of the South. The price of a mule was the main barrier between share and fixed-rent tenancy, and it appears that this barrier was rising faster than earnings, even while the landownership barrier was becoming a little more surmountable. One would expect the trends to diverge for the two assets, because land can be purchased in small and inferior lots, whereas mules are less divisible.[13]

The rising barriers to the acquisition of mules, tools, and fixed-rent tenure had important social consequences as well, because there is reason to believe that the sharecroppers of 1910 had less of the day-to-day independence and decision-making scope described by Ransom and Sutch for the 1880s (pp. 94–99). The continuity in the names of census

---

[13] It is difficult to determine from the available literature the precise reasons for the fluctuations in mule prices. Since three-fifths of U.S. mules were used in the South, one would expect that the cotton boom itself is part of the story. But mules were raised outside of the cotton areas, and the parallel trend in the price of horses (less than one-quarter of which were used in the South) suggest that supply-side pressures or competing demands must also have been involved. Lamb (1963) is less informative than one would like.

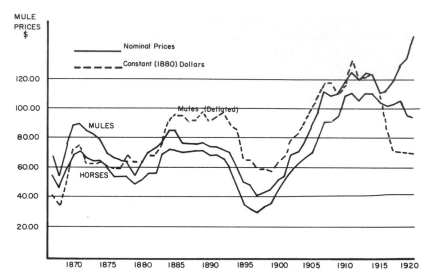

FIG. 5.2. Average prices, U.S. mules and horses, 1866–1920. Source: U.S. Bureau of the Census (1975), Vol. I, pp. 200–201, 519–520.

categories may in this respect be quite misleading. R. P. Brooks, writing in 1913, insisted that a sharecropper was little more than a share-wage day-laborer, and criticized earlier writers (notably Banks and M. B. Hammond) for treating sharecropping as a tenancy.[14] Brooks, like many subsequent historians, may not have appreciated the changing and evolving character of Southern economic and racial relationships. We cannot be sure, because we lack detailed knowledge of the degree of centralization of production decisions in either the earlier or later period, and we cannot safely rule out the possibility that black and white sharecropping were two quite different things with the same name. But if Ransom and Sutch are essentially correct in their account of the "one kind of freedom" which the former slaves had achieved by 1880, then the post-1900 reports suggest that even this limited household freedom had been badly eroded, under legal, social and racial pressures, by the time of World War I. Harold Woodman, in a useful discussion of these trends, suggests that the entire period be viewed in terms of "the making of a working class" of wage laborers, by analogy to the evolution of class relationships in industrial capitalism (Woodman, 1977, pp. 551–554). Applying Occam's razor once again, however, I suggest that the more immediate reason for these developments was the renewed acceleration in world cotton demand after 1900. If this is right, then we have another example of the pattern which

[14] Brooks, 1914, esp. pp. 66–68. Compare Banks, 1905; M. B. Hammond, 1897.

began with slavery, an inverse relationship between the demand for labor and the legal and social status of laborers without property.

The most important constraints to identify are the feasible limits to Southern economic progress in the 19th century. This is not the main focus of *One Kind of Freedom,* and their concluding chapter is largely a listing of various growth inhibiting effects with which, in qualitative terms, it is difficult to disagree. But the overall emphasis of the book, coupled with the statement that "the core of the problem of underdevelopment is institutional," carries with it the implication that the performance of the agriculture sector could have made a significant difference in regional progress, and it is worth noting that there is room for doubt on this score. Did the region possess "all the requisite conditions for rapid economic growth" (p.7)?

The hard economic facts of the Southern economy were that black and white fertility rates were far above the national average, and that between the Civil War and the turn of the century the natural growth of the rural population averaged nearly 2% per year—about as fast as the growth of world cotton demand during this period, and substantially faster than the growth of land on farms. Outmigration from agriculture made very little dent in these rates. Rubin (1975) makes a strong case that geography seriously constrained Southern efforts at diversification, and the unfortunate truth is that the harshest critics of cotton were unable to suggest an alternative source of cash income for farmers. A broadening of land-ownership and self-sufficiency in food crops would have been equitable and humane, and might even have raised cotton prices; but there is not much reason to believe that such a program would have generated sustained progress. As Engerman has stressed, the examples of emancipations where the freedmen had access to land do not encourage optimism that the dictates of equity and progress will necessarily coincide. We can all agree that Southern agriculture could have been more progressive; but rapid productivity growth in the cotton sector would have been of little help to rural incomes if labor had no outlet. One of the reasons (among many) for the slow development of the mechanical cotton picker was the inventors' belief that the machine would inflict misery on the Southern poor (Street, 1957, pp. 62–64).

To understand Southern poverty, therefore, we will have to look into the determinants of population growth, the obstacles to Southern industrialization and the course of migration to Northern jobs. It may well be that the institutions of Southern agriculture have a role to play on each of these points, and such a study will be able to build on the research of Ransom and Sutch. But the connections remain to be developed precisely, and the full story will have to include American immigration policies and the labor and investment strategies of American business. To understand fully the roots of Southern poverty, we will need a national and international perspective.

CHAPTER 6

Accumulation and Discrimination in the Postbellum South

STEPHEN J. DeCANIO

Any effort to provide a unified and balanced account of postbellum Southern economic history must confront the two dominant facts about the late 19th-century Southern economy: the inequality between blacks and whites within the South, and the persistent income gap between the South and the rest of the nation. It is obvious that economic inequalities associated with race were an important element in the South's unhappy record of social discord and political tension. What is not known is whether the economic gap between whites and blacks was created and sustained by racial antipathies and prejudices transmitted through the market mechanism, or whether the unequal material conditions of whites and blacks merely reinforced social and psychological attitudes already entrenched in the minds of Southerners. The large postwar income differential between the South and the North is also a puzzle for economic historians. Relative Southern backwardness after the abolition of slavery has been attributed to microeconomic inefficiency in Southern agriculture (Ransom and Sutch, *One Kind of Freedom*, 1977), a slowdown in the rate of growth of world demand for cotton (Wright, 1974, 1978), the after-effects of the Civil War (Goldin and Lewis, 1975), or a combination of all three factors (Temin, 1976). Racial inequalities within the South may also have been directly related to the South's apparent lag in aggregate performance. Mellman (1975) has shown that income per farm operated by whites in the South was comparable to income per farm in the North, and

The author wishes to acknowledge the excellent research assistance of Joseph M. Trojanowski. William N. Parker, Paul Krugman, and Gerald Jaynes have offered useful advice and suggestions. The research was supported by the National Science Foundation, Grant No. SOC 75-08056.

MARKET INSTITUTIONS AND ECONOMIC PROGRESS
IN THE NEW SOUTH 1865–1900

that Southern manufacturing wages were similar to Northern manufacturing wages. These findings imply that part of the gap between Northern and Southern per capita income must have been due simply to blacks' lower incomes within the South, since blacks constituted such a large fraction of the Southern population.

The blacks' relative poverty in the postbellum period has recently received a great deal of direct and indirect attention from economic historians. (See, for example, *One Kind of Freedom*, Higgs, 1977; DeCanio, 1974a; and Hopkins, 1978). Two kinds of explanations of the blacks' poverty emerge from this literature: those based on *discrimination* and those based on the *initial conditions of emancipation*. The discrimination view sees the denial of equal employment and educational opportunities to blacks, supplemented by discrimination in the credit, factor, and retail markets, as the continuing source of relatively low incomes of blacks in the postbellum economy. The initial conditions hypothesis focuses on the failure of emancipation to be accompanied by the transfer of any land or other property to the ex-slaves, and concentrates on the resulting wealth inequality as the primary determinant of the subsequent relative levels of blacks' and whites' incomes in the South. These two explanations appear with varying degrees of emphasis in the writings of the cliometricians. Ransom and Sutch suggest many "roots of Southern poverty" in *One Kind of Freedom*, but both discrimination and the initial conditions of emancipation form important parts of their total explanation. They write, for example, "emancipation removed the legal distinction between the South's two races, but it left them in grossly unequal economic positions. The blacks lacked assets; they lacked education; they lacked skills. From the outset there were whites who sought to preserve the social and political inequalities between the races, and these white supremacists perceived that to do so they would have to maintain the economic inequalities as well. . . . Southerners erected an economic system that failed to reward individual initiative on the part of blacks and was therefore ill-suited to their economic advancement. As a result, the inequalities originally inherited from slavery persisted" (pp. 185–186). Nevertheless, the disadvantages deriving from freedmen's initial wealth position is subordinated in *One Kind of Freedom* to the continuing effects of racism and discrimination. This emphasis is reflected in the book's concluding paragraph: "The legacy of slavery persists. Racism, racial phobia, racial prejudice, racial animosities still survive. They continue to poison our society and to weaken and distort our economy. The result of the economic advancements achieved by blacks since World War I is not, as we know all too well today, parity with whites. The progress made to date has been painfully slow. At every step it has been resisted by racists, impeded by the force of law, and held back by economic institutions that continue to discriminate on the basis of race" (p. 199). Higgs also incorporates both themes in his schematic account of the blacks' economic history after the Civil War. He first points out that blacks' initial location in the war-devastated South, their lack of education, and of any property "except the clothes on their backs" (Higgs, 1977, p. 4) would have had consequences for their subsequent economic progress even in the absence of discrimination. He goes on to argue that "black economic history in the half century after emancipation makes sense only when interpreted as an interplay of two systems of behavior: a competitive economic system and a coercive racial system. . . . [That blacks'] advance was less than spectacular is easy to understand. To swim in the sea of a dynamic and highly competitive economic system was difficult enough without the weight of racial discrimination forever pulling downward" (p. 13).

Recognizing with these authors that both the initial lack of wealth and economic discrimination were realities of the freedmen's lives, questions remain: What is the relative quantitative importance of these two influences in explaining the white/black income differential and its course in the years following emancipation? Were blacks' efforts to accumulate property hindered, either by discrimination or by other forces affecting patterns of wealth accumulation in the postbellum South? Despite the apparent complexity of the issues, it is possible to approach some reasonable quantitative answers to these questions. In this paper, a decomposition of the sources of inequality shows that the freedmen's lack of tangible property at the time of emancipation was the overriding cause of their low income relative to Southern whites. This lack of property was itself a direct result of the slaves' legal incapacity to accumulate wealth and of the failure of Reconstruction to compensate for that injustice. Even if all markets had operated perfectly and no discrimination had been practiced against the freedmen either in wage payments or in their access to occupations, this initial gap in tangible capital would have produced by itself most of the gap in income between blacks and whites throughout the late 19th and early 20th centuries. Since it takes time to accumulate wealth, it would have taken many years for blacks to approach economic parity with whites even under the best of circumstances (i.e., no discrimination). However, the actual rate of wealth equalization was slower than it would have been without discrimination and with identical savings behavior on the part of blacks and whites, thereby lengthening the time required to eradicate the effects of the initial wealth inequality.

It is a relatively simple matter to partition postbellum Southern income differences into a part due to wealth inequality and a part due to discrimination. Let Y_a = the total income of whites in a typical period and Y_b = the corresponding income of blacks.[1] Then

$$
\frac{Y_b}{Y_a} = \frac{\displaystyle\sum_{i=1}^{n} w_{bi}L_{bi} + \sum_{j=1}^{m} r_{bj}K_{bj}}{\displaystyle\sum_{i-1}^{n} w_{ai}L_{ai} + \sum_{j=1}^{m} r_{aj}K_{aj}} , \tag{1}
$$

where w_{bi} = the wage rate of blacks in the ith employment category, L_{bi} = the number of black workers in occupation i, r_{bj} = the rate of return on capital of the jth type owned by blacks, K_{bj} = the amount of the jth type of capital (including land) owned by blacks, and the a-subscripted variables are the same for the whites. This relationship is not based on any particular theory of wage rate determination, asset pricing, or aggregation. Equation (1) is perfectly general (since the occupational and capital structure can be represented in full detail by a sufficiently large number of n and m categories); in fact it is an algebraic identity. It can be further expanded into labor and property ownership components as follows:

$$
\frac{Y_b}{Y_a} = \frac{\displaystyle\sum_i \frac{w_{bi}}{w_i}\frac{w_i}{w}w'\frac{L_{bi}}{N_b}\frac{N_b}{N}\frac{N}{L_i}\frac{L_i}{L}L + \sum_j \frac{r_{bj}}{r_j}\frac{r_j}{r}r\frac{K_{bj}}{K_j}\frac{K_j}{K}K}{\displaystyle\sum_i \frac{w_{ai}}{w_i}\frac{w_i}{w}w'\frac{L_{ai}}{N_a}\frac{N_a}{N}\frac{N}{L_i}\frac{L_i}{L}L + \sum_j \frac{r_{aj}}{r_j}\frac{r_j}{r}r\frac{K_{aj}}{K_j}\frac{K_j}{K}K} , \tag{2}
$$

where N_b and N_a are the numbers of blacks and whites in the total population N, w_i is the wage that would prevail in occupation i in the absence of discrimination, L_i is the employment in occupation i in the absence of discrimination, r_j is the return to capital of type j in the absence of discrimination, and K_j is the total value of this type of capital in the nondiscriminatory situation. The values of the wages, rates of return, numbers employed, and capital stocks which would prevail if there were no racial discrimination are not known, of course, but it will be seen that **they do not need to be known to carry out the partitioning of the sources of inequality. The quantities L and K are simply aggregate employment and total value of the capital stock in the nondiscriminatory world ($L = \Sigma_i$**

---

[1] Here and throughout, the distribution of income and wealth among whites and among blacks is being ignored. Thirty-eight percent of all United States whites in 1870 were without substantial wealth (i.e., had a total estate valued at less than $100) [Soltow, 1975, p. 60] and consequently had lower incomes than white owners of large properties, but this has no effect on the validity of the comparison developed here of the average incomes of the whites and blacks as groups.

L_i and $K = \Sigma_j K_j$), and w and r are the (weighted) average wage and rate of return in the absence of discrimination ($w = (1/L) \Sigma_i w_i L_i$ and $r = (1/K) \Sigma_j r_j K_j$). Rearranging to take certain unindexed terms outside the summations and dividing numerator and denominator by total income in the nondiscriminatory world,

$$
\frac{Y_b}{Y_a} = \frac{S_L P_b \sum_i \dfrac{w_{bi}}{w_i} \dfrac{w_i}{w} \dfrac{(L_{bi}/N_b)}{(L_i/N)} \dfrac{L_i}{L} + S_K \sum_j \dfrac{r_{bj}}{r_j} \dfrac{r_j}{r} \dfrac{K_{bj}}{K_j} \dfrac{K_j}{K}}{S_L P_a \sum_i \dfrac{w_{ai}}{w_i} \dfrac{w_i}{w} \dfrac{(L_{ai}/N_a)}{(L_i/N)} \dfrac{L_i}{L} + S_K \sum_j \dfrac{r_{aj}}{r_j} \dfrac{r_j}{r} \dfrac{K_{aj}}{K_j} \dfrac{K_j}{K}},
\tag{3}
$$

where S_L = labor's share of income in the absence of discrimination, S_K = capital's share of income in the absence of discrimination, and P_b and P_a are the actual shares of blacks and whites in the total population. Now define

$$
I_b = \sum_i \frac{w_{bi}}{w_i} \frac{w_i}{w} \frac{(L_{bi}/N_b)}{(L_i/N)} \frac{L_i}{L},
$$
$$
J_b = \sum_j \frac{r_{bj}}{r_j} \frac{r_j}{r} \frac{K_{bj}}{K_j} \frac{K_j}{K},
\tag{4}
$$

and define I_a and J_a for whites similarly. Then the ratio of the per capita income of blacks to the per capita income of whites may be expressed as

$$
\frac{y_b}{y_a} = \frac{S_L P_b I_b + S_K J_b}{S_L P_a I_a + S_K J_a} \cdot \frac{N_a}{N_b},
\tag{5}
$$

where $y_b = Y_b/N_b$ and $y_a = Y_a/N_a$. The index I_b may be interpreted as an index of discrimination against blacks in the labor markets. The terms w_{bi}/w_i represent the ratios of the wage paid to blacks in each occupation to the wage in that occupation in the nondiscriminatory world, and the ratios $(L_{bi}/N_b)/(L_i/N)$ are the ratios of the participation rates of blacks in each occupation to the nondiscriminatory participation rate in that occupation. Discrimination takes the form of less pay for equal work ($w_{bi}/w_i < 1$) or of exclusion from certain occupations ($(L_{bi}/N_b)/(L_i/N) < 1$ in high-wage occupations). These measures of wage and labor participation discrimination in each occupation i are weighted by the extent to which i is a high-wage or low-wage occupation (w_i/w), and by the relative importance of i in total employment (L_i/L). Ordinarily, I_b would be thought to decline with increasing discrimination against blacks, but discrimination in some occupations (or income inequality from other sources) might tend to drive up the participation rates of blacks in other occupations, tending to increase I_b. It is unambiguously the case, however, that in the complete absence of discrimination and with no differences in participation rates, $I_b = I_a = 1$. Similarly, J_b represents a combination of discriminatory rates of return to capital owned by blacks (r_{bj}/r_j) and a measure of the amount of each type of capital owned by blacks (K_{bj}/K_j), weighted appropriately by (r_j/r) and (K_j/K). Any distortions in capital values resulting from discrimination will also be subsumed in J_b.

Equation (5) allows calculation of blacks' and whites' relative per capita income at the time of emancipation or shortly thereafter, assuming the only source of income inequality to be the initial discrepancy in property ownership. Blacks were freed without any tangible assets, so (ignoring the insignificantly small amount of property owned by the blacks who were free during the antebellum period) $J_b = 0$ and $J_a = 1$. No discrimination and identical labor participation by blacks and whites at the time of emancipation would have implied $I_a = I_b = 1$. Thus

$$
\begin{aligned}
(y_b/y_a)^* &= \frac{S_L P_b}{S_L P_a + S_K} \cdot \frac{N_a}{N_b} \\
&= \frac{S_L P_a}{S_L P_a + S_K} .
\end{aligned}
\tag{6}
$$

The asterisk indicates the hypothetical per capita income ratio that would have prevailed in the absence of discrimination. The population proportions P_a and P_b are known for the South as a whole or for any subregion; to calculate the nondiscriminatory per capita income ratio it is only necessary to determine the nondiscriminatory labor share S_L (since $S_K = 1 - S_L$). The nondiscriminatory labor share is a hypothetical concept, so it cannot be calculated directly. Estimates of the labor share for the United States as a whole in the late 19th century may provide bounds for the Southern nondiscriminatory S_L. In addition, production functions have been estimated for both antebellum and postbellum Southern agriculture. Since agriculture was the dominant sector in the postbellum South,[2] these production function estimates can be used to further narrow the range of plausible values of S_L.

The most recent estimate of the actual share of gross output received by labor in the United States during the latter half of the 19th century is that of Abramovitz and David (1973). They report average gross labor shares of 0.55 for 1869/1873–1889/1892 and 0.54 for 1888/1892–1903/1907. These labor shares are somewhat less than the labor share of 0.68 employed by Gallman in his decomposition of 19th-century growth into its factor

---

[2] In the five cotton states—South Carolina, Georgia, Alabama, Mississippi, and Louisiana—the rural population constituted 90% of the total population in 1880 and 85% of total population in 1900 (computed from U.S. Bureau of the Census (1975), referred to hereafter as *Historical Statistics*, Series A-195, A-203); the farm population was 55% of total population in 1890 (the first year for which farm population is available by state) and 60% of total population in 1900 (*Historical Statistics*, Series A-195, K 17-81).

growth and productivity components (Davis et al., 1972, pp. 38–39; the property share for 1840–1900 computed from column 1 of Table 2.11) or Budd's "service income" (nonproperty income) shares of 0.61 (excluding unpaid family workers) or 0.65 (including unpaid family workers) averaged over the four census years 1869–1870 through 1899–1900 (Budd, 1960, Table 7, p. 382).

These United States averages must be upper bounds on the Southern nondiscriminatory labor share because of the predominance of agriculture in the South and the values of the labor elasticity in the Southern agricultural production function. The only estimates of agricultural production functions based on postbellum data are those of DeCanio (1974a). These are production functions estimated for each of the 10 cotton-producing states of the former Confederacy for each of the four census years 1880, 1890, 1900, and 1910. For the five cotton states of the Deep South, the unweighted average of the labor elasticities is 0.312 or 0.334, depending on how the land and labor inputs are specified (Group I Variant II estimates, p. 168; and Group II Variant II estimates, p. 207). These estimates are computed from county aggregate data and therefore the only formal statistical test which can be based on them is whether the county data are consistent with the null hypothesis of competition in the factor markets. The data are consistent with the competitive hypothesis, however, and therefore the hypothesis that the estimated labor coefficients represent the actual values of the technological labor input elasticities cannot be rejected on statistical grounds.

Hopkins (1978) and Schmitz and Schaefer (n.d.) have estimated production functions for Southern agriculture in 1860. The problem with determining a nondiscriminatory labor share based on their data is that slavery was still in existence in 1860. Both sets of estimates are based on farm-level data, however, and therefore provide information about the technology of the production process regardless of the competitiveness of the factor markets. Hopkins, allowing slaves and free workers to exhibit different levels of productivity, reports a labor input elasticity of 0.534 for the cotton South as a whole; if the productivity levels of slaves and free workers are constrained to be equal, he estimates a labor elasticity of 0.622. (1978, regressions (1) and (5)). The scale parameters of these two production function estimates are 0.94 and 1.06, respectively. Input elasticities do not correspond to competitive factor shares in any simple way in the absence of constant returns to scale (Nerlove, 1965), but if the input elasticities are simply divided by the scale estimates, implied factor shares of 0.568 and 0.587 are obtained. This procedure for determining the labor share given nonconstant returns is the same as that employed by Fogel and Engerman, so aside from rounding error, Hopkins' constrained estimate is the same as Fogel and Engerman's estimate (1974). Similar S_L estimates are found for Hopkins' subregions as well. Hopkins' production functions are specified to be of generalized Cobb–Douglas form, while Schmitz and Schaefer specify a CES form. Nevertheless, the Schmitz and Schaefer factor share estimates are similar to the Cobb–Douglas factor shares. For the sample of all farms in the Cotton South, the competitive labor share at the point of means is 0.582. For free farms in the same region the labor share is 0.464. [3] The importance of coercion in setting the pace of work, gang labor, and the task system in antebellum slave agriculture suggest that the free farm estimates are closer to the postbellum norm than the all-farm estimates, but on the other hand geographical differences between slave and free farms would not have disappeared with emancipation. Caution is obviously indicated in transferring antebellum factor share estimates to postbellum agriculture.

Estimates of the labor share in agriculture may also be obtained from evidence on actual factor payments in the postbellum period. The sample of agricultural contract terms reported in DeCanio (1974a) shows the labor share actually paid to be between 0.25 and 0.5, averaging 0.415. Ransom and Sutch also report a half-and-half division of the outputs in sharecropping arrangements, and agricultural laborers receiving one-fourth to one-third of the crops under a system of tenure they refer to as "share wages" (*One Kind of Freedom*, p. 92). By including housing services, pork production, and garden produce, Ransom and Sutch find labor's share on black tenant farms to have been 55.8% (p. 216). These labor shares may have represented a discriminatory situation in the labor and land rental markets, but the sharecrop contracts in any particular locality do not appear to differ according to the race of the farmer (DeCanio, 1974a, p. 91). Also Higgs (1977, pp. 64–66) reports only very small differentials in wages paid to blacks and whites as agricultural laborers in the South around the turn of the century, further suggesting an absence of discrimination in the agricultural labor market at that time.

These production function and factor share estimates indicate that the nondiscriminatory S_L in the Southern economy during the postbellum period must have been somewhere between 0.3 and 0.7, with the range 0.4 to 0.6 being the most plausible. Since the values of the hypothetical S_L can never be known with certainty, the partitioning of inequality will be carried out assuming alternative S_L values from 0.3 to 0.7. It will be seen that the major conclusions regarding the relative importance of discrimination and the initial conditions of emancipation are unchanged for S_L values in this range.

---

[3] The functional form estimated by Schmitz and Schaefer is $\ln Q = a_0 + a_1 \ln L + a_2 \ln K + a_3 [\ln(K/L)]^2$. Given this specification the marginal product of labor is $a_1 (Q/L) - 2 a_3 (Q/L) \ln (K/L)$. The Schmitz–Schaefer input data were scaled so that $K/L = 1$ at the point of sample means, hence the marginal product of labor at this point is simply $a_1 (Q/L)$. The labor share figures in the text were obtained by dividing the labor input elasticity by the estimated returns to scale.

nodiscriminate labor shares

TABLE 6.1
Initial Per Capita Income Ratio in the Absence of Discrimination

S_L	0.3	0.4	0.5	0.6	0.7
$(y_b/y_a)^*$ *observed disc*	0.170	0.242	0.323	0.418	0.527

Sources: $P_a = 0.478$ from U.S. Bureau of the Census (1975), Series A-199, A-200; see text.

Table 6.1 contains estimates of the nondiscriminatory per capita income ratio of blacks to whites computed from Eq. (6). The population proportions of 1880 (the first reliable postwar census) are used, and the estimates pertain to the five cotton states of the Deep South (South Carolina, Georgia, Alabama, Mississippi, and Louisiana).

It is evident that whatever the nondiscriminatory labor share, blacks' per capita income could not have been more than about half of Southern whites' per capita income during the Reconstruction period. If the competitive labor share was between 0.4 and 0.6 (the most plausible range), then the per capita income ratio would have been between 0.24 and 0.42, even in the complete absence of any racial discrimination. Clearly, the initial tangible wealth discrepancy between blacks and whites coupled with the large fraction of blacks in the population must have resulted in a very large amount of income inequality in the Reconstruction period.

Higgs' estimate of the actual black/white income ratio prevailing in 1867–1868 is 0.24. This estimate is based on scattered sources containing information on blacks' incomes and on the aggregate per capita income level in the United States. Higgs postulates a 25% margin of error around his estimate of blacks' per capita income, giving bounds to the 0.24 figure of 0.18 and 0.30 (1977, pp. 95–102, 146). Taking the bounds of Higgs' estimate and the most extreme estimates of Table 1, it follows that at least 58% and at most 119% of the 1867–1868 income gap is explained by the initial wealth inequality between blacks and whites alone. For the Higgs estimate of 0.24 and S_L values of 0.4 through 0.6, between 77% and 100% of the income gap is explained by Eq. (6).[4] Higgs' y_a is for all United States whites, not only Southern whites. If the per capita income of Southern whites was lower than that of United States whites (due to greater urbanization and industrialization in the North, or to higher Northern farm incomes), the actual y_b/y_a ratio for the South would be larger than the ratio calculated by Higgs, and thus an even greater fraction of the black/white income gap would be attributable to the initial conditions rather than to discrimination.

The nondiscriminatory per capita income differences between blacks and whites in the South also accounts for most of the difference between Southern per capita income and average United States per capita income

[4] The fraction of the gap explained is computed as: $[1 - (y_b/y_a)^*]/[1 - (y_b/y_a)_{Higgs}]$.

in the late 19th century. The per capita income ratio of the cotton South to the rest of the country may be expressed as

$$\frac{y_{SO}}{y_{US}} = \frac{P_{aSO}\,y_{aSO} + P_{bSO}\,y_{bSO}}{P_{aUS}\,y_{aUS} + P_{bUS}\,y_{bUS}} \qquad (7)$$

where the "a" and "b" subscripts pertain to whites and blacks, the "SO" and "US" subscripts are for the South and the United States, and the y's and P's are the appropriate per capita incomes and population proportions. This can be rewritten as

$$\frac{y_{SO}}{y_{US}} = \frac{P_{aSO} + P_{bSO}\,(y_{bSO}/y_{aSO})}{P_{aUS} + P_{bUS}\,(y_{bUS}/y_{aUS})} \cdot \frac{y_{aSO}}{y_{aUS}} \,. \qquad (8)$$

The South/United States per capita income ratio that would have prevailed, if there had been no racial discrimination and if the only thing different about the South had been its large population of poor and propertyless blacks, may then be calculated by assuming $y_{aSO} = y_{aUS}$ and $y_{bSO}/y_{aSO} = y_{bUS}/y_{aUS} = (y_b/y_a)^*$. This yields[5]

$$(y_{SO}/y_{US})^* = \frac{P_{aSO} + P_{bSO}\,(y_b/y_a)^*}{P_{aUS} + P_{bUS}\,(y_b/y_a)^*} \,. \qquad (9)$$

Table 6.2 shows the values of $(y_{SO}/y_{US})^*$ corresponding to different values of Southern S_L for 1880 values of the population proportions. The actual ratio of per capita income in the five cotton states to average United States per capita income was 0.52 in 1880. (Easterlin, 1957). Table 2 suggests that for the middle range of Southern S_L values (0.4 to 0.6), the initial black/white wealth differential accounts for between about one-half and two-thirds of the actual income gap between the South and the rest of the nation (calculated as $[1 - (y_{SO}/y_{US})^*]/[1 - (y_{SO}/y_{US})]$). If $y_{aSO}/y_{aUS} = 0.9$, either because of lower Southern farm income (Mellman's estimates admit the possibility of a North/South white farm income difference of

---

[5] Mellman (1975, p. 87) has shown that "counter to all claims about the poor state of Southern agriculture and the enormous number of poor whites, . . . during the period 1890–1910, average Southern net white farm income was nearly the same as average Northern net farm income. And contrary to similar claims of low Southern urban incomes . . . during the 1890–1910 period, Southern white urban manufacturing wages were at about the same level of Northern urban manufacturing wages." A straightforward modification of Mellman's calculation shows that average white farm per capita income (including rents) was approximately the same in the five deep South cotton states as in the eight Northern states in his sample. Any discrepancy between Northern and Southern whites' per capita incomes must therefore be due to the greater degree of urbanization and industrialization in the North, combined with the universally observed farm/nonfarm per capita income differential (Kuznets, 1952; David, 1967; Bellerby, 1956).

TABLE 6.2
The South/United States Income Ratio in the Absence of Discrimination

S_L	0.3	0.4	0.5	0.6	0.7
$(y_{so}/y_{us})^*$	0.636	0.672	0.710	0.754	0.803

Sources: U.S. Bureau of the Census (1975), Series A-92, A-93, A-99, A-100, A-199, A-200; see text.

this magnitude) or because of the lower levels of Southern urbanization and industrialization, the fraction of the South/United States income gap explained rises to between 67 and 82%.

The initial wealth inequality between blacks and whites was decisive in establishing the distribution of Southern income in the early postbellum period, and the black–white wealth difference accounts for most of the regional difference in per capita incomes in the late 19th century. The initial wealth discrepancy had dynamic consequences as well. Even if all markets in the postbellum South had functioned perfectly, the incomes of blacks and whites would have been slow to equalize because of the time needed to accumulate property. The time required for blacks to accumulate wealth would have coincided with an extended period during which Southern income was certain to lag behind income in the rest of the country. This conclusion is unaltered if trade and factor mobility worked to equalize factor prices between the South and the rest of the nation. In the case of trade and factor price equalization, the blacks' lack of wealth would have influenced the pattern of regional specialization, with the South concentrating on relatively labor-intensive activities such as cotton production, but wealth and income inequalities would have persisted whatever the pattern of specialization. In the case of factor mobility, the capital stock per worker would tend to be equalized across regions, but racial and regional incomes would *not* be equalized due to the "repatriation" of profits to the capital-owning whites in the North.

The dynamics of the wealth accumulation process must be approached in the setting of a growth model that allows for differences in the wealth holdings of groups. Such a model has been developed by Stiglitz (1969). The Stiglitz model is a neoclassical growth model with perfect factor markets, so it cannot automatically be assumed to represent the Southern growth experience accurately. The model can, however, provide a standard of performance against which the actual history of accumulation in the South can be judged. It will be seen that even under the ideal conditions of the Stiglitz model without discrimination, the initial wealth inequality between blacks and whites precluded rapid equalization of wealth and income following emancipation.

The Stiglitz growth model with heterogeneous wealth holdings is based on a simple neoclassical specification of technology and savings. The basic assumptions of the model are: a constant returns production function satisfying the Inada conditions with two factors of production, labor and capital; a homogeneous labor force (all workers receiving the same wage) with perfect competition in the factor markets and marginal product factor pricing; a linear savings function identical for all individuals; labor force growth at the "natural rate" n, the same for all groups; no intermarriage among groups; and equal division of wealth among heirs. Stiglitz demonstrates that in such an economy, the following conditions hold: (1) In general there are two balanced growth equilibria, the one with the higher aggregate capital/labor ratio being locally stable and the one with the lower aggregate capital/labor ratio being locally unstable. (2) If the economy converges to the upper equilibrium in the long run, there must eventually be an egalitarian distribution of wealth. The second conclusion follows from the fact that the savings function is linear and identical for all individuals. Since an individual's income consists of wage income plus a return to wealth owned, the rate of growth of per capita wealth in any of the distinct groups in the population at time t will be positively related to the ratio of the wage to the per capita wealth in that group at time t. Wealth grows fastest when present wealth per capita is lowest, and therefore the per capita wealth holdings of all groups tend to equalize if the economy achieves aggregate balanced growth.

Stiglitz develops the consequences of relaxation of the assumptions in some detail, but only the basic model is of concern here.[6] The model is sufficiently rich to allow rough calculation of the speed at which wealth and income would equalize under conditions of balanced growth. Stiglitz defines a measure of wealth inequality V as

$$V = \sum_i a_i[c_i(t) - k]^2, \qquad (10)$$

where a_i is the proportion of each group i in the labor force, $c_i(t)$ is the per capita wealth of group i at time t, and k is the aggregate capital/labor ratio. Now V can be rewritten as

$$V = k^2 \sum_i a_i[(c_i/k) - 1]^2 = k^2H. \qquad (11)$$

It is preferable to work with H rather than V because H is expressed entirely in terms of *ratios*. Harrod-neutral productivity growth has to be added to the model (since capital per *man* cannot realistically be taken as constant in the steady state). If the labor-augmenting productivity growth

---

[6] As might be expected, the tendency toward equalization is weakened or eliminated by different rates of reproduction across groups, heterogeneous labor, class savings behavior, primogeniture, life cycle savings, and stochastic elements. The tendency towards equalization is not overturned by nonlinear savings functions or savings as a function of wealth and income, however.

applies equally to members of all groups, these productivity terms will cancel out of the a_i and c_i/k ratios in H, allowing H to be expressed in terms of capital per man rather than capital per effective labor unit. Thus, in the case of only blacks and whites,

$$H = P_b \left(\frac{K_b/N_b}{K/N} - 1 \right)^2 + P_a \left(\frac{K_a/N_a}{K/N} - 1 \right)^2 \tag{12}$$

Some algebraic manipulation yields

$$\left(\frac{K_b}{K} - P_b \right)^2 = \frac{H}{(1/P_a) + (1/P_b)} . \tag{13}$$

Now $K_b/K < P_b$ until wealth equalization is achieved, so

$$\frac{K_b}{K} = P_b - \left(\frac{H}{(1/P_a) + (1/P_b)} \right)^{\frac{1}{2}}. \tag{14}$$

If $K_b/K = 0$, the initial value of H would be P_b/P_a. Obviously, as full equalization is approached, $K_b/K \to P_b$, so $H \to 0$. Finally, the nondiscriminatory per capita income ratio can be expressed as a function of H. In the nondiscriminatory situation with homogeneous labor and capital, Eq. (5) becomes

$$(y_b/y_a)^* = \frac{S_L + (S_K/P_b)(K_b/K)}{S_L + (S_K/P_a)(K_a/K)} \tag{15}$$

so that

$$(y_b/y_a)^* = \frac{S_L + (S_K/P_b) \left[P_b - \left(\frac{H}{(1/P_a) + (1/P_b)} \right)^{\frac{1}{2}} \right]}{S_L + (S_K/P_a) \left[P_a + \left(\frac{H}{(1/P_a) + (1/P_b)} \right)^{\frac{1}{2}} \right]}, \tag{16}$$

since $K_a/K = 1 - (K_b/K)$. In the computationally simple case[7] of $P_a = P_b = 0.5$, Eq. (16) becomes

$$(y_b/y_a)^* = \frac{S_L + S_K - S_K(H)^{\frac{1}{2}}}{S_L + S_K + S_K(H)^{\frac{1}{2}}} . \tag{17}$$

In order to calculate $(y_b/y_a)^*$ at various times according to (16) or (17), it is necessary to know how the wealth inequality index H is changing over time. The clearest illustrations are obtained if aggregate balanced growth

[7] In the five cotton states, $P_a = 0.478$ in 1880 and 0.562 in 1920 (*Historical Statistics*, Series A-195 and A-200). None of the results is altered substantially if either of these values of P_a together with Eq. (16) is used to calculate $(y_b/y_a)^*$ instead of Eq. (17).

$(\dot{k} = 0)$ prevails. Aside from computational convenience, there is an additional reason for making the balanced growth assumption. Under any conditions, the rate of change of H depends on n, the natural growth rate of the economy. This natural rate of growth is the sum of the rate of population growth and the rate of growth of Harrod-neutral technical progress.[8] Any calculation simulating the course of Southern inequality over time requires some estimate of this rate of technical progress. However, the growth rate of the Harrod-neutral component of n is virtually impossible to estimate directly, given the existing 19th-century data. Indirect estimation of n from output, capital stock, or total labor productivity data requires the balanced growth assumption. Therefore in the numerical examples that follow, the assumption that the Southern economy had achieved balanced growth will be made, not because the assumption necessarily is realistic, but in order to indicate by relatively simple calculations the inertia of Southern inequality resulting from the great initial wealth discrepancy between blacks and whites.

In balanced growth, the rate of growth of Harrod-neutral technical progress equals the rate of growth of simple labor productivity. If $\dot{k}/k > 0$, then the rate of growth of ordinary labor productivity will even overstate the rate of growth of purely labor-augmenting technical progress, strengthening the conclusions presented below.[9] Parker (1979) has estimated a 35% increase in labor productivity in cotton production from 1840–1860 to 1900–1920. This translates into an annual rate of growth of 0.0050. However, Parker's initial period data are drawn from plantation diaries and overseers' sheets, indicating that the labor input estimates pertain to slaves. Yet the productivity gain he measures takes no account of the differences in the intensity and organization of the labor effort of slaves compared to free workers. If Hopkins' estimate that one slave worker was roughly the equivalent of two free workers (1978, p. 4) is applied to the initial productivity estimate, the true rate of productivity growth implied by the Parker data is 0.0166.[10] The drawback of these estimates is that they apply only to the cotton-producing sector; their advantage is that they are independent of the aggregate income and capital stock estimates used below. In any case, the actual and adjusted Parker labor productivity growth estimates, combined with the actual population growth rate in the five cotton states of

---

[8] It should be recalled that with Cobb–Douglas technology, any technical progress can be put into Harrod-neutral form (Solow, 1970). It will also be necessary to assume a Cobb–Douglas production function to derive the equations used below to calculate the rate of change of wealth inequality in the Stiglitz model.

[9] It seems likely that any bias in the estimates of n from labor productivity data in the postwar period will run in this direction, because of the war-related destruction of physical capital in the South and the "portfolio disequilibrium" of former slaveholders whose wealth in slaves was wiped out by emancipation (Higgs, 1971, pp. 113–114).

[10] $(Q_0/2N_0)e^{\alpha(60)} = (Q_0/N_0)e^{(0.0050)(60)}$, which implies that $\alpha = 0.0166$.

0.0146 per annum over the period 1880–1920 (*Historical Statistics*, Series A-195),[11] imply that $n = 0.0196$ or $n = 0.0312$.

It is also the case that during balanced growth, n is equal to the rate of growth of output and the rate of growth of the capital stock. Easterlin's estimates of personal income for the five cotton states yield an undeflated $\dot{Y}/Y$ of 0.0476 over the period 1880–1920 (1957, Table Y1), and his wealth estimates for the same states imply an undeflated $\dot{K}/K$ of 0.0490 over the same period (1957, Table 4.6, with wealth of the five states calculated as their percentage of total United States wealth times total United States wealth). Estimation of n as the rate of growth of real output or capital requires taking account of price changes, however. The ratio of the BLS wholesale price index in 1920 to its value in 1880 implies $\dot{P}/P = 0.0206$ (U.S. Bureau of the Census, 1966, Series B-69); the BLS consumer price index over the same period indicates $\dot{P}/P = 0.0182$ (*Historical Statistics*, Series E-135). The four possible combinations of these estimates yield values of n of 0.0284, 0.0308, 0.0270, and 0.0294. In addition, total wealth in Georgia obtained from a different source (the Georgia tax data described below) increased from \$240 million in 1880 to \$1,181 million in 1920, a rate of increase of real wealth of 0.0193 or 0.0217 per annum, depending on which price index is used as the deflator.

Thus the estimates of n range from 0.0193 to 0.0312, averaging 0.0259.[12] Taken together, they strongly suggest that the natural rate of growth of the economy of the cotton South between 1880 and 1920 was in the neighborhood of 0.02 to 0.03. It is relatively easy to use these estimates of n to calculate the per capita income ratio that would have prevailed at successive points of time in the absence of discrimination. Stiglitz shows that if the economy is in aggregate balanced growth, the production function is Cobb–Douglas with labor elasticity S_L, and the savings function is of simple proportional form, then the proportional rate of change of V may be expressed simply as

$$d \ln V/dt = -2S_L n. \tag{18}$$

Since $\dot{k} = 0$, $\dot{V}/V = \dot{H}/H$ from (11), and therefore

$$H(t) = H_0 e^{-2S_L n t}. \tag{19}$$

[11] The black and white populations in the five states were growing at annual rates of 0.0102 and 0.0186, respectively, over the 1880–1920 period. Assuming a common rate of productivity growth, the slower rate of increase of the black population should imply even a more rapid rate of equalization of wealth and income than predicted by the Stiglitz model. This direction of bias in the predicted rate of equalization will strengthen the conclusion that forces were operating which impeded the equalization of wealth.

[12] Estimates of real $\dot{K}/K$ based on the Georgia tax data allowing assessed values to approach market values only with a lag yield estimate of 0.0251 or 0.0235. These estimates are fully consistent with those reported in the text.

Thus (17) may be rewritten as

$$(y_b/y_a)^*_t = \frac{1 - (1 - S_L)(H_0)^{\frac{1}{2}}e^{-S_L nt}}{1 + (1 - S_L)(H_0)^{\frac{1}{2}}e^{-S_L nt}} \tag{20}$$

and $(y_b/y_a)^*_t$ may be calculated for any t given the initial value if the inequality index H, the nondiscriminatory labor share S_L, and n. Since aggregate balanced growth must be assumed to derive (20), it is realistic to begin the simulation of $(y_b/y_a)^*$ at least a few years after the cessation of military hostilities and the end of the uncertainties of Reconstruction. The Hayes–Tilden compromise took effect in 1877, so 1880 is a convenient year to take as the starting point for balanced growth.

The value of H in 1880 can be computed from the Georgia tax data on wealth holdings of blacks and whites (see below), on the assumption that per capita wealth of blacks and of whites in Georgia were typical of these per capita wealth values in the cotton South as a whole. In Georgia in 1880, $K_b/N_b = \$8.00$ and $K_a/N_a = \$286$, implying that $H_{1880} = 0.894$ with $P_a = P_b = 0.5$. Table 6.3 contains hypothetical per capita income ratios in 1880, 1900, 1920, and 1970 for various n and S_L combinations,

TABLE 6.3

$(y_b/y_a)^*$ at Various Times under Conditions of Identical Savings Behavior by All Individuals, No Discrimination, $H_{1880} = 0.894$, and Aggregate Balanced Growth Commencing in 1880

n	S_L				
	0.3	0.4	0.5	0.6	0.7
			1880		
	0.203	0.276	0.358	0.451	0.558
			1900		
0.01	0.232	0.313	0.401	0.498	0.604
0.02	0.260	0.348	0.442	0.541	0.647
0.03	0.288	0.383	0.481	0.582	0.686
0.04	0.315	0.416	0.519	0.621	0.721
			1920		
0.01	0.260	0.348	0.442	0.541	0.647
0.02	0.315	0.416	0.519	0.621	0.721
0.03	0.368	0.480	0.588	0.689	0.782
0.04	0.419	0.539	0.650	0.747	0.831
			1970		
0.01	0.329	0.433	0.537	0.639	0.738
0.02	0.443	0.567	0.678	0.772	0.851
0.03	0.545	0.677	0.782	0.861	0.918
0.04	0.633	0.763	0.855	0.916	0.955

Notes. The underscored values in each part of the table represent the most plausible values of the per capita income ratios; see text.

assuming that balanced growth began in 1880. Since blacks had accumulated very little wealth by 1880, the per capita income ratios of Table 3 are very close to the values of those ratios at the time of emancipation and 20, 40, and 90 years following emancipation, if it were assumed that aggregate balanced growth began immediately following emancipation. It is evident from Table 3 that even under the ideal nondiscriminatory, identical savings behavior, balanced growth conditions of the Stiglitz model, a considerable income gap between Southern blacks and whites would have persisted for a very long time. The initial wealth discrepancy also accounts for a large (though decreasing) fraction of the subsequent income inequality between blacks and whites actually observed. Higgs estimates (y_b/y_a) in 1900 to be 0.35 (1977, p. 146). The actual (y_b/y_a) ratio in 1970 was 0.55 (computed from U.S. Department of Labor, 1975, Table 181, and *Historical Statistics*, Series A-92, A-93, A-94, A-99, A-100, A-101).[13] For $n = 0.03$ and $S_L = 0.5$ or 0.6, the values of $(y_b/y_a)^*$ given in Table 3 are 0.481 or 0.582 in 1900, and 0.782 and 0.861 in 1970.[14] These numbers imply that the initial wealth inequality alone accounts for between 64 and 80% of the 1900 per capita income gap and between 31 and 48% of the 1970 income inequality between blacks and whites.[15] These percentages are only rough approximations, but they do indicate the long-lasting consequences of the freedmen's initial lack of property, even if racial discrimination had not further hindered blacks' progress towards equality.

It is also possible to compare the actual pace of equalization of wealth and income in the postbellum South with the ideal of the Stiglitz neoclas-

---

[13] "Blacks" here includes "other races" who constituted 1.3% of the total population in 1970.

[14] Abramovitz and David (1975) give aggregate labor shares for 1903/1907–1925/1929 and 1925/1929–1965/1969 of 0.54 and 0.57, respectively. They also report 20th-century annual rates of growth of output between 0.032 and 0.033, and an average growth rate of the capital stock between 0.020 and 0.024. Gallman's (in Davis et al., 1972, p. 35) comparable figures for the period 1900–1960 are 0.031 and 0.026, respectively. These figures suggest a "steady state" rate of growth of the aggregate economy somewhere in the vicinity of 0.03 per annum, if indeed the economy was in a "steady state" (which it may not have been, since the growth rates of output and the capital stock appear to be different). The capital stock is notoriously difficult to measure, so the steady state assumption will be maintained here with $n = 0.03$. Obviously, calculations of the type reported in the text need to be qualified with the usual observation that 90 years is a long time for a real economy to remain in a steady state with unchanging parameters of the underlying technological and demographic processes.

[15] Maintaining the $P_a = P_b = 0.5$ assumption throughout these and the subsequent calculations is equivalent to making comparisons of the initial black population of the five states of the cotton South and their descendants to the original white population of those states and their descendants. Obviously, as time went on, these groups became intermixed in the black and white populations of the United States as a whole. The United States average of (y_b/y_a) for 1970 is therefore used as a substitute for exact knowledge of the ratio for the two groups of descendants.

sical growth model. The annual *Report*[s] *of the Comptroller-General of Georgia* beginning in the 1870s (referred to throughout this paper as the Georgia tax data) provide an extensive amount of information on the wealth holdings of blacks and whites over time. These data are disaggregated to the county level, and include statistics on a variety of different types of property holdings by race. The data are available through the Great Depression, and can be used to provide an empirical perspective on the questions of the dynamics of inequality being considered here.

A brief description of the data and its sources is in order.[16] Statistics were originally collected at the individual level in order to assess the Georgia property tax. As with all data gathered for purposes of taxation, there are problems of reliability and completeness. Property assessments were returned by the individual taxpayer to the "tax-receivers" in each county, who forwarded copies of the lists to the Comptroller-General of the state, the "ordinary" who performed the duties of a board of county commissioners, and the tax collector. "Defaulters" who did not return their property were subject to a double tax, and the tax collectors were also empowered to ascertain taxable property not returned to the receivers. In addition, the justices of the peace were required to furnish the tax-receivers with a list of all taxpayers in their districts.

The assessments themselves were subject to two kinds of scrutiny. The receivers could revise assessments upwards, and if the taxpayer appealed, his entire valuation was left to three disinterested persons, one selected by the taxpayer, one by the receiver, and the third selected by the first two. Furthermore, *any* taxpayer could lodge a complaint against the assessment of *any* property, with a new assessment made as in the case of an appeal of a receiver's revisions. Despite these checks, Schmeckebier states that "the general property tax has worked but little better in Georgia than in the other states where it has been employed" (p. 230). Election of receivers and collectors, inconsistencies from county to county and between urban and rural property, and double counting of mortgages and mortgaged property for tax purposes were some of the difficulties alluded to by Schmeckebier.[17] Attention here will also be restricted to the relative wealth holdings of blacks and whites and to rates of change of wealth holdings, so that the perennial problem with assess-

---

[16] This discussion is summarized from Schmeckebier (1900).

[17] One of the most severe problems, the undervaluation of consumer durables, is actually no problem in the present application, since the emphasis is on productive capital. The choice of whether to count the purchase value of consumer durables or the stream of imputed returns from them as income is arbitrary. Since the blacks were emancipated without any substantial stock of consumer durables, the procedure followed here is to treat consumer durables as part of the capital stock or wealth of a group.

ment data—the determination of the implicit ratio of assessed to market value—is not serious.[18]

The Georgia statewide wealth totals are roughly consistent with the dynamics of the Stiglitz model. For the period 1880 to 1920, blacks were accumulating at a faster rate than whites. The ratio of blacks' per capita wealth to total per capita wealth was 0.051 in 1880 and rose steadily (except during the 1890s) to a level of 0.139 in 1920.[19] Blacks' rate of accumulation also appears to have slowed down over the period. The 20-year rate of change in blacks' real per capita wealth holdings was 1.06 over the period 1880–1900, while the same proportional change was only 0.52 from 1900 to 1920, despite the fact that blacks' per capita wealth accumulation virtually ceased during the agricultural depression of the 1890s (computed from Georgia tax data deflated by the BLS wholesale price index).

Values of the H index may also be computed directly from the Georgia tax data, assuming the actual Georgia values of per capita wealth of blacks and whites and that $P_b = P_a = 0.5$. The actual rate of change of H can then be estimated. The result for the 1880–1920 period, assuming a first-order autocorrelated disturbance to avoid a biased estimate of the standard error of the trend coefficient, is[20]

---

[18] These data were used by DuBois in his study, "The Negro Landholder in Georgia" (1901). DuBois held that the self-assessment procedure "gives rise to wholesale undervaluation, especially in the case of the rich, and to overvaluation in the case of the very small estates of the poor" (p. 649), but this conjecture did not prevent him from judging that the data, particularly if disaggregated to the individual level, "would form a complete and invaluable source of information" (p. 649). DuBois also believed that "perhaps there could be found no other single index of the results of the struggle of the freedman upward so significant as the ownership of land" (p. 648).

[19] As argued earlier, a starting date of 1880 assures that any structural change associated with Reconstruction would be over. The 1920 closing date for the comparison requires more justification. After 1920, the black/white per capita wealth ratio fell slightly and remained steady through 1937. This change in the behavior of the wealth ratio probably occurs because the 1920s marked the peak of the first large-scale black outmigration from Georgia. Northern opportunities began to be opened to blacks during and after World War I. (In some of the other Southern states, the first peak of outmigration occurred during the 1910–1920 decade.) There is no reason to believe that migrating blacks would necessarily have sold their fixed assets to other blacks, so that the Georgia wealth ratio might have stagnated while blacks originating from Georgia continued to accumulate at a faster rate than whites. The magnitude of this migration effect can be seen by observing that net intercensal migration of blacks from Georgia as a fraction of total Georgia black population averaged −0.011 over the three decades beginning in 1880; the rate was −0.072 over 1910–1920; then it more than tripled to −0.257 during the 1920s [computed from Lee (1957)]. This massive outmigration of the 1920s suggests that the Georgia wealth data in isolation can safely be used to chart the course of blacks' accumulation patterns only through about 1920.

[20] The ordinary least squares estimate of $\dot{H}/H$ is −0.0049.

$\ln H_t = 10.3 - 0.00554\,t;$
$$(0.00063)$$

$$\hat{\rho} = 0.9,\ R^2 \text{ of transformed equation} = 0.551. \quad (21)$$

It is evident that the actual rate at which Southern wealth inequalities were being eliminated was lower than the rate predicted under the ideal conditions of the Stiglitz model. Even with $n = 0.0146$ (the rate of population growth) and $S_L = 0.3$, Eq. (19) would predict $\dot{H}/H = -0.00876$, which is outside the 99% confidence interval for $\dot{H}/H$ according to the estimate of Eq. (21). It follows that at least one of the premises of the Stiglitz model or of the procedures used to estimate n must be false. The most likely possibilities are (1) there was enough discrimination in the factor and asset markets to slow wealth equalization significantly, (2) savings behavior of blacks and whites was not identical, blacks having a lower marginal propensity to save, (3) the Southern economy was not experiencing balanced growth after 1880, or (4) the rate of productivity growth in the Southern economy was lower than estimated here. It should be noted that the second of these possibilities does not require discrimination if savings propensities were directly related to income levels, and that discrimination need not have been responsible for sluggish Southern productivity growth. Nevertheless, discrimination against blacks in their efforts to accumulate property is consistent with the Georgia tax data.

The hypothetical per capita income ratios of blacks and whites can be calculated for various times, given the value of $\dot{H}/H$ estimated in Eq. (21). Again beginning in 1880, the (y_b/y_a) ratios resulting from $\dot{H}/H = -0.00554$ combined with the initial 1880 wealth ratio are shown in Table 6.4. The per capita income ratios of Table 6.4 are, of course, lower than those of Table 6.3 because of the lower absolute rates of decline of H underlying Table 6.4. It is interesting to observe that the plausible $S_L = 0.4$ through $S_L = 0.6$ values of (y_b/y_a) from Table 6.4 bracket the Higgs estimate of 0.35 for the income ratio in 1900. Also, for $S_L = 0.6$, the hypothetical (y_b/y_a) ratio in 1970 from Table 6.4 is 0.545, compared with the actual 1970 ratio of 0.55. There is some suggestion in this comparison that the rate of equalization may have improved slightly at some point after 1920 if the true value of S_L is lower than 0.6.

TABLE 6.4

Hypothetical Per Capita Wealth Ratios, $\dot{H}/H = -0.00554$ from Eq. (21)

Year	S_L	0.3	0.4	0.5	0.6	0.7
1900		0.230	0.301	0.382	0.473	0.577
1920		0.256	0.326	0.405	0.494	0.595
1970		0.319	0.387	0.462	0.545	0.638

Source: Equations (17), (21); see text.

As a final illustration, the consequences of emancipation accompanied by the redistribution of "40 acres and a mule" to each freed household can be examined. To make the comparison, it is first necessary to determine the size of the proposed initial wealth transfer. Rather than attempting to recover land and mule prices for the chaotic years just following emancipation, the relative size of the initial transfer will be calculated as the total value of 40 acres and a mule for each black household in 1880 as a fraction of total wealth in 1880. This only amounts to assuming that the relative size of the grant at the time of emancipation was the same as the relative size of the grant had it been made in 1880. This fraction can be determined for Georgia because of the availability of total wealth data, and of land and livestock prices for that state. Higgs (1977, p. 78) assumes one-fifth of the freedmen would have been heads of households eligible to receive the wealth transfer.[21] The Georgia black population was 725,000 in 1880, so 40 acres to each household at $2.94 per improved acre (the price given in the Georgia tax data) totals $17,052,000. The price of a mule in Georgia in 1880 was $77 (USDA, 1937), but it is necessary to correct this price by an assessment ratio.[22] The total value of horses, mules, hogs, all cattle, and stock sheep in Georgia in 1880 was $30,871,000 (USDA, 1938, pp. 96–97). The assessed value of all livestock from the Georgia tax data was $23,183,000, yielding an assessment ratio for livestock of 0.751 and an "assessed" mule price of $57.82. Total assessed value of a mule for each black household was therefore $8,348,510. Thus the ratio of the total assessed value of 40 acres and a mule for each black household to the total assessed value of tangible wealth in Georgia was 0.106 (computed from text and the Georgia tax data). Blacks constituted 0.470 of the Georgia population in 1880, so the ratio K_b/K then would have been 0.113 if blacks had formed 50% of the population. $((K_b/N_b)/(K/N) = (K_b/K)/(N_b/N) = 0.2255$, so holding per capita wealth of blacks constant, if $N_b/N = 0.5$, then $K_b/K = 0.113$.) This initial K_b/K allows calculation of H_0 from (13), yielding $H_0 = 0.599$. The implied per capita income ratios at the time of emancipation for the various values of S_L are given in Table 6.5.

Comparison with Table 6.1 shows that 40 acres and a mule would have considerably improved blacks' income position as compared to emancipation without property, but that even with the redistribution, blacks' per capita income level would have been markedly lower than that of the whites. Improved land plus livestock comprised only 0.460 of total Georgia wealth in 1880 (computed from Georgia tax data), and if the freedom

---

[21] In 1890, black population ÷ black households = 5.3. *Historical Statistics* Series A-93, A-100, A-321.

[22] Since the denominator of the wealth ratio (total Georgia wealth) is also obtained from the Georgia tax data, the land price obtained from the assessed value of land does not need to be adjusted by the assessment ratio.

TABLE 6.5
$(y_b/y_a)^*$ at the Time of Emancipation, Given a Redistribution of
40 Acres and a Mule to Each Black Household

S_L	0.3	0.4	0.5	0.6	0.7
$(y_b/y_a)^*$	0.297	0.366	0.442	0.527	0.623

Source: See text.

dues had amounted to the same fraction of total wealth that 40 acres and a mule were of improved acres and livestock, K_b/K would initially have been 0.113/0.460 = 0.246. This implies $H_0 = 0.259$. The $(y_b/y_a)^*$ ratios corresponding to $S_L = 0.3$ through 0.7 for this value of H_0 are 0.475, 0.532, 0.594, 0.662, and 0.735. Even for S_L between 0.4 and 0.6, this larger wealth redistribution would have raised the initial level of blacks' per capita income to only about half or slightly more than half the per capita income of whites.

Even though 40 acres and a mule for each black household would not have come close to eliminating the income gap immediately, a wealth redistribution of this type would have considerably speeded blacks' progress towards economic parity. Given the same assumptions as those underlying Table 6.3 (i.e., actual rates of accumulation through 1880, balanced growth and the other assumptions of the Stiglitz model after that date), the relative per capita income level that could have been achieved immediately after emancipation with 40 acres and a mule would not actually have been reached until sometime between 1891 ($S_L = 0.6$, $n = 0.03$) and 1905 ($S_L = 0.4$, $n = 0.02$). (The absolute level of blacks' per capita income would have reached the emancipation-with-redistribution level sooner than this, of course.) If equalization after 1880 took place at the rate of $\dot{H}/H$ estimated in Eq. (21), the inital per capita income ratio achieved with the wealth grant to the freedmen would not have been reached until 1952. Alternatively, given the actual $\dot{H}/H$ together with an initial (1867) grant of 40 acres and a mule to each freed household, the 1970 (y_b/y_a) ratio with $S_L = 0.6$ would have been 0.622 as compared with 0.545 in Table 6.4 or with the actual value of 0.55. The more generous freedom dues of 0.246 of total wealth, on the other hand, would have implied $(y_b/y_a) = 0.735$ in 1970 under the same assumptions. A payment of freedom dues would have hastened blacks' progress towards economic equality, but given the operation of those forces that retarded the equalization of per capita wealth, the initial grant would have had to have been larger than the hypothesized 40 acres and a mule to each freed household to have been able to affect dramatically the closure of the income gap.

IV. SUMMARY

The main conclusion that can be drawn from these calculations is that the unequal ownership of property by blacks and whites in the postbellum South was the chief source of race-related economic inequality. The blacks' emancipation with zero wealth accounts for most of the gap in income between blacks and whites during the Reconstruction period. This large black/white income gap, together with the high concentration of blacks in the South, accounts for most of the North/South regional income differential which persisted through the end of the nineteenth century. Furthermore, quite a long time would have been required for substantial progress of blacks relative to whites to have become manifest even under the best of circumstances (i.e., no discrimination, homogeneous savings behavior, etc.). The actual wealth holdings of blacks and whites were tending towards equality, at least until the 1920s, but at a slower rate than in the ideal case. Whether direct discrimination against blacks in the acquisition of property, indirect discrimination in the form of less protection of blacks' property rights, occupational discrimination, low rates of savings by blacks, or low Southern productivity growth was the cause of the low rate of wealth equalization remains a matter of conjecture, but what is established without doubt is that emancipation without property condemned the blacks to a lengthy period of economic disadvantage. Although payment of freedom dues would not have instantaneously closed the relative per capita income gap, it would have shortened the time required for blacks to reach any particular level of relative per capita income. A grant more generous than 40 acres and a mule probably would have been required to counteract effectively the forces retarding equalization. Large-scale confiscation and redistribution of wealth would have involved a drastic upheaval in the political and economic life of a nation already convulsed with civil war, but the Emancipation Proclamation and the military defeat of the Confederacy had prepared the way for a complete realignment of Southern society and economic institutions in any case. Some sort of substantial distribution of tangible wealth to the freedmen at the time of emancipation need not have been a revolutionary measure, and would have spared the nation many of the worst consequences of slavery's enduring injustice.

CHAPTER 7

Growth and Welfare in the American South in the Nineteenth Century

ROGER L. RANSOM

AND

RICHARD SUTCH

The history of the American economy has been largely one of expansion and steadily improving standards of living. This fortunate history, it would seem, has simplified the tasks of economic historians to make inferences about what has happened to the American people from aggregate indexes of per capita income, output, and productivity—the same measures used to chart the course of American economic growth. At least, it seems to be widely believed among economists that welfare disputes should be less complex and troublesome in an economy that is expanding in a smooth and balanced fashion. In principle, each group in such a society can experience an improvement in personal income per capita without coming into direct conflict with other groups over the distribution of the national product. Conflict between groups is made even less likely in the context of the American political–legal structure, which, according to North, was designed to make it "unprofitable" for groups to use the political process to redistribute wealth (1978, pp. 967–70). This made it more likely that groups and individuals would turn their energies

This chapter incorporates some materials originally presented to the conference entitled "The First and Second Reconstructions: The Historical Setting and Contemporary Black–White Relations, 1860–1978," held in St. Louis on February 15–17, 1978. The conference was sponsored by the University of Missouri-St. Louis and the Missouri Committee for the Humanities. We are grateful to the conference sponsors and to conference participants at both Duke University and the University of Missouri, St. Louis, for their helpful comments.

127

toward increasing their economic productivity rather than dissipate it in efforts to gain political advantage. If we combine these arguments with the economist's propensity to equate measures of personal income per capita with economic welfare, one can understand the preoccupation with economic growth and the comparative neglect of welfare issues in the field of American economic history.

The indirect approach to the issues of relative welfare is less defensible, however, when the historian's attention is directed away from the broad sweep of the American past and toward the narrower topic of the American South of the nineteenth century. In *One Kind of Freedom* we present evidence that agricultural output per capita in the South declined substantially during the decade of the 1860s, and that it was virtually stagnant after 1872 for the balance of the century (pp. 9–12 and Appendix F). In an economy experiencing stagnation or decline, an improvement in one group's welfare can only come at the expense of some other group's well-being. Furthermore, if the constitutional system is designed to frustrate direct political attempts to redistribute income, then the various groups in society would be more likely to turn to extralegal methods to advance their economic position. Obviously, the welfare issues in such societies must be dealt with in their own right, rather than by the facile equation of growth and welfare.

The case of the American South presents a number of unique features which make an explicit study of welfare not only more important and potentially more illuminating, but also more complex and less straightforward than it might at first appear. We can begin with the obvious point that, in any context, aggregate measures such as per capita income reveal nothing about the distribution of total income to the various members of the population. Any examination of changes in the *average* standard of living must be interpreted in light of whatever shifts in the distribution of income accompanied those changes. In the South of the nineteenth century, this point is particularly relevant. During the first half of the century, under slavery, the blacks are widely believed to have experienced a decline in the material conditions of their existence. Although the statistical bases supporting this view are weak, it is certain that the living standards of slaves was well below the average for southern whites, and, even if the prevailing view were incorrect, it remains highly unlikely that slaves experienced as great an improvement in living standards as did the free population. Not only did the slave economy generate a highly skewed distribution of income, but that distribution also undoubtedly became more unequal over the first half of the century.

Emancipation of slaves following the Civil War, on the other hand, was accompanied by a significant redistribution of income in favor of the blacks. Estimates we have presented in *One Kind of Freedom* indicate that the black population experienced nearly a 30% increase in their material income per capita as a consequence of freedom (Table 1.3, p. 7, and Appendix A). Within an appropriate context, equating the increase in blacks' personal income with an improvement in their welfare might be valid. But in this case the context is inappropriate for such an equation. Economists have long been aware of the dangers inherent in cross-cultural or intertemporal comparisons of economic welfare that are based on relative income measures. Although our own interest is not cross-cultural, and the span of time we wish to examine is not unusually long, we are nevertheless faced with a similar situation. The Civil War and emancipation so altered the institutional framework of the South that comparisons of income statistics before and after the war may be a very misleading way to begin a study of the changes in economic welfare.

To illustrate the point, we make two observations. Approximately one-half of the Southern population was enslaved throughout the first half of the century, and as slaves these people were denied the economic freedoms which are assumed in making the standard argument that more income should allow its recipient to enjoy a higher level of welfare. The transition from slavery to free labor poses the second problem. Generally, slaves were obligated to work harder and longer than they would have chosen to do voluntarily in a free labor market. Therefore, the high levels of per capita output observed with slavery were obtained—at least in part—by overruling the slaves' preference for leisure over income at the margin. Once free, the black population predictably withdrew a substantial amount of their labor from production for the market. The statistician observes a drop in per capita output, but there was no corresponding fall in welfare.[1]

It follows from these thoughts that an analysis of welfare in the nineteenth century South must maintain the distinction between per capita income and welfare and ought to at least attempt an assessment of the impact of the changes in these averages on the different groups and classes within society.

This chapter reviews what is known about growth and welfare in the South, and addresses several issues which have been raised in the course of the recent debates on slavery and the post-emancipation economy. The result is far from a complete examination of the issues. Nevertheless, we hope this chapter will serve to clarify some points left unclear by our earlier discussion in *One Kind of Freedom*, and to extend our earlier arguments further along the lines we pursued there.

[1] These issues have been dealt with extensively. See Fogel and Engerman (1974, Vol. 1, pp. 191–209; Vol. 2, pp. 126–142), David and Temin (1976, pp. 202–223), Gutman and Sutch (1976, pp. 55–93), Ransom and Sutch (1975a), and *One Kind of Freedom* (Chap. 3 and Appendix C).

REGIONAL ANALYSIS AND INTERREGIONAL MIGRATION

As North has observed, any study of growth and welfare must be based on theoretically relevant quantitative evidence (1974, p. 2). In this spirit, we present our estimates of the trends in Southern agricultural production and use them to build up new estimates of the relative welfare of blacks and whites. It should be pointed out that the estimates that we present here, like those originally presented in *One Kind of Freedom*, are for the five-state region comprising South Carolina, Georgia, Alabama, Mississippi, and Louisiana. These were the major cotton-producing states of the deep South. We chose to concentrate our attention on them because all of the ingredients of the uniquely "Southern" economy were there in the purest form: plantation slavery and cotton factors before the war, tenancy and credit merchants afterward, white landowners, black laborers, and black-belt soil. If this is the recipe for economic backwardness, then we believe that here is where to study its chemistry first hand.

While we confine our statistical research to this region, one should not lose sight of the fact that these five states were embedded within a larger South, and that that larger South was an integral part of the national economy. If the American economy of the nineteenth century had been smoothly functioning and fully integrated, the economic trends in each of its states and regions would in theory have been identical, and this point would make little difference. Of course, as we know from Richard Easterlin's pioneering work on regional income trends, this was not the reality (Easterlin, 1960a, 1960b, 1961). Yet, while impediments to factor mobility, high information and transportation costs, and the continuing disequilibrium generated by the westward movement of population produced sufficient independence between the regional economies to make separate regional studies interesting and fruitful, the movements of factors between regions were sufficiently important that they must be considered in any regional economic analysis.

This is particularly true when examining the issue of economic growth. Productivity growth, after all, is produced by factor mobility. When a manufacturer changes from one technology to a superior one, when a worker leaves one job for a higher-paying one, or when an investor risks capital only in the more promising ventures, productivity will rise and economic growth takes place. Within an integrated economy, factor mobility can also be geographical. When labor leaves one state for higher-paying jobs in another, or when capital flows between regions in pursuit of highest returns, productivity improvements and growth in per capita income are generated which are no less real than those caused by any other form of mobility. Nevertheless, we have intentionally designed our analysis of economic growth to focus on that growth in per capita income caused by all factors other than interregional migration.

To understand the reason why we deliberately ignored growth generated by interregional migration, consider the hypothetical case of two regions set side-by-side, both economically stagnant in terms of per capita income. If the standards of living in the two regions are different, labor will have an incentive to move from the low-income to the high-income region. Per capita income in the two regions when they are considered together will be seen to rise as a consequence of the population movement, since the productivity of the migrants is enhanced. However, unless the population flow itself somehow alters the underlying economic situations, each region will remain stagnant when viewed separately.

Interregional migration can only make a transitory contribution to economic growth, and it is for that reason that we wish to separate the growth produced by interregional migration from that generated by forces working within each region. As soon as significant numbers become involved in the migration streams, the underlying economic situations within each region cannot remain unchanged. The destination region will become sufficiently supplied with labor that incomes there will be depressed. Meanwhile, the increasing scarcity of labor in the origin region is unlikely to improve the situation there. Since migration is selective of the young, well-educated, highly skilled, and affluent, the poorer region will experience declines in its per capita income as it loses the best and the brightest of its population. Soon the influence of the falling incomes within each region will overcome the gains achieved by interregional mobility and aggregate per capita income will cease to grow.

The narrower regional focus that obscures the transitory growth caused by interregional mobility is useful because it directs attention to the underlying economic institutions of each region that must change if there is to be self-sustaining economic growth *within* each of the twin economies.

The trick in performing this type of regional economic analysis lies in the careful delineation of the region to be studied so that the investigator is certain that the economic institutions it encompasses are homogeneous. The idea is to minimize in the statistics the type of growth which is generated by migration from one distinct set of economic institutions to another. In that way, the growth-generating capacity of the set of institutions under study can be examined free from such interference. In selecting the appropriate region, one could err by making it too large, but not by making it too small. Thus, in our own attention to the heartland of the cotton South, we hope to have avoided choosing too large a region for meaningful analysis, but at the same time to have focused on a set of institutions that have broad relevance to the economic conditions experienced throughout the South.[2]

---

[2] See *One Kind of Freedom*, Appendix G, particularly pp. 273–283, for a discussion of the procedures we followed to define the region to be examined.

ESTIMATES OF PER CAPITA CROP OUTPUT, 1839–1899

Our measures of the trends in per capita output for the agricultural sector of the five cotton states are given in Table 1 and charted in Fig. 1. They are based upon estimates which include only primary agricultural production; manufacturing and other nonagricultural income is excluded. The nonagricultural portion of the economy in these states was comparatively small. But in any case, we wish to exclude the nonagricultural sector in order to concentrate upon agriculture and the economic institutions which served that sector of the economy. Any growth which occurred because of the transfer of resources from agriculture to manufacturing is intentionally left out of our analysis. The figures are best described as estimates of real crop output per member of the rural population (including slaves) rather than as estimates of per capita income. To eliminate the influence of price fluctuations on the trends, we have reported all values in terms of 1859 prices.

It should be noted that the level of per capita crop output falls short of a measure of the level of per capita income, since the latter includes the value added by economic activity in animal husbandry, home manufactures, garden crop cultivation, and capital investment in agriculture as well as all incomes generated outside of the agricultural sector. Therefore, crop output is also an incomplete measure of agricultural income per capita. Our interest in this article, however, is focused upon the shifts in and rates of change of per capita income, not in its absolute level. Our examination of the available information on trends in income generated by non-crop-related agricultural activities suggested to us that none of the noncrop sources of income experienced changes or exhibited trends which would significantly influence the conclusions we reach about economic growth based on our less inclusive measures.[3] The exclusion of the noncrop sources of income, however, may influence the welfare comparisons we discuss later. In particular, the estimates exclude incomes generated for Southerners by investments they may have made outside of the region. Since extraregional investment is more likely to have been made by the wealthy, its exclusion will make the income distribution appear less unequal than it actually was.

The figures given in Table 7.1 are benchmarked to the estimate of the value of per capita crop output in 1859 presented in *One Kind of Freedom* (Table F.2, p. 258). This estimate—$84.89 to be exact—includes the census-enumerated production of 10 crops (cotton, corn, sugar, sweet potatoes, wheat, rice, oats, Irish potatoes, rye, and tobacco) evaluated at farmgate prices. The population used to deflate the aggregate value in-

---

[3] The reader is warned that, because these statistics were developed specifically for the arguments made in this chapter our estimates of per capita output may not be suited for other purposes. A close examination of the techniques and data underlying our estimates is recommended for anyone who wishes to employ them elsewhere.

TABLE 7.1

Agricultural Output per Member of the Rural Population, Five Cotton States, Prices of 1859

Year[a]	Average annual output
1839	$66.28
1857	74.28
1859	84.89
1867	38.07
1868	44.07
1869	49.26
1870	49.30
1871	52.42
1872	50.88
1873	53.72
1874	53.81
1875	54.16
1876	55.82
1877	55.41
1878	57.42
1879	60.13
1880	59.94
1881	63.65
1882	61.24
1883	62.50
1884	59.88
1885	60.22
1886	63.00
1887	62.92
1888	67.40
1889	69.42
1890	72.28
1891	68.28
1892	65.99
1893	68.04
1894	71.20
1895	73.04
1896	73.36
1897	76.98
1898	76.22
1899	71.28

[a] For all observations after 1859, the figure given is a 3-year moving average centered on the year stated. Source: See text.

cludes the total white, free black, and slave inhabitants living outside of towns and cities with populations of 2500 or more. Census figures for 1860 were extrapolated backward to 1859 assuming that the rural population grew as fast between 1859 and 1860 as the aggregate population grew over those 2 years.[4]

[4] See *One Kind of Freedom*, Appendix F, especially pp. 263–264 and Table F.2, p. 258, for details and references.

The benchmark estimate of $84.89 in 1859 agrees closely with Stanley Engerman's estimates of personal income per capita in 1860. For the South Atlantic region (Virginia, including present-day West Virginia, North Carolina, South Carolina, Georgia, and Florida) Engerman estimated an income per capita of $84; for the East South Central region (Kentucky, Tennessee, Alabama, and Mississippi) he reports a figure of $89.[5]

Our estimate of per capita crop output for 1839 (measured in the prices of 1859) was obtained by extrapolating the 1859 benchmark backward assuming a growth rate of 1.245% over the 20-year period. That rate of growth was estimated by averaging the rate of growth of real personal income per capita for the South Atlantic region (1.21% per year) with that for the East South Central region (1.28% per year) as measured by Engerman.[6] We have chosen to average the rates of growth in these two subregions rather than to use the rate of growth calculated by Engerman for The South as a whole (1.67% per year). The pace of growth in Engerman's South actually exceeded that of any of its component subregions. This counterintuitive phenomenon is the result of interregional migration of labor of the type which we discussed above. Since the overall growth rate is affected by the migration-induced growth, it is hoped that the rate of 1.25% per year which we have chosen will more accurately reflect the trend of per capita income within the five cotton states.

As illustrated in Fig. 7.1, per capita agricultural income probably grew at substantially less than 1% per annum between 1839 and 1857, since much of the growth between 1839 and 1859 came in a spurt during the last 2 years of that 20-year period. Our estimate—admittedly crude—is that per capita crop output grew at a rate of 0.64% per year in the years before 1857. This estimate was obtained by adjusting the level of crop output observed in 1859 downward to eliminate the influence of the unusually high level of cotton output in that year. Several investigators have noted that 1859 is a poor year to choose as representative of late antebellum agricultural productivity. Not only was cotton output unusually high in

[5] Engerman (1971, Table 2, p. 287). Engerman's figures are based on works by Richard Easterlin (1961) and Robert Gallman (1960, 1966) that were in turn based on the census returns of 1860. The census enumerations of crops and manufacturing were for 1859, thus Engerman's estimates are properly labeled estimates for 1859 rather than 1860. See *One Kind of Freedom*, pp. 264–269, for details. It is not possible to adopt Engerman's methodology to estimate per capita income for the five states in which we are interested, since Easterlin's relative income measures for 1860 are unavailable at the state level.

[6] Engerman (1971, p. 287), and *One Kind of Freedom* (Table F.6, p. 267). There is good reason to suspect that these figures may exaggerate the true rate of growth between 1840 and 1860, and, if so, our 1839 figure may well be too low. See Gunderson (1973, 1975), Gallman (1975), and *One Kind of Freedom* (pp. 264–269).

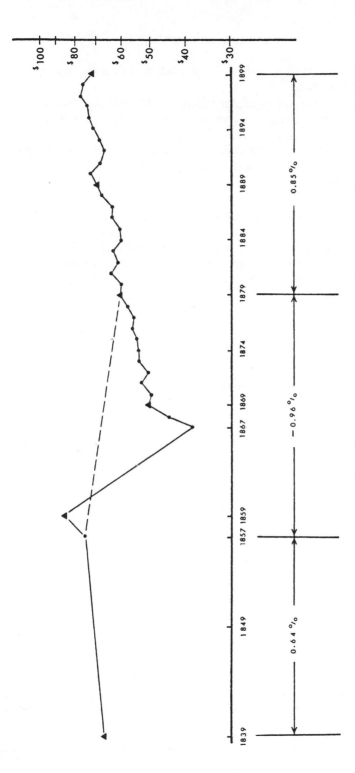

FIG. 7.1. Agricultural output per member of the rural population in prices of 1859 for the period 1839–1899 in the five cotton states. Ratio scale with annual rates of growth for three subperiods. Source: Table 7.1.

that year, but the price of cotton did not fall significantly in response to the extraordinary crop.[7]

Other than annual figures of American cotton output, there is little to rely upon when attempting to estimate per capita crop output for a more representative year—such as 1857. The best we can hope for is a rough guess. Cotton output in 1859 was 31.3% above a simple trend line extrapolating the annual crop production recorded between 1849 and 1858. The value of cotton produced per capita in the United States in 1857 was only 64% of the level achieved in 1859.[8]

Of course, the unusually high cotton output in 1859 could have been the result of a shift of resources from other crops to cotton, in which case aggregate crop output would not require as extensive an adjustment as the cotton statistics at first suggest.[9] Alternatively, the large crop may be a reflection of unusually favorable weather which improved yields per acre, in which case other crops may have benefited from the favorable conditions as well. If this were the situation, then aggregate crop output would have to be adjusted by an even larger amount than the cotton figures above indicate.[10] Given the uncertainty about the direction of change of the output of crops other than cotton between 1857 and 1859, we have assumed for our rough calculations that the per capita output of those crops did not change.[11]

Although the per capita real value of cotton produced in the entire South in 1857 was only 67% of the 1859 level, we have made a more cautious adjustment. We have assumed that per capita cotton output in 1857 in the five cotton-producing states was 75% of its 1859 level. Since cotton output represented approximately one-half of aggregate crop out-

[7] Sutch (1965, pp. 372–373), Gavin Wright (1976, pp. 313–315; 1978, pp. 104–106), and *One Kind of Freedom* (pp. 6–7). It should be noted that the income and welfare measures for slaves in 1859 presented in *One Kind of Freedom* were based on estimates which were not adjusted for the unusual crop that year (Tables 1.1, 1.2, and 1.3, pp. 3–7). We did allude to the unusual crop in our discussion of labor productivity (p. 7).

[8] *One Kind of Freedom* (p. 7) and James Waktins (1895, pp. 3, 8, and 10).

[9] This possibility has been suggested by Fogel and Engerman (1977, pp. 281–282), Hopkins (1978), and Goldin (Chapter 1). While such a possibility remains to be tested, we do not accept the suggestion by Fogel and Engerman that our figures on output per capita (*One Kind of Freedom*, Table 8.1, p. 152) can be used to support their contention that there was a decline in the number of acres devoted to foodstuffs.

[10] This possibility was suggested by Gavin Wright (1978, p. 165). Wright cites evidence from contemporary reports of crop conditions referred to by Gallman (1970, p. 8) to support his interpretations.

[11] The plausibility of our assumption may be enhanced by noting that the per capita production of food crops in 1859 was within 5% of the level 10 years earlier (*One Kind of Freedom*, Table 8.1, p. 152). The estimates by Albert Fishlow of the South's imports of foodstuffs for 1857 and 1860 do not suggest that Southern producers experienced unusually large deficits of food crops as a consequence of the harvest of 1859 (Fishlow, 1964, Table 3, p. 360).

put (50.6% in 1859), we calculate the 1857 crop output per capita to be 87.5% of that reported in 1859.

Annual estimates of per capita crop output for the five cotton-producing states following the Civil War are presented in *One Kind of Freedom*. For the purposes of this chapter, the annual series has been converted into 3-year moving averages to emphasize the trends in the data. The figures presented in *One Kind of Freedom* were expressed in 1899–1908 prices. We converted these figures to 1859 prices using a two-step procedure. The published estimates of physical crop output were first shifted to a base of 1879–80 prices. [12] The values thus estimated were then converted to 1859–60 prices using the cost-of-living index for 1879–80 calculated in *One Kind of Freedom*. [13] The cost-of-living index which was used to place the postwar estimates on a comparable basis with the antebellum figures is a conservative choice. Had we used the implicit price index of crop output, the measured deflation between 1859 and 1879–80 would have been less than that indicated by the cost-of-living measure (the index number of 1879–80 would be 96.2 rather than 86.2), and the dollar values for the postwar years would have been even lower than those given here.

The result of these calculations are displayed in Fig. 7.1, which shows that income per capita fell dramatically over the Civil War decade. Indeed, according to our estimates, per capita production in 1866–68 was 55.2% below the prewar peak. In the years immediately after the war, economic recovery was rapid; the South reorganized her disrupted economy and restored much of the significant damage wrought by the fighting. [14] Yet this initial recovery was far from complete; even by 1879 (2 years after the last federal troops left the South, and 14 years after the end of the war) per capita output was only 81% of its 1857 level and 71% of its 1859 level. As Fig. 7.1 shows, between 1857 and 1879, per capita income shrank at the rate of 0.96% per year. We feel confident that this decline represents a reliable estimate of the magnitude of the fall in per capita crop output between the late antebellum era and the immediate post-Reconstruction period.

Most, if not all of this decline can be explained by the abolition of slavery. As we noted above, output per capita in the slave economy was high partly because so much labor was devoted to production. In *One*

---

[12] The constant-dollar crop output series is presented in *One Kind of Freedom*, Table F.3, p. 259; the current-price series in Table F.2, p. 258. By comparing these two series, an implicit price deflator for the current-dollar series can be calculated. With 1899–1908 equal to 100, the index for the year 1879 is 113.2; the index for 1880 is 115.5. Averaging these gives an index for the period 1879–80 of 114.3.

[13] *One Kind of Freedom* (Table A.9, p. 218). The index based on cash prices in 1879–80 was 86.2, with 1859–60 defined as 100.

[14] See Ransom and Sutch (1975a) and *One Kind of Freedom* (Chap. 3) for a discussion of this recovery period and the impact of the damage from the Civil War.

Kind of Freedom we presented evidence that the quantity of labor supplied by the black population declined by between 28 and 37%.[15] Given the differential labor force participation rates between blacks and whites, this suggests that the total labor supply fell by as much as 20 to 26%. Not surprisingly, output per capita declined as a consequence.[16]

THE RELATIVE INCOME OF THE SOUTH, 1867–1879

After the economic reorganization was complete—and it was nearly so by 1873—the South settled into a long period of slow and slowing growth. Between 1873 and 1879 southern agriculture grew at the rate of 1.78% per year; from 1879 to 1889 it grew at an annual rate of 0.97%; and from 1889 to 1899 it grew at the rate of 0.79% per annum.[17] These rates are substantially below the pace of economic growth in the entire United States economy. Table 7.2 presents the comparisons originally presented in *One Kind of Freedom*. Over the entire period from the quinquennium 1869–1873 to the quinquennium 1902–1906, the United States economy grew 2.74% per year, while Southern agricultural output grew at only 1.17% annually—about half as fast.

These figures for United States gross national product are based upon the estimates of Simon Kuznets (1961). Kuznets' figures for the period after 1891 were adjusted to make them comparable to the U.S. Department of Commerce definition of gross national product by John Kendrick (1961). The Kuznets–Kendrick estimates are the best known GNP series for the late nineteenth century, and are those reproduced in such standard sources as *Historical Statistics of the United States* (U.S. Bureau of the Census, 1975, Vol. 1, Series F-4, p. 224). Robert Gallman.suggests that

[15] *One Kind of Freedom* (Table 3.3, p. 45; Appendix C, pp. 232–236).

[16] See *One Kind of Freedom* (p. 9 and note 13, p. 318). As we noted above, output per capita fell 18 to 29% of its prewar level. If the nature of the agricultural production function was such that the possibility of further substitutions of capital, land, and workstock for labor was not possible, and if no changes in productivity of labor per effective man-hour took place, then the decline of output per capita should equal the percentage decline in labor supplied per capita. In Ransom and Sutch (1975a) we argued that capital-labor substitutions have been pushed to their limit, therefore the figures we present are consistent with a modest expansion in labor productivity. This is a point we first made in *One Kind of Freedom* (p. 7).

[17] These growth rates have been estimated by calculating the slope of a linear trend line which minimizes the sum of squared residuals from logarithms of the annual data in *One Kind of Freedom* (Table F.3, p. 259). We believe that the regression method of calculating growth rates is the most appropriate when annual data is available. Had we calculated the rates of growth from end point to end point of each period using the data of Table 1, the annual growth rates would be: 1.90% for 1873–79; 1.45% for 1879–89; and 0.26% for 1889–99 (c.f. *One Kind of Freedom*, Table 1.4, p. 10). The rather large differences obtained underscores the sensitivity of growth rates calculated over short intervals to the method of calculation.

TABLE 7.2

Annual Rates of Growth in per Capita Constant-Dollar Values of Gross National Product of the United States and Gross Crop Output of the Five Cotton States, 1869–1873 to 1902–1906[a]

| | Annual percentage rates of growth | |
Interval[b]	United States gross national product[c]	Gross Southern crop output[d]
1869–73 to 1872–76	4.43	1.85
1872–76 to 1877–81	5.18	1.33
1877–81 to 1882–86	2.72	1.31
1882–86 to 1887–91	0.74	2.28
1887–91 to 1892–96	1.60	−0.18
1892–96 to 1897–1901	2.70	1.04
1897–1901 to 1902–06	2.78	0.83
1869–73 to 1902–06	2.74	1.17

[a] Source: *One Kind of Freedom* (Table 9.13, p. 194).

[b] The original Kuznets GNP data was presented for the quinquenniums indicated. The figure for gross crop output for each quinquennium were calculated from the annual series in constant dollars presented in *One Kind of Freedom* (Table F.3, p. 259). All growth rates are calculated from quinquennium to quinquennium as indicated.

[c] Gross national product per capita is calculated on the basis of the total resident population of the United States averaged over each quinquennium.

[d] Southern crop output per capita is calculated on the basis of the rural population of the five cotton states.

the estimates of GNP constructed by Kuznets and Kendrick imply too high a rate of growth for the U.S. in this period (Gallman, 1966, pp. 40–41; 1978, pp. 1040–41). Annual rates of growth based on Gallman's alternative estimates are compared with the rate of growth of Southern crop output in Table 7.3. Direct comparison of the two GNP series is complicated by the fact that Gallman presented his data as overlapping decade averages beginning in years ending in four and nine. Annual estimates prepared by Kendrick, however, do allow a direct comparison of the rate of growth over the entire interval 1869–78 to 1899–1908. Gallman estimated the rate of growth over the 30-year period at 2.01%, which is significantly lower than the 2.52% implied by Kendrick.[18] Nevertheless, the conclusion that the Southern economy lagged well behind the rest of the country is supported by the Gallman estimates of GNP. In every interval for which Gallman provides estimates—except for the interval 1879–88 to 1889–98—the rate of growth of GNP was substantially higher than the rate of growth in Southern crop output. Over the

[18] This growth rate was calculated from series F-4 in U.S. Bureau of the Census (1975), Vol. 1, p. 224.

TABLE 7.3

Annual Rates of Growth in per Capita Constant-Dollar Values of Gross National Product of the United States and Gross Crop Output of the Five Cotton States, 1869–1879 to 1899–1908[a]

	Annual percentage rates of growth	
	---	---
Interval[b]	United States gross national product[c]	Gross Southern crop output[d]
1869–78 to 1879–88	2.79	1.57
1874–83 to 1884–93	1.91	1.14
1879–88 to 1989–98	0.96	1.51
1884–93 to 1894–1903	1.15	0.97
1889–98 to 1899–1908	2.30	0.21
1869–78 to 1899–1908	2.01	1.10

[a] Sources: Gallman (1966, Table A-1, p. 26), U.S. Bureau of the Census (1975, Vol. 1, Series A-7, p. 8), and *One Kind of Freedom* (Table F.3, p. 259).

[b] The original Gallman GNP data were presented for the overlapping decades indicated. The figures for gross crop output for each decade were calculated from the annual series in constant dollars presented in *One Kind of Freedom* (Table F.3, p. 259). All growth rates are calculated from decade to decade as indicated.

[c] Gross national product per capita is calculated on the basis of the total resident population of the United States averaged over each decade.

[d] Southern crop output per capita is calculated on the basis of the rural population of the five cotton states.

entire 30-year period covered in Table 3, Southern output grew at the rate of 1.1%, while Gallman's estimates of GNP grew at 2.01%.

POSTWAR ECONOMIC GROWTH

Our finding, first reported in Ransom and Sutch (1975a, p. 5), that the rate of growth in southern agriculture was relatively slow, particularly after 1873, is somewhat controversial. As early as 1971 Robert Higgs claimed that

> Scholars have too often exaggerated the problems of Southern development. Statistics themselves—it would be more accurate to say *naively interpreted* statistics—are partly to blame for a fascination with Southern "backwardness" and "stagnation". . . . Contrary to assertions of Southern "stagnation" in the post-Civil War era, the South did not lag behind the rest of the nation after 1880. (Higgs, 1971, pp. 108–109; emphasis in original)

The data which Higgs presents to support this claim are those developed by Easterlin. Easterlin's calculations imply that per capita income grew at 1.59% per year in the South between 1879 to 1899. Our own estimate of per capita crop output, by contrast, places the rate of growth at only 0.85% per year.[19] More recently, Claudia Goldin and Frank Lewis pre-

[19] Easterlin's estimates of income are presented in Easterlin (1960b, p. 185; 1961, p. 528).

sented estimates of per capita consumption for the Confederate South, also based on the work of Easterlin, which reflect a growth of 1.18% per year between 1879 and 1899 (Goldin and Lewis, 1975, Table 12, p. 324).

The estimates of growth offered by Higgs and Goldin and Lewis, unlike our own, are for an inclusive 13-state region which Easterlin called "the South." The rate of growth in this larger area incorporates that growth which was generated by the migration from one subregion of the South to another. As we discussed above, growth caused by interregional migration cannot be used to dismiss an argument that the institutions within a region are hindering economic development. Moreover, Easterlin's figures are as large as they are because his definition of the South incorporates the rapidly growing frontier states of Florida and Texas, together with several non-cotton states that also experienced growth substantially above the average. In Table 7.4 we present state-by-state estimates of the rate of growth in real per capita personal income between 1879 and 1899 calculated from Easterlin's data—the same data which underlie the figures reported by Higgs. In the table, the states are ranked from those states with lowest growth rates to those with the highest growth rates. The five cotton states highlighted in our analysis are the slowest-growing states in the table. Other cotton-raising states, such as North Carolina, Arkansas, and Tennessee, that had many institutional features in common with those fives states, also grew at rates substantially below those of Texas and Florida. Even more revealing are Easterlin's estimates of agricultural service income per worker in each of the Southern states. The rates of growth in these statistics between 1879 and 1899 are also presented in the table. Four of the cotton-growing states (Arkansas, Mississippi, Tennessee, and Alabama) actually experienced declines in agricultural income per worker. Four other cotton states (Louisiana, Georgia, South Carolina, and North Carolina) recorded only miniscule gains; none grew faster than 0.4% per year. The one cotton-growing state which exhibited a respectable rate of growth in agricultural income per worker was Texas, the only state of the nine which had made progress toward diversifying its agriculture. Not only was there a significant cattle industry in Texas by the turn of the century, but it was also the first state to be infested by the boll weevil. By 1900 Texas had begun to reduce its dependency on cotton in response to the insect's threat to the cotton crop.[20]

Table 7.4 also presents the subtotals for the five cotton states which formed the basis of our own analysis. Easterlin's figures on per capita personal income for that subregion grew at the rate of 0.86% per year; our own estimate based on crop output, put the rate at 0.85% per year. It is

Easterlin—and therefore Higgs—reports figures for the census years 1880 and 1900. The data, however, refer to the calendar years 1879 and 1899, respectively. The rate of growth of our crop output series is calculated between 1879 and 1899 from Table 1.

[20] For a discussion of the boll weevil's impact, see *One Kind of Freedom* (pp. 171–174).

TABLE 7.4

Annual Rates of Growth in Constant-Dollar Values of per Capita Personal Income and of Agricultural Service Income per Worker between 1879 and 1899, by States[a]

	Annual percentage rates of growth	
State	Per capita personal income	Agricultural income per worker
Louisiana	0.44	0.28
Georgia	0.81	0.32
Mississippi	0.96	−0.47
South Carolina	0.98	0.33
Alabama	1.14	−0.02
Five Cotton States[b]	0.86	0.09
North Carolina	1.38	0.40
Kentucky	1.42	0.78
Arkansas	1.43	−0.77
Tennessee	1.89	−0.23
Virginia	2.15	1.43
West Virginia	2.26	1.04
Texas	2.53	2.63
Florida	2.64	1.80
Total, 13 states[b]	1.59	0.74
United States	1.59	0.85

[a] Source: Easterlin (1960b, pp. 185, 187).

[b] The regional averages were calculated by using the population weights given in Lee (1957, p. 349).

obvious that there is no real inconsistency between our estimates and Easterlin's. Therefore, whatever controversy exists must be one of interpretation of the regional rates of growth, not one of statistical methodology. This being the case, we shall turn to the implications of the remarkable fall in per capita output associated with the Civil War decade for the relative welfare of blacks and whites in the South.

THE REDISTRIBUTION OF INCOME AND WEALTH FOLLOWING EMANCIPATION

According to Table 7.1, the level of per capita crop output in 1878–80 was 81% of the 1857 level. A 19% fall in income is not insignificant, and the distribution of that loss influenced the attitudes of both whites and blacks in the post-emancipation era. The large aggregate decline is even more remarkable when considered together with the findings we reported in *One Kind of Freedom* that the material income of freed blacks in the postwar years must have exceeded that of slaves by a substantial margin. A careful study of the provisions afforded slaves toward the end of the antebellum period produced an estimate of per capita slave "income" in 1859 of $28.95.[21] In 1879, our estimates place per capita incomes of black tenant farmers at $42.22 in 1859–60 dollars. This represents an increase in real income of 45.8%.[22] The figure would be even higher if we took account of the value of the leisure time which blacks enjoyed as one of the fruits of their emancipation.[23] But on the other hand, this estimate of postwar income takes no account of the exploitation inherent in the credit monopoly of the rural merchant.[24]

Now it should be obvious that if aggregate income fell, while blacks' income rose substantially, then there must have been a sharp fall in the incomes received by whites. While we have no direct estimate of the decline in the per capita incomes of whites, we can at least set a lower bound on the fall, calculating whites' income in 1859 as a residual by subtracting our estimate of the slaves' share of income from the aggregate level. Our estimate of slave "income" is likely to overstate the share of output consumed by black slaves. Thus our estimate of white income before the war will be understated. This bias works toward diminishing the estimated decline in income received by whites. Our calculation of the residual suggests that the per capita income of all whites in 1857 must have been more than $124.79 if the aggregate level of per capita income was $74.28, as indicated in Table 7.1.[25] Our estimate of the per capita income for blacks in 1879 is for family members of black-operated tenant farms, and probably understates the average income received by all blacks. Thus, the average income of all whites—computed as a residual—will exaggerate that figure. Nevertheless, making the calculation suggests that whites' income must have fallen to at least $80.57; a decline of 35.4%.[26]

---

[21] *One Kind of Freedom* (Table A.5, p. 211). This figure is given in 1859 prices, and, as we noted in the discussion on pages 210–212, it is probably a generous estimate. The use of the term "income" to characterize this estimate of the provision of material goods and services to slaves should not be allowed to obscure the fact that the quantity, quality, and selection of items included in the slaves' consumption was entirely under the control of the slave owner, not the blacks themselves.

[22] One Kind of Freedom (Table A.10, p. 219).

[23] For a discussion of this point see *One Kind of Freedom* (pp. 4–7). This omitted welfare is considerable; we estimated the value of free time gained by blacks to be between $16 and $25, an increase of 40 to 60% in the "income" of blacks in 1879.

[24] See Chapter 4 for a discussion of this form of exploitation. The redistributive impact of this institution is touched upon below. Also see Ransom and Sutch (1975b).

[25] These calculations are based on the proportion of the rural population of the five cotton states (i.e., excluding the residents of towns with a population of 2500 or more) which was reported as slave in 1860 (52.7) in U.S. Census Office (1860b, pp. 9, 74, 195, 271 and 452). (Incidentally, the slave population of Columbia, S.C., was not given in the 1860 Census; we estimated it to have been 2000 slaves.)

[26] This calculation is based on the proportion of the rural population which was black in 1880 (53.3%), computed for the five cotton states from Lee (1957, pp. 357–360).

Drastic changes in an individual's economic fortunes will usually have a significant impact on their outlook on life generally, and there is no question but that the Civil War and emancipation brought about rather powerful shifts in the fortunes of Southerners. Blacks' income rose by 46% while whites' income fell by 35%. This shift in the distribution of income is, we believe, of greater significance to Southern history than the absolute decline in aggregate output. The numbers are not known with precision, of course, but we are confident of their order of magnitude. Whites' income may have fallen only 30%, or alternatively, they may have lost as much as 50%; either situation represents a very significant fall.

The pre- and post-Civil War estimates of average income by race are contrasted in Fig. 7.2. Note that despite the large redistribution of income, it did not imply a reversal in the relative income positions of the two races. In 1879 the typical black received only 52% as much income as the typical white person. The gap in measured income had been narrowed; however, it remained very large.

In fact, the actual transfer of income from whites to blacks was probably less than Fig. 7.2 suggests. Our calculations are based on production figures—they are not consumption estimates. Since it is probable that blacks—inexperienced and without legal protection afforded whites—were more susceptible to being cheated or defrauded by the unscrupulous, the income they were actually able to enjoy may have been less than what they produced. Indeed, we have discussed one form of such redistribution at considerable length in *One Kind of Freedom*. Rural merchants in the South exploited their customers by charging exhorbitant prices for the goods they sold on credit. The territorial local monopolies which these merchants held and protected allowed them to successfully divert a significant fraction of their customers' income into their own hands. We estimate that the income of black tenant farmers who were caught in the merchant's trap was reduced by 13.5% (*One Kind of Freedom*, p. 169). One might argue that as much as 37% of this transfer represented "legitimate costs" for the credit provided by the merchant, but even so, the customers' income would have been reduced by 8.5% (*One Kind of Freedom*, p. 243 and Table 7.2, p. 130). In the case of blacks, this would imply that their 1879 level of income per capita would have been reduced to $38.63, about one-third above the 1857 level of $28.95. Not all blacks were exploited by merchants, and not all the people who were exploited were black, so these figures cannot be taken as averages for the black population. Nor can they be used without further information to estimate the impact of this transfer on the average income of whites. Emancipation, then, can be said to have effected a major redistribution of income from former slave owners to former slaves, but the net effect of other changes in the postwar period was to push the income of whites higher than they otherwise would have been.

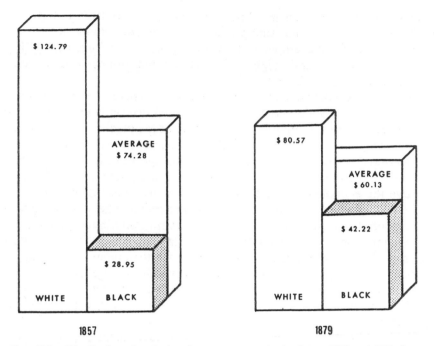

FIG. 7.2.   Distribution of agricultural output per capita by Race, 1857 and 1879. Source: See text.

The major cause of the dramatic redistribution of income pictured in Fig. 7.2 was the uncompensated emancipation of the slaves. We know that slave owners exploited the labor of their slaves. Indeed, over 50% of the output which might legitimately be called the "product of labor" on slave plantations was denied the slaves by their owners.[27] When slaves were freed, they gained the right to retain all the income they might earn, and their former masters lost the stream of income which slaveownership had previously bestowed upon them. This transfer alone would have been a quite substantial fraction of the total white income in the prewar period. Before emancipation, nearly 60% of the property income earned by whites in agriculture was attributable to their holdings of slaves. Since approximately 71% of whites' income in 1860 was generated from property ownership (including slave property), the loss of their slaves could have reduced whites' income by as much as 42%.[28] As it stands, our

[27] *One Kind of Freedom* (Table 1.1, p. 3). By the share "due" labor we mean that portion of the total output which is not required to remunerate the owners of other factors of production: land, capital, and management.

[28] The aggregate value of wealth (all white-owned, of course) and its composition is given in *One Kind of Freedom* (Table 3.5, p. 53). Slave capital (assumed to be exclusively in agriculture) comprised 59.4% of the aggregate capital invested in agriculture. The aggregate wealth of the agricultural South in 1860 was 2.677 billion dollars. If that capital returned an average income of 6.9% (which is the best estimate of the rate of return on slaves we have; Foust and Swan, 1970, Table 6, p. 55), the average white would have received $104.24 of

estimate of the reduction in whites' income between 1857 and 1879 is 35.5%; somewhat less than that predicted by our estimated loss from the expropriation of slave·property. It would appear, therefore, that whites actually managed to shift slightly the income distribution in their favor during the early postwar period.

This is not a particularly surprising conclusion. There is ample evidence that whites used a wide variety of coercive and discriminatory tactics in an attempt to thwart economic advancement of the blacks. Black artisans were actively discouraged from practicing their trade, and black farmers often worked poorer land with fewer animals and farm implements than did their white counterparts.[29] The effect of such actions would be to improve the economic position of the whites vis-a-vis the blacks.

There is an additional point worth making explicit. The loss that emancipation produced for whites was very unevenly distributed among the white population. There were only 154,491 slave owners in the five cotton states in 1860, representing about 40% of the white families living in those states.[30] It was this slave-owning minority which lost the most with the abolition of slavery. Other whites may even have gained. The relative wage of laborers and artisans rose following the war because of the severe labor shortage which itself was a consequence of the withdrawal of labor by blacks after emancipation. Owners of nonslave farms before the war seem to have been relatively unaffected by the changes which occurred, though the value of their farmland probably fell with the general fall in land prices immediately after the end of hostilities.[31]

To summarize the argument of this section: the material well-being of blacks unquestionably rose substantially after emancipation; that of white laborers and artisans probably rose moderately; the income of slaveless farm owners was largely unaffected; and the white slaveowning class suffered both a substantial loss of income and a sizable decline in the value of their real property. It would be a mistake, however, to argue that the ex-slaveowners were forced into poverty. A number of studies—the most recent by Jonathan Wiener (1975, 1976, 1978)—clearly establish that the planter class retained both its landholdings and their social and political control of southern society as well. And, as our 1879 estimates of per

property income in 1859. Our estimate of the aggregate income per capita for whites in 1859 is $147.22.

[29] See Ransom and Sutch (1973) and *One Kind of Freedom* (Chap. 9) for a discussion of the manner in which discriminatory practices limited the economic opportunity for blacks in the Reconstruction Period.

[30] This figure assumes an average size for white families of 4.6 members. Statistics on slave ownership are from U.S. Census Office (1860a, p. 247).

[31] While comprehensive data on the value of land before and after the war are not available, it seems beyond question that land values in the South fell substantially between 1860 and 1870, and that the decline was not subsequently made up by increasing prices of land later in the period. See Ransom and Sutch (1975a, pp. 16–17) and *One Kind of Freedom* (p. 51).

capita income demonstrate, the average income for whites in that year was still substantially above that of the blacks.

THE RELATIVE INCOME OF BLACKS, 1879–1899

As we have seen, blacks greatly improved their relative income position when they were set free in 1865. However, they made only limited advances thereafter. Though data on income by race is very incomplete, what evidence we have suggests that the disparity in income levels of blacks and whites did not lessen after 1879. Figures for the value of farm output per family member in that year show that the per capita output on farms operated by blacks was only about 56.3% the level produced on farms operated by whites.[32] The ensuing two decades brought no appreciable improvement in this situation. The published census data for 1899 allow us to identify the value of farm output by the race of the farm operator. Dividing this total by the rural population of each race allows us to construct an income relative for 1899 which can be cautiously compared to our estimate from the sample of farms in the Cotton South for 1879. In 1899 the value of output per capita produced on farms operated by blacks was only 55.8% that achieved by whites on their farms.[33] This comparison should not be pushed too far, since the ratios provide a crude index of the relative income position of whites and blacks. Moreover, the 1879 figures refer to a sample of farms in the "Cotton South," while the 1899 figures are based on aggregate data for farms in the five cotton states.

However, we need not rely solely on this rough comparison to conclude that blacks made little or no gains between 1879 and 1899. Our series on aggregate per capita crop output shows that very little growth occurred over the two decades. It would be surprising if blacks were able to make substantial gains at a time when any gains could only come at the expense of further declines in the incomes of white southerners.

Notwithstanding this point, several writers have suggested that blacks substantially improved their income position in the late nineteenth century. Although their interpretation differs from ours, the evidence they present is not inconsistent with our own data. Robert Higgs has offered conjectural estimates for per capita income of blacks in 1867–68 and 1900 which imply a rate of improvement of about 2.69% per year (1977, pp. 98–102). This, Higgs notes, would be "considerably greater" than the growth rate of the overall American economy (1977, p. 102).

---

[32] The value of farm output per family member reported in 1879 was $84.89 on farms operated by blacks; $150.76 on farms operated by whites. For a discussion of the sample of farms and the data collected in the 1880 census, see *One Kind of Freedom* (Appendix G, pp. 283–294).

[33] The value of output for farms, by race of the farm operator, is from U.S. Census Office (1900, Part II, Tables 13 and 14, pp. 158–85). The rural population figure for 1899 is given in *One Kind of Freedom* (Table F.2, p. 258). It was partitioned by race on the basis of proportions for 1900 given in Lee (1957, pp. 357–360).

We have serious doubts concerning the method by which Higgs derives his estimates—particularly for the earlier years which are based on the money wages of hands hired by the month in 1867 and 1868, as reported by the USDA.[34] One of the problems with using this data as the basis for calculating average incomes of blacks immediately following the Civil War is that the annual wages for 1868 had declined by 25 to 40% from their level in the previous year. The comments of Horace Capron, Commissioner of Agriculture, suggest that the wages in 1868 cannot be thought of as typical for the early Reconstruction period.[35] We argued in *One Kind of Freedom* that this decline in wages was in response to the disastrous crop failures of 1867 (pp. 64–65). Had Higgs based his estimates on the more representative data from 1867, the implied rate of growth in income of rural blacks would have been closer to 2.15% per year than to 2.7%. This would give a figure only slightly higher than the rate of growth between 1867 and 1899 in aggregate income per capita in the five cotton states calculated from our estimates. The data presented in Table 7.1 indicate a growth rate of 1.98% per year. However, these high rates of growth are misleading, as an examination of Fig. 7.1 quickly reveals. Two-thirds of the absolute growth which occurred over the period which Higgs examined took place between 1867 and 1879. The evidence at hand suggests that the rate of growth of agricultural income in the South after 1879 was actually below 1% per year, and the calculations we have made of the value of crop output per family member suggest that movements in blacks' per capita income roughly paralleled those of whites between 1879 and 1899. Therefore, no significant convergence of incomes occurred in the last two decades of the nineteenth century.

RACISM AS AN IMPEDIMENT TO BLACK PROGRESS

In Chapter 6 this volume, Stephen DeCanio argues that incomes of blacks and whites converged during the period, but that because the initial disparity of wealth positions between blacks and whites was so large, the rate of convergence was very slow. We have no doubt that the initial differences in wealth were large, and it is hardly surprising that blacks accumulated what wealth they could only very gradually. However, De-Canio presents no historical data on the actual trends of black incomes. His estimates are entirely hypothetical, generated by the simulation of a simple growth model. As such, they can hardly be used to contradict the empirical data which we employed in our calculations of per capita crop output. DeCanio does raise an interesting question: To what extent was the failure of blacks' income to converge rapidly to parity with whites

[34] See Higgs (1977, Table 3.1, p. 44) and also U.S. Department of Agriculture (1868, p. 416).

[35] U.S. Department of Agriculture (1868, p. 416). Also see the extensive wage data in U.S. Department of Agriculture (1912), that illustrate the unusual level of level of wages in 1868.

attributable to the initial inequality of the distribution of wealth, and to what extent did other factors—such as racial discrimination—play a major role? To our way of thinking, however, DeCanio's approach oversimplifies the issue. In his model, only two factors are allowed to influence the rate of growth of per capita income of blacks: the rate at which blacks accumulate wealth through saving and the extent to which a single and a very specific form of racial discrimination lowered blacks' income. In DeCanio's analysis, the rate at which blacks would have saved had there been no racial discrimination is assumed to be equal to the rate of saving for society as a whole. Although this assumption is convenient in that it simplifies the calculations, it can hardly be realistically applied—even in a counterfactual sense—to the case at hand. When blacks were emancipated from slavery, they were able to earn income generated by their own labor, but they owned virtually no capital or land. Economic theories of consumption and saving behavior suggest that in such a situation with no racial discrimination blacks would attempt to save a considerably higher fraction of their income than would whites, who began the postwar period with endowments of capital and land.[36]

DeCanio's treatment of racial discrimination also greatly simplifies the economic reality. He focuses only on those forms of racism which reduced labor's share of output, thus the model he employs excludes those racial restrictions which affected savings behavior, capital–labor ratios, or land–labor ratios. If our own interpretation is correct, the most economically significant forms of racial discrimination were those that denied blacks equal access to credit markets, compelled them to labor with less capital per hand and fewer total acres per worker, and those that denied the blacks opportunity to acquire human capital.[37] Racial discrimination which took the more direct form of paying blacks lower wages than were paid to whites for comparable work, played only a minor role, a point which Robert Higgs has particularly emphasized.[38]

DeCanio acknowledges the possibility that forms of discrimination working in the asset markets might have slowed wealth equalization, but only after the model he employed failed to predict the rate of convergence. While he does not develop this line of analysis further, it is nevertheless

[36] It is well known that both life-cycle and permanent-income models of consumption imply the existence of some equilibrium ratio of wealth to income. If so, the black population would choose to adopt higher rates of saving than otherwise in order to build up wealth holdings to a level commensurate with their income position. Unless the income of blacks was so low as to preclude such savings behavior, one would expect a more rapid convergence of black and white income levels than would be predicted by DeCanio's growth model, since he takes no account of the disequilibrium relationship between income and wealth that had been produced by emancipation.

[37] Our approach to the impact of racism in the South is outlined in Ransom and Sutch (1973) and One Kind of Freedom (Chap. 9).

[38] See Higgs (1972, 1978) and Roberts and Higgs (1975).

worth asking how a more general view of racism might be incorporated into an economic analysis. Unfortunately, in our opinion, the standard theory of racism has provided very little help to economic historians because it considers racism as an external phenomenon quite apart from the economic system. The major conclusion reached by this approach is that discriminatory behavior in the marketplace will be discouraged through the imposition of "costs" charged the discriminator. The racist employer who pays white employees a higher wage than comparable black workers increases his costs (and thereby lessens his competitive position) by his discrimination. The landlord who turns down higher offers of rent from blacks simply because he dislikes blacks reduces his effective market for land and lowers his own return in the process. The market, by this reasoning, will tend to mitigate the effects of race prejudice by making it expensive to discriminate.[39]

Such a model is useful in that it cautions us against completely ignoring the fact that discrimination can be "costly," and that those costs will tend to discourage some discriminatory acts. However, as Robert Higgs notes, "the model applies more to a kind of tea-party discrimination than to the blood and steel of the Southern racial scene" (1977, p. 9). Consequently, Higgs develops a modified version of the theory to more closely fit the situation in the American South. Racist pressures meant that blacks were less able to protect their claims to property and to have their contracts enforced than was the case for whites. Higgs incorporates these difficulties into the economic analysis by considering them as "costs" which must be borne by blacks, but not by whites. Particularly crucial to his analysis were the added costs imposed on blacks seeking land or education. Racist threats increased the costs (or reduced the expected return) to the point where blacks were discouraged from investing in these activities. In Higgs' interpretation, the failure of blacks' income to converge more rapidly than they did with whites' stems from this added burden imposed by the costs of racism (1977, pp. 11–13).

Higgs' revision of the economic model of discrimination makes it considerably more useful to the analysis of Southern history. However, in this view, the economic and racial factors still remain separate, and indeed, in tension with each other. Economic history of the Reconstruction period, according to Higgs, "makes sense only when interpreted as an interplay of two systems of behavior: a competitive economic system and a coercive racial system."[40] We take exception to this approach. The

---

[39] The model of economic discrimination discussed in the text is summarized by Higgs (1977, pp. 6–13). His discussion draws upon the analysis developed by Gary Becker (1971).

[40] Higgs (1977, p. 13). This tension between the market forces and social and political forces is the basic theme of Higgs' book. Such a view seems to have been accepted by several contributors to this volume. In particular, Joseph Reid (Chapter 3) has argued that it was the political coercion of the state which held back black progress, and Claudia Goldin (Chapter 1) endorses a similar view. This issue is dealt with from a historian's perspective by Harold

racial and economic "systems" were, in our view, inseparable, and reinforced each other. Racist expectations and prejudices were an integral part of the "information" which determined the prices in the marketplace. Moreover, the initial inequality of wealth not only had the direct role which DeCanio emphasized, but it was also indirectly important in preserving the economic disparity between blacks and whites. In the first place, the wealth and income of antebellum planters was reduced as a consequence of emancipation, but they remained at the top of the social and economic hierarchy. It is of great significance that the very class which lost the most as a consequence of the South's ill-advised war was the group which ultimately had the most to say about the nature of the economic institutions which replaced those destroyed in the conflict. Whites insisted on institutional arrangements that protected their own economic and social position from further deterioration and that served to keep the black "in his own place." In the economic realm this meant that blacks were denied the right to hold land or practice certain professions reserved for whites. Whites also exploited their political power to limit the availability of educational facilities, and ultimately to deprive blacks of their vote. By the end of the century, a complex system of segregation had been imposed on blacks through the passage of the infamous "Jim Crow" laws. These developments were not economically "neutral", and it is not helpful to treat them as divorced from the economic mechanisms. There was no separation of the "systems" of competition and coercion. The two melded together in such a fashion that the economic institutions did not conflict with the social values of the dominant group; rather they reinforced them.

There is a second way in which the economic system and the racially coercive social system worked to reinforce each other. Factor markets generally rely upon a contracting process which requires the consent of both partners. Blacks initially found themselves at a disadvantage in bargaining in such markets because of their lack of land, capital, and skills. A freedman in 1866 was almost certain to be illiterate, have no skills, and very little experience with independent employment. As a consequence, blacks found many employment opportunities closed. White employers were simply unwilling to consider black applicants for skilled positions. By closing opportunities to blacks, employers insured that the correlation between race and productivity would persist. The market prices offered for their labor would continue to reflect the belief that blacks were less productive than whites. There would be little incentive for blacks to gain skills as long as the color of their skin would signal to any prospective employer that they were a member of a low-skill class. Thus the belief that blacks were not skilled would be reinforced.[41]

Woodman in his thorough review of the recent scholarship on the economic and social history of the postbellum South (Woodman, 1977).

[41] See Ransom and Sutch (1973, pp. 134–139) and One Kind of Freedom (pp. 176–186).

STAGNATION AND RELATIVE WELFARE

intro

Our review of the issues surrounding the topics of growth and welfare of the American South after 1839 has focused on the heartland of the Cotton South. Viewed in isolation, this region did not exhibit any propensity for sustained economic growth. To be sure, there were a few short periods in which the rate of increase of per capita income exceeded 1.5% per year—the few years preceeding the American Civil War, and a recovery period following the war which lasted less than a decade. But even that postwar readjustment failed to restore per capita income to its prewar level, and afterward the rate of growth fell to an unimpressive 0.85% per year and lagged considerably behind the growth of the United States as a whole.

This characterization of the Southern economy should come as no surprise to someone familiar with the historical literature dealing with the southern experience, for the South of the nineteenth century has long been regarded as a backward and stagnant region. More recently, however, economists such as Stanley Engerman (1971) and Robert Higgs (1977) have taken a more optimistic view of Southern economic growth. Engerman has characterized the pre-Civil War period as one of satisfactory economic growth, while Higgs has suggested that the postwar era was also one of economic expansion. Our review of the statistical evidence which supports the "new view" has shown that their numbers are not inconsistent with our own. In part, the difference in interpretation is attributable to a difference in perspective. We have consistently focused on five black-belt cotton-producing states, while Engerman and Higgs refer to a much larger 13-state "South." To those who might feel that we have "stacked the empirical deck" by concentrating our attention only on the slowest-growing states, we would answer that this is not only intentional but necessary in order to separate the contribution of interregional migration to economic growth from the total.

Another difficulty with the view that the American South exhibited rates of growth close to the national average during the nineteenth century is that it seems to ignore the sizable fall in output per capita which accompanied, and was substantially caused by, the freeing of the slaves. Engerman has examined the period 1839–59, while Higgs measured the rate of growth between 1867 and 1900. But it was during the unexamined period 1860 to 1866 that output fell so dramatically. Moreover, two-thirds of what growth did take place during the period Higgs investigated occurred during the postwar economic recovery; that is, before 1879. After that date, the rate of growth in per capita output in the agricultural sector of the Cotton South was below 1% per annum.

Whether or not a rate of economic growth below 1% is so low as to warrant characterizing the economy as "stagnant" is, of course, a semantic issue. In this case we feel that use of the term is justified, since a rate of growth of 0.85% would require the elapse of 82 years before per capita income would double. By contrast, the rate of growth of 2.9% would double per capita income within a generation, and 1.5% would produce a doubling within two generations. Rates of growth below 1% would not double income within the life-span of even a long-lived individual. Contemporaries who studied the problem of economic expansion in the Cotton South saw the situation in the same light. An 1895 report of the U.S. Senate on precisely this issue, entitled "Present Conditions of Cotton-Growers of the United States Compared with Previous Years," wryly commented that

> Immobility, or even that slow advance which is perceptible to laborious statisticians only, and is unfelt and unseen by the masses, produces discouragment and discontent." (U.S. Congress, 1895, p. iv)

The lack of perceptible economic progress must have been particularly unsettling to those familiar with the standards of living and the rate of economic expansion in the North. If we set the level of per capita personal income in the United States as an index of 100, the five cotton states would stand at a relative level of 51.7% in 1879 and at 44.8% in 1899.[42]

The lack of economic progress during this period obviously made it less likely that black Southerners would gain relative to whites. While the evidence we have presented is not conclusive, and more research on the relative welfare of blacks and whites in 1900 is definitely called for, one should view with some skepticism any suggestion that rural southern blacks were economically better off at the end of the nineteenth century than they had been a quarter of a century earlier.

References

Abramovitz, M., and David, P. A. (1973), "Reinterpreting Economic Growth: Parables and Realities." *American Economic Review* **63**, 428–439.

Bain, J. S. (1968), *Industrial Organization,* 2nd ed. New York: John Wiley and Sons.

Banks, E. M. (1905). "The Economics of Land Tenure in Georgia." *Studies in History, Economics and Public Law,* **23**, 1–142.

Barnett, G. E. (1911), *State Banks and Trust Companies Since the Passage of the National Bank Act.* Publications of the National Monetary Commission, Vol. 7. Washington: Government Printing Office.

Barzel, Y. (1977), "An Economic Analysis of Slavery." *Journal of Law and Economics* **20**, 87–110.

Becker, G. S. (1971), *The Economics of Discrimination,* 2nd ed. Chicago: University of Chicago Press. 1st ed., 1957.

Bell, C., and Zusman, P. (1976), "A Bargaining Theoretic Approach to Cropsharing Contracts." *American Economic Review* **66**, 578–588.

Bellerby, J. R. (1956), *Agriculture and Industry: Relative Income.* New York: St. Martin's Press.

Berthoff, R. T. (1951), "Southern Attitudes Toward Immigration, 1865–1914." *Journal of Southern History* **17**, 328–360.

Brooks, R. P. (1914), "The Agrarian Revolution in Georgia, 1865–1912." Madison: *Bulletin of the University of Wisconsin,* History Series 3. Pp. 393–521.

Brown, W. W., and Reynolds, M. O. (1973), "Debt Peonage Re-examined." *Journal of Economic History* **33**, 862–871.

Budd, E. C. (1960), "Factor Shares, 1850–1910." In National Bureau of Economic Research, *Studies in Income and Wealth,* Vol. 24: *Trends in the American Economy in the Nineteenth Century.* Princeton: Princeton University Press.

Bull, J. P. (1952), "The General Merchant in the Economic History of the New South." *Journal of Southern History* **18**, 37–59.

Cheung, S. N. S. (1969), *The Theory of Share Tenancy, with Special Application to Asian Agriculture and the First Phase of the Taiwan Land Reform.* Chicago: University of Chicago Press.

Clark, T. D. (1943), "Historical Aspects of Imperfect Competition in the Southern Retail Trade after 1865." *Journal of Economic History* **3**, 38–57.

Clark, T. D. (1944), *Pills, Petticoats, and Plows: The Southern Country Store.* Indianapolis: Bobbs–Merrill.

Crafts, N. F. R. (1977), "Industrial Revolution in England and France: Some Thoughts on the Question, 'Why Was England First?' " *Economic History Review* **30**, 429–441.

David, P. A. (1967), "The Growth of Real Product in the United States before 1840: New Evidence, Controlled Conjectures." *Journal of Economic History* **27**, 151–197.

David, P. A., and Temin, P. (1976), "Slavery: The Progressive Institution?" In P. A. David *et al.*, *Reckoning with Slavery: A Critical Study in the Quantitative History of American Negro Slavery*. New York: Oxford University Press. Pp. 165–230.

Davis, L. E. (1965), "The Investment Market, 1870–1914: The Evolution of a National Market." *Journal of Economic History* **25**, 355–399.

Davis, L. E., et al. (1972), *American Economic Growth: An Economist's History of the United States*. New York: Harper & Row.

DeCanio, S. J. (1973), "Cotton 'Overproduction' in Late Nineteenth-Century Southern Agriculture." *Journal of Economic History* **33**, 608–633.

DeCanio, S. J. (1974a), *Agriculture in the Postbellum South: The Economics of Production and Supply*. Cambridge: MIT Press.

DeCanio, S. J. (1974b), "Productivity and Income Distribution in the Post-Bellum South." *Journal of Economic History* **34**, 422–446.

DeCanio, S. J. (1979), "Review of *One Kind of Freedom: The Economic Consequences of Emancipation.*" *Economic History Review* **32**, 455–457.

Dew, C. B. (1971), "Critical Essay on Recent Works." In C. V. Woodward, *Origins of the New South, 1877–1913*, Reprinted edition. Baton Rouge: Louisiana State University Press. pp. 517–628.

Dong, F., (1976), "Debt Peonage and Economic Efficiency." Harvard University. mimeograph.

Dowell, R. (1977), *Risk Diversification and Land Tenure in United States Agriculture, 1890 to 1970*. Ph.D. Dissertation, University of Chicago.

DuBois, W. E. B. (1901), "The Negro Landholder of Georgia." *Bulletin of the U.S. Department of Labor*, **6**, 647–677.

DuBois, W. E. B. (1935), *Black Reconstruction in America, 1860–1880*. Cleveland: Meridian; reprinted, New York: Harcourt, Brace and Company, 1964.

Easterlin, R. A. (1957), "State Income Estimates." In S. Kuznets et al., *Population Redistribution and Economic Growth, United States, 1870–1950*, Vol. I, *Methodological Considerations and Reference Tables*. Philadelphia: American Philosophical Society.

Easterlin, R. (1960a), "Interregional Differences in Per Capita Income, Population, and Total Income, 1840–1950." In National Bureau of Economic Research, *Studies in Income and Wealth*, Vol. 24: *Trends in the American Economy in the Nineteenth Century*. Princeton: Princeton University Press. Pp. 73–140.

Easterlin, R. (1960b), "Regional Growth of Income: Long-Term Tendencies, 1880–1950." In S. Kuznets *et al.* (Eds.), *Population Redistribution and Economic Growth, United States 1870–1950*, Vol. 2: *Analyses of Economic Change*. Philadelphia: American Philosophical Society. Pp. 140–287.

Easterlin, R. (1961), "Regional Income Trends, 1840–1950." In S. E. Harris (Ed.), *American Economic History*. New York: McGraw-Hill.

Edwards, T. J. (1913), "The Tenant System and Some Changes Since Emancipation." *Annals of the American Academy of Political Science* **49**, 38–46.

Elkins, S. M. (1959), *Slavery*. Chicago: University of Chicago Press.

Engerman, S. L. (1966), "The Economic Impact of the Civil War." *Explorations in Entrepreneurial History* Second Series **3**, 176–199.

Engerman, S. L. (1971), "Some Economic Factors in Southern Backwardness in the Nineteenth Century." In J. F. Kain and J. R. Meyer (Eds.), *Essays in Regional Economics*. Cambridge: Harvard University Press. Pp. 279–306.

Engerman, S. L. (1977a), "Notes on the Patterns of Economic Growth in the British North American Colonies in the Seventeenth, Eighteenth, and Nineteenth Centuries." mimeograph.

Engerman, S. L. (1977b), "Quantitative and Economic Analysis of West Indian Slave Societies: Research Problems.' In V. Rubin and A. Tuden (Eds.), *Comparative Perspectives on Slavery in New World Plantation Societies*. New York: New York Academy of Science.

Fishlow, A. (1964), "Antebellum Interregional Trade Reconsidered." *American Economic Review* **54**, 352–364.

Fogel, R. W., and Engerman, S. L. (1974), *Time on the Cross*, Vol. 1: *The Economics of American Negro Slavery;* Vol. 2: *Evidence and Methods: A Supplement*. Boston: Little, Brown.

Fogel, R. W., and Engerman, S. L. (1977), "Explaining the Relative Efficiency of Slave Agriculture in Antebellum South." *American Economic Review* **67**, 275–296.

Foust, J. D., and Swan, D. E. (1970), "Productivity and Profitability of Antebellum Slave Labor: A Micro-Approach." *Agricultural History* **44**, 39–62.

Gallman, R. E. (1960), "Commodity Output, 1839–1899." In National Bureau of Economic Research, *Studies in Income and Wealth*, Vol. 24: *Trends in the American Economy in the Nineteenth Century*. Princeton: Princeton University Press. Pp. 13–67.

Gallman, R. E. (1966), "Gross National Product in the United States: 1834–1909." In National Bureau of Economic Research, *Studies in Income and Wealth*, Vol. 30: *Output, Employment, and Productivity in the United States after 1800*. New York: Columbia University Press, Pp. 3–76.

Gallman, R. E. (1970), "Self-Sufficiency in the Cotton Economy of the Antebellum South." *Agriculture History* **44**, 5–23.

Gallman, R. E. (1975), "Southern Ante-bellum Income Reconsidered." *Explorations in Economic History* **12**, 89–99.

Gallman, R. E. (1978), "Review of *One Kind of Freedom*." *Journal of Economic History* **38**, 1039–1041.

Gallman, R. E., and Anderson, R. V. (1977), "Slaves as Fixed Capital." *Journal of American History* **64**, 24–46.

Georgia, Department of Agriculture (1878–1891), *Publications of the State Department of Agriculture* (From September 1878 through 1890). 13 volumes. Atlanta: J. P. Harrison and Company.

Goldin, C. D., and Lewis, F. D. (1975), "The Economic Cost of the American Civil War: Estimates and Implications." *Journal of Economic History* **35**, 299–326.

Goldin, C. D., and Lewis, F. D. (1978), "The Postbellum Recovery of the South and the Cost of the Civil War: Comment." *Journal of Economic History* **38**, 487–492.

Greenhut, M. L. (1970), *A Theory of the Firm in Economic Space*. New York: Appleton–Century–Crofts.

Greenhut, M. L., and Ohta, H. (1975), *Theory of Spatial Pricing and Market Areas*. Durham: Duke University Press.

Griffin, R. W. (1964), "Reconstruction of the North Carolina Textile Industry, 1865–1885." *North Carolina Historical Review* **41**, 34–53.

Gunderson, G. (1973), "Southern Ante-bellum Income Reconsidered." *Explorations in Economic History* **10**, 151–176.

Gunderson, G. (1975), "Southern Income Reconsidered: A Reply." *Explorations in Economic History* **12**, 101–102.

Gutman, H., and Sutch, R. (1976), "Sambo Makes Good, or Were Slaves Imbued with the Protestant Work Ethic?" In P. A. David *et al.*, *Reckoning with Slavery: A Critical Study in the Quantitative History of American Negro Slavery*. New York: Oxford University Press. Pp. 55–93.

Hammond, H. (1883), *South Carolina: Resources and Population, Institutions and Industry*. Charleston: Walker, Evans & Cogswell.

Hammond, M. B. (1897), *The Cotton Industry: An Essay in American Economic History, Part I. The Cotton Culture and the Cotton Trade*. New York: American Economic Association and Macmillan Company.

Hammond, M. B. (1909). "Agricultural Credit and Crop Mortgages." In *The South in the Building of the Nation*. Richmond: Southern Historical Society. Vol. B.

Helper, H. R. (1857), *The Impending Crisis of the South*. New York: Collier Books, 1963.

Hibbard, B. (1913), "Tenancy in the Southern States." *Quarterly Journal of Economics* 27, 482–496.

Higgs, R. (1971), *The Transformation of the American Economy, 1865–1914: An Essay in Interpretation*. New York: John Wiley & Sons.

Higgs, R. (1972), "Did Southern Farmers Discriminate?" *Agricultural History* 46, 325–328.

Higgs, R. (1973), "Race, Tenure and Resource Allocation in Southern Agriculture, 1910." *Journal of Economic History* 33, 149–169.

Higgs, R. (1974), "Patterns of Farm Rental in the Georgia Cotton Belt." *Journal of Economic History* 34, 468–82.

Higgs, R. (1977), *Competition and Coercion: Blacks in the American Economy, 1865–1914*. New York: Cambridge University Press.

Higgs, R. (1978), "Racial Wage Differences in Agriculture: Evidence From North Carolina in 1887." *Agricultural History* 52, 308–311.

Hilgard, E. W. (1884), *U.S. Census Office, Tenth Census, Report on Cotton Production in the United States*. Two vols. Washington: Government Printing Office.

Holmes, G. K. (1893), "The Peons of the South." *Annals of the American Academy of Political and Social Science* 4, 65–74.

Hopkins, M. M. (1978), "Emancipation: The Dominant Cause of Southern Stagnation." Paper presented to the Cliometrics Conference, University of Chicago, May 1978.

Hotelling, H. (1929), "Stability in Competition," *Economic Journal* 39, 41–57.

Jones, W. N. (1887), *First Annual Report of the Bureau of Labor Statistics of the State of North Carolina*. Raleigh: Josephus Daniels.

Kendrick, J. W. (1961), *Productivity Trends in the United States*. New York: National Bureau of Economic Research.

Kousser, M. (1974), *The Shaping of Southern Politics: Suffrage Restriction and the Establishment of the One Party South, 1880–1910*. New Haven: Yale University Press.

Kousser, M. (1977), "Progressivism for Middle-Class Whites Only: The Distribution of Taxation and Expenditures for Education in North Carolina, 1880–1910." California Institute of Technology, Social Science Working Paper No. 177.

Kuznets, S. (1952), "Long-Term Changes in the National Income of the United States of America since 1870." In International Association for Research in Income and Wealth, S. Kuznets (Ed.), *Income & Wealth of the United States: Trends and Structure*. Baltimore: Johns Hopkins Press.

Kuznets, S. (1961), *Capital in the American Economy: Its Formation and Financing*. New York: National Bureau of Economic Research.

Lamb, R. B. (1963), *The Mule in Southern Agriculture*, Berkeley: University of California Press.

Lee, E. S. (1957), "Migration Estimates." In S. Kuznets *et al.*, (Eds.), *Population Redistribution and Economic Growth, United States, 1870–1950*, Vol. 1: *Methodological Considerations and Reference Tables*. Philadelphia: American Philosophical Society. Pp. 9–362.

Lösch, A. (1954), *The Economics of Location*. New Haven: Yale University Press.

Marshall, A. (1920). *Principles of Economics*, Eighth ed. London: Macmillan Company.

McGuire, R., and Higgs, R. (1977). "Cotton, Corn and Risk: Another View," *Explorations in Economic History* 14, 167–182.

Mellman, R. E. (1975), *A Reinterpretation of the Economic History of the Post-Reconstruction South, 1877–1919*. Unpublished Ph.D. Dissertation, Massachusetts Institute of Technology.

Metzer, J. (1975), "Rational Management, Modern Business Practices, and Economies of Scale in the Ante-Bellum Southern Plantations." *Explorations in Economic History* 12, 123–150.

Mitchell, B. (1921), *The Rise of the Cotton Mills in the South.* Baltimore: Johns Hopkins Press.

Morehead, S. D. (1929), *Merchant Credit to Farmers In Lousiana.* Russellville, La.: Privately Printed.

Nerlove, M. (1965), *Estimation and Identification of Cobb–Douglas Production Functions.* Chicago: Rand McNally.

North, D. C. (1974), *Growth and Welfare in the American Past: A New Economic History,* 2nd ed. Englewood Cliffs: Prentice Hall.

North, D. C. (1978), "Structure and Performance: The Task of Economic History." *Journal of Economic Literature* **16,** 963–978.

Otken, C. H. (1894), *The Ills of the South, or Related Causes Hostile to the General Prosperity of the Southern People.* New York: G. P. Putnam's Sons.

Parker, W. N. (1979), "Labor Productivity in Cotton Farming: The History of a Research." *Agricultural History* **53,** 228–244.

Prunty, M., Jr. (1955), "The Renaissance of the Southern Plantation." *The Geographical Review* **45,** 459–491.

Ransom, R. L., and Sutch, R. (1972), "Debt Peonage in the Cotton South After the Civil War." *Journal of Economic History* **32,** 641–669.

Ransom, R. L., and Sutch, R. (1973), "The Ex-Slave in the Post-Bellum South: A Study of the Economic Impact of Racism in a Market Environment." *Journal of Economic History* **33,** 131–148.

Ransom, R. L., and Sutch, R. (1975a), "The Impact of the Civil War and of Emancipation on Southern Agriculture." *Explorations in Economic History* **12,** 1–28.

Ransom, R. L., and Sutch, R. (1975b), "The 'Lock-in' Mechanism and Overproduction of Cotton in the Postbellum South." *Agricultural History* **49,** 405–425.

Ransom, R. L., and Sutch, R. (1977), *One Kind of Freedom: The Economic Consequences of Emancipation.* New York: Cambridge University Press.

Ransom, R. L., and Sutch, R. (1978a). "Sharecropping: Market Response or Mechanism of Race Control?" In G. C. Sansing (Ed.), *What was Freedom's Price?* Jackson: University Press of Mississippi. Pp. 51–69.

Ransom, R. L., and Sutch, R. (1978b), "Economic Dimensions of Reconstruction: An Overview." Paper presented to the conference: *The First and Second Reconstructions: The Historical Setting and Contemporary Black–White Relations, 1860–1978.* University of Missouri, St. Louis, February 1978.

Reid, J. D., Jr. (1973), "Sharecropping as an Understandable Market Response: The Post-Bellum South." *Journal of Economic History* **33,** 106–130.

Reid, J. D., Jr. (1976a), "Antebellum Southern Rental Contracts." *Explorations in Economic History* **13,** 69–83.

Reid, J. D., Jr. (1976b), "Sharecropping and Agricultural Uncertainty." *Economic Development and Cultural Change* **24,** 549–576.

Reid, J. D., Jr. (1979), "The Evaluation and Implications of Southern Tenancy." *Agricultural History* **53.**

Reid, J. D., Jr. (in press), "Sharecropping and Tenancy in American History." In J. Roumasset, (Ed.), *Risk and Uncertainty in Agriculture.* Berkeley: University of California Press.

Roark, J. (1977), *Masters Without Slaves.* New York: Norton.

Roberts, C. A., and Higgs, R. (1975), "Did Southern Farmers Discriminate: An Exchange." *Agricultural History* **49,** 441–447.

Robinson, J., and Eatwell, J. (1973), *An Introduction to Modern Economics.* London: McGraw–Hill.

Rosengarten, T. (1975), *All God's Dangers: The Life of Nate Shaw.* New York: Knopf.

Rubin, J. (1975), "The Limits of Agricultural Progress in the Nineteenth-Century South." *Agricultural History* **49,** 362–373.

Sanderson, W. C. (1974). "Does the Theory of Demand Need the Maximum Principle?" In P. A. David, and M. W. Reder (Eds.), *Nations and Households in Economic Growth.* New York: Academic Press.

Schmeckebier, L. F. (1900). "Taxation in Georgia." In J. H. Hollander, (Ed.), *Studies in State Taxation, with Particular Reference to the Southern States,* Johns Hopkins Studies in Historical and Political Science, Series XVIII. Baltimore: Johns Hopkins Press.

Schmitz, M. D., and Schaefer, D. F. (n.d., 1978?), "Slavery, Freedom, and the Elasticity of Substitution." Department of Economics, North Carolina A & T University.

Scitovsky, T. (1976). *The Joyless Economy.* New York: Oxford University Press.

Seagrave, C. E. (1971), *The Southern Negro Agricultural Worker: 1850–1870.* Ph.D. Dissertation, Stanford University.

Shlomowitz, R. (1975), "The Transition from Slave to Freedman labor Arrangements in Southern Agriculture, 1865–1870." Ph.D. Dissertation, University of Chicago.

Sisk, G. L. (1955), "Rural Merchandising in the Alabama Black Belt." *Journal of Farm Economics* **37**, 705–715.

Sjaastad, L. (1962), "The Costs and Returns of Human Migration." *Journal of Political Economy,* Supplement, 80–93.

Smith, R. S. (1960), *Mill on the Dan.* Durham: Duke University Press.

Solow, R. (1970), *Growth Theory: An Exposition.* New York: Oxford University Press.

Soltow, L. (1975), *Men and Wealth in the United States, 1850–1870.* New Haven: Yale University Press.

Sonnenschein, H. (1973), "The Utility Hypothesis and Market Demand Theory." *Western Economic Journal* **11**, 404–410.

Stampp, K. (1956), *The Peculiar Institution.* New York: Knopf.

Stiglitz, J. E. (1969), "Distribution of Income and Wealth among Individuals." *Econometrica* **37**, 382–397.

Stover, J. F. (1955), *The Railroads of the South: 1865–1900.* Chapel Hill: University of North Carolina Press.

Street, J. H. (1957), *The New Revolution in the Cotton Economy.* Chapel Hill: University of North Carolina Press.

Sutch, R. (1965), "The Profitability of Slavery—Revisited." *Southern Economic Journal* **31**, 365–377.

Sutch, R. (1975), "The Frontiers of Quantitative Economic History, Circa 1975." In Michael Intrilligator (Ed.), *Frontiers of Quantitative Economics.* Vol. IIIB. New York: North–Holland. Pp. 399–416.

Sylla, R. (1969), "Federal Policy, Banking Market Structure, and Capital Mobilization in the United States, 1863–1913." *Journal of Economic History* **29**, 657–686.

Swierenga, R. P. (1976), *Acres for Cents: Delinquent Tax Auctions in Frontier Iowa.* Westport: Greenwood Press.

Taylor, R. H. (1943), "Post-Bellum Southern Rental Contracts." *Agricultural History* **17**, 121–128.

Taylor, R. H. (1953), "Fertilizers and Farming in the Southeast, 1840–1950." *North Carolina Historical Review* **30**, 307–328.

Temin, P. (1976), "The Postbellum Recovery of the South and the Cost of the Civil War." *Journal of Economic History* **36**, 898–907.

U.S. Bureau of the Census (1922), *Fourteenth Census of the United States, Agriculture, 1920.* Washington: Government Printing Office.

U.S. Bureau of the Census (1960), *Historical Statistics of the United States, Colonial Times to 1957.* Washington: Government Printing Office.

U.S. Bureau of the Census (1966), *Long Term Economic Growth, 1860–1965.* Washington: Government Printing Office.

U.S. Bureau of the Census (1975), *Historical Statistics of the United States, Colonial Times to 1970*, Two volumes. Washington: Government Printing Office.

U.S. Census Office, Eighth Census (1860a), *Agriculture of the United States in 1860, Compiled from the Original Returns of the Eighth Census*. Washington: Government Printing Office, 1864.

U.S. Census Office, Eighth Census (1860b), *Population of the United States in 1860, Compiled from the Original Returns of the Eighth Census*. Washington: Government Printing Office, 1864.

U.S. Census Office, Twelfth Census (1900), *Census Reports: Agriculture*, Two parts. Washington: Government Printing Office, 1902.

U.S. Congress, Senate Committee on Agriculture and Forestry (1895), "Present Condition of Cotton-Growers of the United States Compared with Previous Years." *Report on the Committee on Agriculture and Forestry on Conditions of Cotton Growers in the United States, the Present Prices of Cotton, and the Remedy; and on Cotton Consumption and Production*, Senate Report Number 986, 53rd Congress, 3rd Session, two volumes. Washington: Government Printing Office.

U.S. Department of Agriculture, Horace Capron (1868), "Southern Agriculture." In *Report of the Commissioner of Agriculture for the Year 1867*. Washington: Government Printing Office.

U.S. Department of Agriculture, Bureau of Statistics (1912), "Wages of Farm Labor: Nineteenth Investigation, in 1909, Continuing a Series that Began in 1866." *U.S.D.A. Bureau of Statistics Bulletin*, Number 99.

U.S. Department of Agriculture, Bureau of Agricultural Economics (1937), "Livestock on Farms, January 1, 1867–1919, Revised Estimates: Number, Value per Head, Total Value, by States and Divisions." Washington: USDA.

U.S. Department of Labor, Bureau of Labor Statistics (1975), *Handbook of Labor Statistics 1975, Reference Edition*. Washington: Government Printing Office.

Vance, R. (1929), *Human Factors in Cotton Culture*. Chapel Hill: University of North Carolina Press.

Vickrey, W. E. (1969), "The Economics of the Negro Migration, 1900–1960." Ph.D. Dissertation, University of Chicago.

Watkins, J. L. (1895), U.S.D.A. Division of Statistics, "Production and Price of Cotton for One Hundred Years." *U.S.D.A. Miscellaneous Bulletin*, Number 9.

Weiher, K. (1977), "The Cotton Industry and Southern Urbanization, 1880–1930." *Explorations in Economic History* **14**, 120–140.

Wharton, V. L. (1947), *The Negro in Mississippi, 1865–1890*. New York: Harper & Row, 1965.

Wiener, J. M. (1975), "Planter–Merchant Conflict in Reconstruction Alabama." *Past and Present* **68**, 73–94.

Wiener, J. M. (1976), "Planter Persistence and Social Change: Alabama, 1850–1870." *Journal of Interdisciplinary History* **7**, 235–260.

Wiener, J. M. (1978), *Social Origins of the New South: Alabama: 1860–1885*. Baton Rouge, Louisiana State University Press.

Woodman, H. D. (1968), *King Cotton and His Retainers*. Lexington: University of Kentucky Press.

Woodman, H. D. (1977), "Sequel to Slavery: The New Economic History Views the Postbellum South." *Journal of Southern History* **43**, 523–554.

Woodward, C. V. (1951), *The Origins of the New South, 1877–1913*. Baton Rouge: Louisiana State University Press, 1971.

Woolfolk, G. R. (1958), *The Cotton Regency*. New York: Bookman Associates.

Wright, G. (1974), "Cotton Competition and the Post-Bellum Recovery of the American South." *Journal of Economic History* **34**, 610–635.

Wright, G. (1976), "Prosperity, Progress, and American Slavery." In P. A. David *et al.*, *Reckoning with Slavery: A Critical Study in the Quantitative History of American Negro Slavery*. New York: Oxford University Press. Pp. 302–336.

Wright, G. (1978), *The Political Economy of the Cotton South: Households, Markets, and Wealth in the Nineteenth Century*. New York: W. W. Norton.

Wright, G., and Kunreuther, H. (1975), "Cotton, Corn, and Risk in the Nineteenth Century." *Journal of Economic History* **35,** 526–551.

Wright, G., and Kunreuther, H. (1977), "Cotton, Corn and Risk in the Nineteenth Century: A Reply." *Explorations in Economic History* **14,** 183–195.

Zepp, T. M. (1976), "On Returns to Scale and Input Substitutability in Slave Agriculture." *Explorations in Economic History* **13,** 165–178.